Lives
OF THE
Courtesans

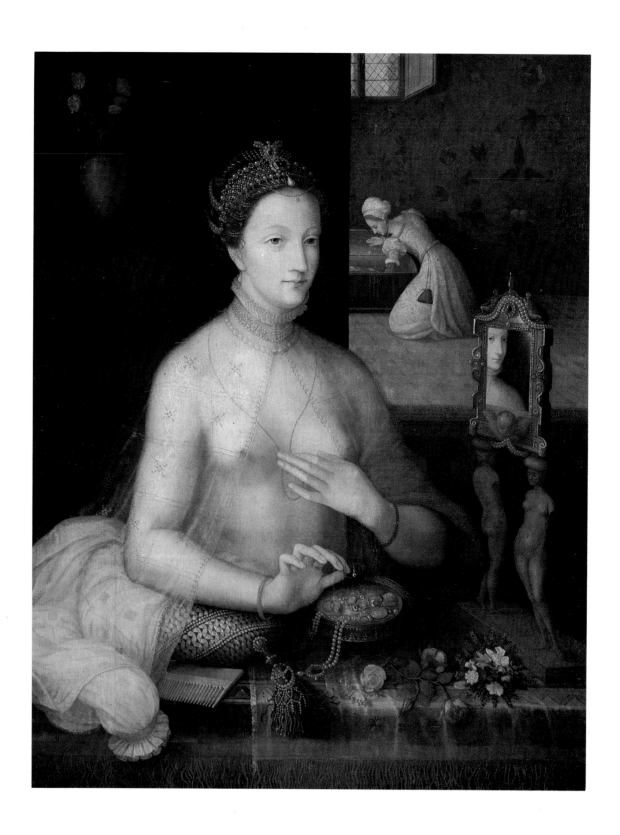

LYNNE LAWNER

LIVES
OF THE
COURTESANS

✳

PORTRAITS OF THE RENAISSANCE

RIZZOLI
NEW YORK

Under dark, transparent veils
one sees here angels from heaven in the flesh.
O Titian, you perfect spirit, paint
their noble semblances, let us feast our eyes on them!
                                        —*Pietro Aretino*

Frontispiece: School of Fontainebleau, *Woman at Her Toilet*.
16th century. Worcester Art Museum, Worcester, Massachusetts

Design by Gilda Hannah
Composition by Rainsford Type, Ridgefield, CT

First published in the United States of America in 1987 by
RIZZOLI INTERNATIONAL PUBLICATIONS, INC.
597 Fifth Avenue, New York, NY 10017

Library of Congress Cataloging-in-Publication Data
Lawner, Lynne.
  Lives of the courtesans.
  Bibliography: p.
  1. Italy—Civilization—16th century. 2. Courtesans—
Italy—History—16th century. 3. Courtesans in art.
4. Courtesans in literature. I. Title.
DG445.L38 1986   945′.06   86–42732
ISBN 0–8478–0738–X

Printed and bound in Hong Kong

·CONTENTS·

·PREFACE·

This is a book about courtesans, both real and fictional, of the sixteenth century, in Italy but also in France, Germany, the Netherlands, and other places, seen as others saw them and as they saw themselves. In this shifting kaleidoscope of images, we shall see that courtesans do not exist, or rather that they exist in such a multiplicity of forms that they can never actually be seized. Yet traces of their lives remain, and the courtesan can be known by knowing many of "her."

The Renaissance was a time of exploring possibilities, of universalizing experience, of imagining and evoking the myriad variations nature and art had
already elaborated out of material reality. Multiplicity was a lure, a way of attracting attention and of perpetuating pleasure: it constituted an aspiration toward the infinite. Artists and writers, as they portrayed the variable, many-sided courtesans, inevitably imitated them. Similarly, by attempting to chart the vagaries of these portrayals, we, too, are driven to construct the "one" artificially from the qualities and features of the "many."

The flowering of the courtesan was essentially a cultural phenomenon, an invention of society, not merely of a caste of women who wanted to get ahead in the world and to assume some of the privileges of the patricians. Courtesans are the final expression of a desire on the part of society as a whole, which began to make itself felt around the beginning of the sixteenth century and was to have reverberations throughout Europe for at least two more centuries.

Society made the courtesan. Art and literature advertised her, occasionally plunging her into the future and perpetuating her. Nevertheless, she also acted as a comment on culture, aware that representations of her revealed only a partial truth. The courtesan depended on artists and writers to propagate her image, to create her and to make that creation known. What she thought about the images may occasionally be discerned in portraiture, in distancing smiles that skirt the edges of a faint sneer and yet remain inviting. At times the courtesan comes alive most vividly in words—in the various *motti* and *arguzie* and wise, high-toned discourses attributed to her in novellas, plays, poems, and dialogues, and in her actual letters, prose, and poetry, projecting an image of herself that blends and contrasts with images others have devised.

An odd dichotomy came to exist in the Renaissance between portrayals of the courtesan in art and in literature. At least in Italy, the visual arts exalted her figure, while literature often viciously undercut that vision. In northern art, the ideal image appears here and there, but genre painting (and prints) give us more often the brothel whore than the salon courtesan. The full-fledged "realistic" version emerges a little later; thus, although most of the art reproduced in this book dates from the sixteenth century, some seventeenth-century examples—and even one from the eighteenth century—are included to complete the story.

It would be foolish to propose that all of the beautiful women in Renaissance painting are courtesans, and if my argument occasionally seems to imply that this is so, it is only because the courtesan has heretofore not been adequately recognized, and in bringing her the recognition she deserves, I may have erred in the direction of overemphasis. This presentation is meant to be no more than a fertile hypothesis, a new way of viewing works whose formal and iconographic elements have sometimes seemed mysterious or at least partly to have withheld their meaning.

If the courtesan is as complex as I paint her, perhaps the mysteries are only compounded. But it is my hope to have at least established a fresh dialogue on the subject in the community of scholars, lovers of Renaissance culture and culture in general, and—not least of all—the lovers of love.

Lynne Lawner
New York
July 1986

THE COURTESAN IN ROME AND VENICE

· THE COURTESAN AT THE PAPAL COURT ·

The Renaissance saw the emergence of several "types" that took on a significance for the whole society—above all, the Courtier and the Prince. Ideals of the statesman and the military leader (the *condottiere*) also were shaped. It could be debated, but the conceptions of the feminine counterparts of these various roles—despite vigorous individual incarnations such as the military Caterina Sforza, the political Caterina de Medici and milder Caterina Cornaro, and the cultural Marguerite de Navarre—were somewhat vaguer and less well formulated. And this is true as well concerning Baldasarre Castiglione's *dama di palazzo*, the suitable companion of his Courtier. Nevertheless, one female figure—the courtesan, the so-called "honest courtesan"—took her place among the major role images of the time. Painters and poets busied themselves fashioning the courtesan's shifting yet dominant image—in a sense, creating her—but were not the Courtier and the Prince also, to some extent, literary-cultural manifestations?

Although other writers of the time devoted their talents to describing and defining the Courtier and the Prince, a Renaissance writer, Pietro Aretino, produced a major treatise on the courtesan. Unlike these works, however, his *I ragionamenti* (*Dialogues*) is not a *galateo* (a book of etiquette and behavior) or a serious description of a profession, but a rollicking social satire written in a deliberately peppery and plebeian language. So powerful is it, however, that it endures as a monumental testimony to a major Renaissance personage.

Aretino's is the best-known portrait of the Renaissance courtesan, particularly in the Anglo-Saxon world, but it is not the only one. In Italy, and to a limited extent in Spain, France, and the Netherlands, a whole literature is dedicated to the courtesan. Some works praise her; some denigrate; most of these accounts are extremely colorful and provide rare information about her existence, the figure she cut, and the great influence she had on the culture and tenor of life in her time. The poetry and prose by Renaissance authors supplies some information about the courtesan, but perhaps the most revealing passages are found in her own literary creations, wherein the courtesan projects an image of herself and—one might say—reflects on her own reflection.

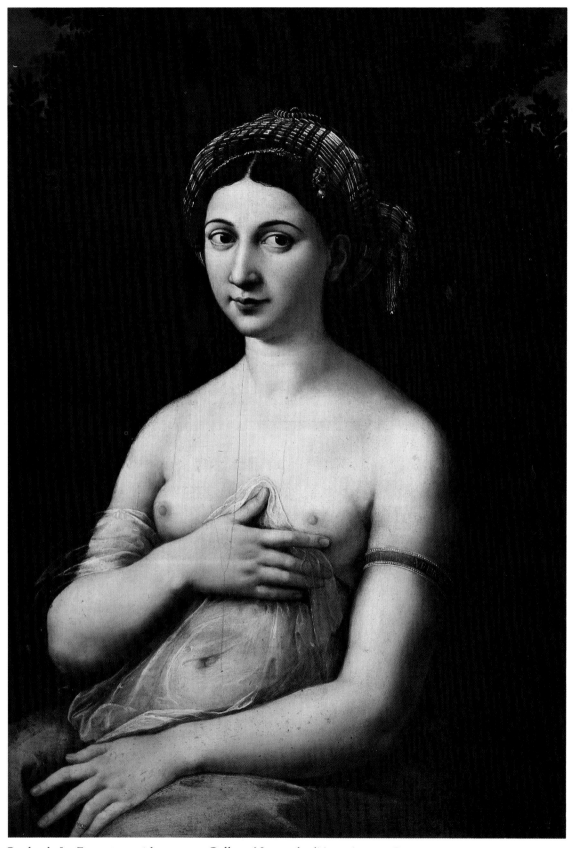

Raphael, *La Fornarina*. 16th century. Galleria Nazionale d'Arte Antica, Rome

Palma Vecchio, *La Violante*. 16th century. Kunsthistorisches Museum, Vienna

This collage of literary portraits and self-portraits, fascinating as it is, would be incomplete without the juxtaposition of another series of works inspired by the ideal of the honest courtesan: paintings for which real flesh-and-blood courtesans served as models. Only by examining both interpretations and speculating on how these literary and artistic representations came about can we begin to see the Renaissance courtesan for what she was—namely, a major social and cultural manifestation. This living ideal was gradually crushed out, of course, by historical forces, foremost the moralistic impulses stemming from the Council of Trent in 1545. Hence the phenomenon is delimited in time and space, but remains all the more intriguing for that reason.

The emergence of the courtesan in the Renaissance is an important subject, for our conception of beauty and style is still affected by Raphael's *La Fornarina*, and Palma Vecchio's *La Violante* and *La Bella*. A whole heritage of pulchritude stares out at us from the most unlikely places—portraits of saints and madonnas, biblical and historical heroines, and allegorical depictions of the Republic of Venice. In addition, our psychological orientation toward romantic love ultimately stems from the Provençal tradition as it filtered through Italy into France and England. It was Renaissance courtesans such as the poet Gaspara Stampa who consciously took up the role of preserving and rendering socially valid those delicate conceptions.

If one was still needed, there is yet another reason for intense interest today in the figure of the courtesan. The courtesan is one of the first examples of modern woman achieving a relatively autonomous economic position. Examining the conditions of her existence, we are able to temper the somewhat voyeuristic curiosity about her physical gifts and amorous prowess, encouraged by the exhibitionistic mode of her presentation in art. However, the two spheres naturally converge, for the courtesan's trade and her art—one and the same endeavor—was primarily the successful production of "self-images."

It took several generations of spirited persons exercising the best qualities of their minds, cultivating feelings about nature, and developing the conception of artfulness in every area of life to produce the cult of female beauty in the High Renaissance. A theoretical Neoplatonism idealizing the female figure as "heaven on earth"—literally the stepping stone to, or shadowy copy of, divine beauty—converged with a practical epicureanism to allow a quite concrete image of the desirable woman to emerge.

But exactly where and when did the courtesan usurp the exclusive privilege of representing this ideal, this concept of beauty? Why did she claim the right to identify herself with Sophia (Wisdom) and to imagine that in her arms a man could have a transcendent experience? What gave her the assurance that the very curves of her body or the perfection of an arched eyebrow or the glitter of blond tresses conformed to a Pythagorean cosmic formula, thus constituting an immense treasure, a repertory of harmonious proportions to be shared with all mankind?

If one thinks that, previous to the emergence, at the end of the fifteenth century, of a distinct class within society of elite prostitutes, mercenaries of love in Italy constituted an amorphous group blurring into the category of female slaves used as concubines (traces of this custom being readily found in Renaissance plays), it is all the more startling to see courtesans accord themselves the greatest honors in an ontological and epistemological sense—that is, as representations of, and ways of letting human intellect have access to, higher realities.

The social forces that sparked the phenomenon of the courtesan converged at a particular time and place—in Rome at the papal court at the end of the fifteenth century. But why the "honest courtesan" came into being at exactly the time painters and writers "needed" her, and bankers, diplomats, and high-placed prelates were willing to pay for her, one can only guess.

At the end of the fifteenth century, Rome was a city of celibates. The capital of Christianity, it was fast becoming the capital of prostitution. It would soon be a literary commonplace to remark that Rome itself had become one vast brothel. First of all, men greatly outnumbered women. Merchants and bankers jockeyed for important positions;

courtiers seeking sinecures and Church benefits crowded around the papal court, and along with them came hordes of low-ranking officials, clerks, and servants in and out of the pay of important personages. All were bent on enjoying the perpetual *vita dulcedo* offered by Rome at that time. A realistic if enormously cynical picture of this world emerges in Aretino's play *La cortigiana* (*The Courtesan*, 1525), in which the figure of the courtesan never appears, although Camilla of Pisa—a famous one—lurks offstage—both prey and predator in a society become a jungle of power and pleasure seekers.

As for the wives of Roman gentlemen, they have not been recorded in history as particularly charming. In the last quarter of the sixteenth century, the French traveler and writer Pierre de Brantôme commented that "Roman ladies copulate like bitches but are silent as stones." According to him, gentlemen who visited Rome had no desire to meet them: although lovely, the wives were "sans âme, sans esprit, et sans parôle" (*La vie des dames galantes*, p. 154). Although Brantôme's words are surely too acrid, they nevertheless offer a clue to the great need filled by the emergent courtesan.

An intellectual flavor permeates this decadence in expansion. What else explains the prominence and ubiquitous presence of the witty, often viciously gossipy buffoons who, together with renowned parasites, appeared at banquets and parties throughout the city and absorbed so much of the pope's own daily life? At the center of this sea of recommendations, influences, favors, bribes, and other corruption, was the courtesan, tossed on waves of hypocrisy, crude ambition, and imperious sensual demands, but sailing valiantly toward her own needs and fulfillment. Reigning as its female deity over an essentially celibate city, serving up her image as something at once august and delectable to be consumed but also conserved, the courtesan embodied a highly evolved conception of refinement. In addition, as a revival of the ancient hetaera, the courtesan emerged into the Roman world blessed, even partly regenerated, by humanism.

Gradually, a kind of aristocracy distinguished itself from the rest—women who saw the advantage of grooming themselves as luxurious objects, suitable companions for high-placed prelates, princes, ambassadors, bankers, and merchants. It was Giovanni Burchard, the chronicler of the court of Alexander VI (Borgia), who may have been the first to use the term *cortesanae honestae*, making explicit its derivation from the papal curia. Differentiating these women from common prostitutes, Burchard recounts the honor accorded them by courtiers and wealthy prelates around the court. At the same time, he offers piquant accounts of some of the boisterous games played with courtesans at social affairs.

The Roman *cortesana honesta*—equivalent of the Venetian diarist Marin Sanudo's term "sumptuous whore" and corresponding to the first of three classes of prostitutes specified in a document in the Archivio di Stato Fiorentino—namely, the "richest" ones, were almost from the beginning social regents and goddesses to be propitiated. The appropriate offerings being at once material and cultural, Roman society was prepared not to stint, what with the presence of such wealthy noblemen as the pope's banker Agostino Chigi of Siena, and a flock of humanists ready to toss off an ode in Latin at the drop of a courtesan's perfumed glove.

But we should not imagine that the honest courtesan held the stage alone. Behind these standard bearers marched a troupe of common prostitutes, their growing numbers becoming, for some, a phenomenon of alarming proportions. By the second decade of the century, a large part of the total population consisted of prostitutes, along with their "managers" and staff.

Stefano Infessura, a chronicler of the period of Innocent VIII claimed, on the basis of the 1490 census, that in a population of less than 50,000, there were 6,800 prostitutes in Rome "in addition to concubines and brothel prostitutes." Under the Spanish popes Calixtus III and Alexander VI, prostitutes flocked to Rome, raising the number considerably. In a humorous passage in the *Lozana andalusa*, a prose dialogue offering a portrait of a Spanish procuress in Rome at the turn of the century, a character named Dovizia offers the preposterous figure of 30,000 prostitutes and 9,000 procuresses.[1] Around 1588 a Dutchman even speaks of 40,000 prostitutes in Rome. But the most reliable opinion is perhaps

Cesare Vecellio, *Courtesan at the Time of Pius V* from
Habiti antichi et moderni di tutto il mondo. Venice,
1590. Houghton Library, Harvard University,
Cambridge, Massachusetts

expulsion of prostitutes and of those who depended on them for their livelihood risked reducing the city's population by no less than 25,000 persons—in other words, by nearly one-half. The pope listened to reason and desisted. Nevertheless, under Pius IV (1559–65) and Pius V (1565–72), courtesans and prostitutes had a much harder time. A glance at the dark, concealing, almost penitential cloak worn by the *Courtesan at the Time of Pius V* in Cesare Vecellio's engraving tells us all we need to know.

Earlier in the century, however, during the reign of Alexander VI, Julius II, and Leo X, Roman courtesans enjoyed what has often been called a "Golden Age." This series of popes, through contributions to the arts and an unbridled hedonism, made the Roman court the most vivacious and attractive on the peninsula. Numerous artists and writers were drawn to the city, among them Raphael, Leonardo da Vinci, Michelangelo, Sebastiano del Piombo (whose nickname derived from his post as Keeper of the Pope's Seal), and Marcantonio Raimondi, the great engraver, who became involved, along with Pietro Aretino, in a cultural scandal under Clement VII, just before the Sack of Rome (1527) brought this radiant era to an abrupt close.

Palaces and villas sprang up based on classical examples and designed to be pleasure houses as well as architectonic and painted homages to a distinguished historical and intellectual past. Agreeable vineyards (the *vigne* where lovers tarried and humanist circles met to discuss philosophy and letters) were transformed into remarkable gardens. Not least among these glorious locations were the dwellings of the Roman courtesans.

The great short story writer from Lombardy, Matteo Bandello, offers an extensive decription of the domestic surroundings of Imperia, foremost of Roman courtesans in the early years of the sixteenth century: "If one judged by the splendid furnishings and number of servants, one might think a princess lived in that palace" (*Novelle* III, 42). Velvet and brocade decorated the living room and boudoir, and precious carpets covered the floors. In the sitting room beside her bedchamber, where the courtesan conversed with her lovers, embroidered cloth of

that of Domenico Gnoli, author of a basic work on the era of Leo X.[2] Basing his estimate on the 1527 census, Gnoli offers the figure of 4,900 out of a population of 55,035, adding that this number is, of course, in addition to hundreds of pimps, procuresses, and others earning a living from prostitution. If these numbers correspond to the truth, then about one-tenth of the Roman population in the first half of the sixteenth century consisted of prostitutes and their associates.

Judging by a well-known episode, the situation stayed much the same throughout the century. When in 1566 Pope Pius V wanted to exile from Rome all courtesans and prostitutes, the conservators of the city formally protested, claiming that the

Palma Vecchio, *La Bella*. 16th century. Thyssen-Bornemisza Collection, Lugano

Anonymous, *Portrait of Imperia* (medal). 16th century

it is troubling to learn that when the ambassador, Enriques de Toledo, returned to make a more intimate visit to Imperia, he gave the distinguished courtesan the same tip (25 ducats) he had given his servant for retrieving a trivial present from the pope. Courtesanry in Rome had a double aspect.

In Renaissance Rome courtesans lived in three main areas of the city: the *rione* (quarter) Ponte, the financial center containing banks, courts, the mint, the prison of Tor di Nona, and the piazza named after Cesare Borgia's flame, Fiammetta; Parione, stretching to Piazza Navona; and Campo Marzio. The highest-class courtesans lived on or near the via dell'Orso at the far end of which. stands the Osteria dell'Orso, a renowned hotel for foreigners, which housed such illustrious guests as Dante Alighieri and, later, Montaigne. Here, fashionable courtesans, such as Matrema-non-vole (Mother-doesn't-want-me-to), Beatrice of Ferrara, Angela Greca, and Lorenzina lived, locked behind high iron grills, as if in castles or fortresses, away from the plebeian throngs (and lovers who might try to avenge themselves). The census accounts of 1517 and 1527 contain colorful details about these dwellings, naming their residents but sometimes describing them in euphemistically indirect wording: "No one will say to whom such-and-such a house belongs, although a proud woman living there claims she is married"; "This house with an iron door belongs to a monsignore from Lucca. A Madonna Credentia who has roomers lives there."[3]

Strewn through these quarters of the city were the *stufe*, or public baths, a reminiscence of ancient times and the setting for much vice orchestrated by the courtesans. The most famous of these was "Pozzo Bianco" (White Well) named after a sarcophagus near the ancient church—long since gone—of Santa Maria in Posterula (today, Piazza della Chiesa Nuova). Originally these baths were small clinics or spas for the treatment of rheumatism and venereal diseases, and for bloodletting, but in the early sixteenth century they became meeting places for prostitutes and their clients, thus gaining a sinister reputation. Divided into dry rooms heated with wood fires and wet ones heated by steam, the baths also contained other chambers where prosti-

gold adorned the walls, and, above those rich folds, a gilded cornice painted with ultramarine served as a support for vases of alabaster, porphyry, serpentine, and many other kinds of precious stone. Around the room lay elaborately carved and inlaid chests and coffers, and in the center of the room stood a beautiful table covered with green velvet on which were placed various musical instruments, books of music, and volumes in Latin and Italian. Clearly culture and opulence were ineffably fused in such a context, and one can well imagine the effect on a foreign visitor when the lavishly garbed owner of all these possessions took up her lute and sang to him alone a madrigal she herself had written.

Bandello's story has a snobbish point. The Spanish ambassador visiting Imperia at home is so amazed by what he sees around him that he finds nowhere homely enough to spit and therefore spits in the face of one of his servants. Related bluntly, much of the wit vanishes, but it is a startling little tale that reveals the elegance and prestige of the courtesan's quarters and her exalted rank. Therefore

tutes could ply their trade. The *stufe* appear often in literature, especially in plays (a comedy by Antonfrancesco Doni is entitled *Lo stufaiolo* [*The Bath Keeper*]). It is said that Michelangelo descended into the underground squalors of the *stufe* in order to study male anatomy for his *Slaves* sculptures.

A great frequenter of the *stufe* is the fictional character, the Lozana Andalusa. Practicing the multifarious trade of procuress, the Lozana offers her services as a one-woman ambulant beauty parlor to clients throughout the city, thus giving the reader the chance to eavesdrop on spicy conversation and to view Rome through her cynical, amused eyes.

Led by her new partner in vice, Rampino, son of a Neapolitan procuress, Lozana is taken on a tour of the courtesan quarters. "Look at this street," Rampino tells her, pointing to what today is called via dei Banchi Nuovi (Street of the New Banks), halfway between the infamous Ponte Sisto and Campo di Fiori; "it's as thick as bees with courtesans."

Through the muddy byways, the two see sauntering mules carrying courtesans and their prelate lovers. Occasionally pigs scramble underfoot. But Rampino tells Lozana to keep her head high: "Raise your eyes and you will see Signora Chiarini, a divine masterpiece," he tells her. "See how beautiful she is, and this other one, too. That one over there is kept by a mighty churchman, and in this building the lovely Portuguese woman lives." Still others stroll past, one courtesan with a large hat accompanied by two maids. A horde issues from the doorways of houses: the courtesans are on their way to Mass where they will lure clients. Meanwhile, police officers move in to collect fines for the night, confiscating jewelry that will be returned upon request for a small fee the next morning.

How did courtesanry actually work? There is no reason to think that what Bandello delineates as their regular practice in Venice was not true for Roman courtesans as well:

There is a custom in Venice . . . namely that a courtesan take six or seven lovers, assigning to each a certain night of the week when she dines and sleeps with him. During the day she is free to entertain whomever she wishes so that her mill never lies idle and does not rust from lack of the opportunity to grind grain. Once in a while, a wealthy foreigner insists on having one of her nights, warning her that otherwise she will not get a cent from him. In this case, it is her duty to request permission from the lover whose evening that would ordinarily be and to arrange to see him during the day instead. Each lover pays a monthly salary, and their agreement includes the provision that the courtesan is allowed to have foreigners as overnight guests (*Novelle* II, 31).

Another interesting clue is contained in a casual passage in a letter written by Francesco Vettori, the Florentine ambassador to Rome, in 1513. Vettori outlines the ascetic life he is leading, reporting that he spends most evenings at home reading ancient Roman authors, and chatting with a male friend or two. He has nevertheless condescended, he says, to entertain a courtesan or two: "I trained one so well that she often came to me of her own free will, and I enjoyed her lovely person and agreeable conversation."

These words raise tantalizing questions. Were such visits made in the afternoon? And were they made by courtesans such as Matrema-non-vole, Isabella da Luna, and others who gave themselves such airs? The most exclusive courtesans held salons in their own palaces and did not deign to receive visitors in their boudoirs unless they were extremely important personages. In order to converse with Matrema at home, the visitor had to sit on the floor on special little cushions, and others of the elite strata no doubt demanded similar forms of homage.

Quite a bit is known about these afternoon salons—who frequented them, the techniques a courtesan used to indicate which lover was her favorite, and so forth. Writers and philosophers were among those who attended, as well as the usual crowd of diplomats and other gentlemen. On these occasions courtesans could display their talents, strumming the lute and singing sonnets and madrigals set to music for them by well-known composers, discoursing about literary matters, and engaging in political gossip.

In Bandello's novella about Imperia, the honest courtesan has not yet spoken; she has simply appeared—distanced and glamorous—chiefly an external insignia. Meanwhile, beneath this surface, work was being done, the drudgery of keeping up appearances, leavened with incessant chatter.

Other novellas provide the information that clothes and furnishings were rented from Jews (upon whom courtesans often bestowed their favors, even though the law forbade it), virgins were sealed again with various astringents, while skillfully tearful courtesans persuaded different lovers to redeem the same pawned necklaces over and over again. Young courtesans, such as Aretino's Pippa, took important lessons from their mothers.

To the personage Nanna in Aretino's dialogues we owe a somewhat jaded picture of the motive and tenor of these salons and dinners. Her daughter Pippa—the courtesan-initiate—is told to show on these occasions an intense interest in the arts, so that paintings and sculptures will be given to her. She is told not to dive into her food or to make other gruesome faux-pas. Everyone will be looking at her and judging her, and other courtesans will be rivaling her. She must shine. But those were also moments that could be used to stir jealousy in a lover who needed to be drawn more tightly into the net, or to pay homage in public to the chosen one, for example by seeking his permission before helping oneself to an extra piece of chicken.

Etiquette on the most basic level is discussed in the anonymous *Dialogo di Maddalena e Giulia* (*Dialogue of Madeleine and Julia*), where a Roman courtesan called "La Tortora" (Turtledove) is held up as an example to others:

In addition to being attractive, La Tortora is always cheerful toward everyone with whom she comes into contact. She knows better than to howl with laughter at inappropriate moments. Her quick ripostes fall like caresses on the ear, making all who hear her smile with pleasure. Knowledgeable about many subjects, she never overdoes the presentation of her ideas. Using a sympathetic tone with everyone, she makes sure never to deceive or lie. Frequenting only those men who promise to give her what she wants, nevertheless she does not insist on getting her payment in advance. Eating and drinking with moderation, she never appears greedy, even when her favorite dishes are set in front of her. Indeed, she eats only a little bit of each course, lifting morsels delicately with the tips of her fingers, chewing slowly on one side of her mouth, and generally exercising restraint (*Dialogo di Maddalena e Giulia*, p. 6).

Life on the margins of respectability—a deft shift-ing between appearance and reality—was the substance of courtesan life. A courtesan had constantly to readjust her position (up, down, high, low, inside, outside), the sexual seldom disjunct from the social, and in addition she could expect that her life would run the classical trajectory from the sublime to the ridiculous, sinking from paradisiacal peaks to hellish depths—or so this existence was painted over and over in satirical and moralistic literary works.

Two of these works—an anonymous prose dialogue, *Il ragionamento dello Zoppino* (*Zoppino's Discourse*), and an ode and palinode called *Il vanto e il lamento della cortigiana ferrarese* (*The Vaunt and the Lament of the Ferrarese Courtesan*)—offer dazzling versions of this "double" existence in which the truth always had to be divined through the elaborate, artificial veils courtesans threw around their shoulders and over their breasts. Zoppino, a pimp-turned-priest, offers lively glimpses into the "Splendeurs" and "Misères" (to use Balzac's terms) of courtesan existence. It is Zoppino who undercuts their genealogical pretensions, while ridiculing the fancy classicizing names they adopted. His miniature biographies of Roman courtesans are fascinating. It may be that, buried in one of them, lies the story of Raphael's *Fornarina*. Parmigianino's *Antea*, whose face was scarred by an unforgiving lover, is mentioned. There are rare details—for example, the courtesans are depicted at the windows of their houses, their arms resting on velvet cushions with gold borders, of the kind carried before cardinals in processions, scrutinizing the economic level of the gentlemen walking by. The dialogue is a gossip column as well: lists of names ripple through it, a sensual delight of melodic sounds—la Farfalla, la Livia, la Tinetta, la Laura, la Diana Romana, la Faustina, and countless others, including illustrious Albina who dined at the table of the greatest dignitaries of the Church.

Zoppino gives us harrowing scenes of childhood poverty and abuse. Even he, he brags, took part in one of the infamous "thirty-ones" (rape by thirty-one men, but sometimes as many as eighty) that launched poor Lorenzina, a baker's daughter who used to carry trays of apples on her head. The Fer-

THE TRUTH ABOUT THEIR BACKGROUNDS

LUDOVICO: Perhaps they're justified in wanting to be surrounded with luxury since they were used to it in their youth.

ZOPPINO: You still imagine they are of noble birth and deserve luxury? I had better draw you a clear picture. Why there isn't a single one on the level of your chambermaid. Let's examine the case of this one here, the proudest and grandest of them all.

[They stand outside of house]

Look at those velvet cushions trimmed in gold set there in the windows, they're the kind that precede cardinals in a procession. Look at her there behind the shutters. Where did she learn those graces? Not from her parents, that's for sure, because from time immemorial this family has been infamously poor.

LUDOVICO: You must be joking. Everyone describes her as a rich Roman patrician. Her family have always given magistrates to Campidoglio.

ZOPPINO: Only if they were tried and hanged did her relatives ever set foot on Campidoglio.

LUDOVICO: You must be teasing me. Everyone says the opposite of what you say.

ZOPPINO: How can she be of noble birth if, until a few years ago, her family was dying from starvation? Who started her off? *I* did! Don't forget the reason why she was given the name Matrema-non-vole [Mother-doesn't-want-me-to], which still sticks to her. I found a lover for her. Indeed, she owes everything to me. Since she was darling and cheerful, I turned over to her many rich men and thus, little by little, helped her to get ahead. As she put on weight (she was very thin to start with) she also accumulated many valuable objects. By frequenting high-placed prelates she learned how to dress and speak like a lady.

LUDOVICO: Like a lady, you say? She goes far beyond that. To me she seems another Cicero. She has memorized all of Petrarch and Boccaccio as well as an infinite number of excellent Latin poems by Virgil, Horace, Ovid, and dozens of others. Most of the gentlemen I know who pride themselves on their literary abilities are less skilled in speaking and arguing than she.

ZOPPINO: What you say is true: Matrema is extremely virtuistic, but this "virtue" is counteracted by the vices she has. She hardly deserves to live in such grand style. . . .

All Giulia del Sole learned from her mother, a fruit and vegetable vendor, and her father, a herdsman, was how to skin others alive. Hoping to marry her off to a notions merchant, her mother sent two other daughters out on the street to earn their bread.

Beatrice was the daughter of an impoverished washerwoman in Campo Marzio whose many daughters would go half-naked, with huge baskets of laundry on their heads, to do the washing in the Tiber. She fell into the hands of a dissolute doctor during the reign of Julius II. This man was the brother of Giovanpietro of Cremona. He used to dress her up as a boy and get his pleasure out of her the backway, the most dishonest way there is. Eventually she took a house. . . .

Cecilia the Venetian from Friuli (this is the name she has assumed) was Jewish twenty years ago. She got baptised, married a scoundrel, then left him to return to Rome with a greedy priest who ended up in prison. She then started to frequent a Sienese banker who set her up again on her feet.

Beatricia, daughter of a poor Spanish woman, was born in Ferrara. [Author here confounds the two Beatrices—Beatrice of Ferrara and Beatrice of Spain.] When her mother came to Rome she brought her with her along with two other daughters. Since Beatrice was the most beautiful and vivacious of the three (even though she was covered with boils), she was placed with a Spanish gentleman, Don Pietro di Bonadiglia. So enamored of her was he that after he returned to Spain he sent her two hundred *scudi*. This was the act of a true chevalier, and after that time she always stayed popular, one of the most elegant courtesans around the curia.

Il ragionamento dello Zoppino, pp. 10–11

Giacomo Franco, *Courtesans Bullbaiting* from *Habiti delle donne venetiane*. Venice, 1628. Biblioteca del Civico Museo Correr, Venice

rarese courtesan of *Il vanto e il lamento*, the description of whose features corresponds to the *Fornarina*, as well as those in a portrait of a courtesan in Moscow by Giulio Romano and who many believe to be Beatrice of Ferrara, tells us in her own words about the miserable end of courtesans, a theme popular for a long time in French and Italian literature.

Whoever she was, the Ferrarese courtesan lived in incredible luxury among silver cabinets; chests and *cassoni* covered with tapestries; exquisite, delicately perfumed linens "whiter than snow"; dresses of cloth of gold, velvet, and silk sewn with precious stones and pearls; pleated shirts of gold and silk; fashionable hose and shoes, and the 200-ducat gold chain she wore around her neck. Only great princes and lords accompanied her as she moved about the city to parties, plays, concerts and bullbaiting, followed by maidservants and lackeys, often arriving in her lavishly adorned coach of inlaid gold drawn by Arabian steeds. Her dinner parties were worthy of kings, what with their partridges, pheasants, quails, and other gourmet dishes, marzipan desserts, and Trebbian and malmsey wines. Above all, in her own person, Beatrice offered a "paradise" to whomever she judged worthy to enjoy it.

Now, the poem laments, her lace is made of cabbage leaves, her pearls are syphilis boils, and she is so hungry that she would willingly dine in a stable. She sleeps outside under benches and begs for a drink of pure water. She once teased wittily; now she is the butt of jokes; and she has descended the social ladder from procuress to laundress, to tavern cook, to vendor of candles in church. Now nothing awaits her but the hospital and Ponte Sisto. Lucky is the courtesan, she says, who does not end up in prison or become a thief or beggar! These are "other times," she cautions. The poem is meant to be a salutary warning, to her sisters in the trade, that men are no longer spending on courtesans as they used to. The lament for an earlier age becomes a cliché of courtesan literature, as if the time of true liberality, when Rome was a *terra da donne*—a place where women had the advantage—receded ever further into the past, a veritable mirage.

We learn from the *Lamento*, the full title of which is *Lament of the Ferrarese Courtesan for Having Been Thrown into the Cart because of Having Contracted Syphilis*, that one of the most common punishments for Roman courtesans fallen into disgrace and who had contracted the dreaded disease of their occupation was *la carretta* (the cart), an image that appears time and again in satirical poems, dialogues, and tracts. Courtesans chosen by the authorities as an example to the public were rounded up and placed in wagons, where—visible to everyone—they were literally carted around the city and finally dumped at the Hospital of the Incurables (San Giacomo in Campo Marzio). Like the ignominious crowning of courtesans and procuresses in San Marco in Venice, this Roman punishment seems to have had little impact on the mores of prostitutes. We know from another novella by Bandello that a prominent Roman courtesan—in this case, Isabella da Luna—could be whipped in public and still go home with her head held high.

Yet the local authorities persisted in prosecuting the more wretched of these creatures, driven by moralistic, economic, and sanitary considerations. Antonia, Pippa's godmother in Aretino's *Dialogues*, comments, "It must be a great consolation to men ruined by courtesans to see these women carried along on carts," and she quotes several lines from the opening of the *Lamento* to reinforce her point, lines in which Beatrice cries out to other prominent Roman courtesans not to follow her example:

> O Matrema-non-vole, o Lorenzina,
> O Angela, o Cecilia, o Beatrice,
> let my misery be a lesson to you!
> (ll. 7–9)

A popular poem called *La carretta*, which contained a list of Roman courtesans already subject to that punishment, was sold as a broadsheet at fairs in the early sixteenth century. During the Carnival of 1525, effigies of Roman courtesans were paraded to the Tiber and, in the presence of the pope himself, tossed into the river. What a futile exercise in exorcism this seems to have been.

But the cart was only a symbol of disgrace, part of a ceremony signifying the end of a glorious career. It was "the bridge or the hospital" that truly menaced; indeed, this phrase becomes a formula in satirical literature about Roman courtesans. Like the skull in Vanity pictures of the seventeenth century, it is proffered as a constant *memento mori*. As many elements in the satires do, it functions ambiguously both as a persuasion to award favors to suitors before it is too late and as an admonishment to give up vice for virtue's sake.

Ponte Sisto, the stone bridge running from the end of via Giulia over the Tiber to Trastevere, constituted one of the last refuges of courtesans fallen into disrepute. On the bridge impoverished women solicited clients and slept in the open air on straw mats. Satirists, many of them former lovers, took pleasure in mentioning these mats, emblematic of the miserable condition of those who had once reclined on silken sheets in beautifully adorned bedrooms. Pimps operated there; indeed a low-class pimp with whom she is negotiating tells the Lozana that if he could benefit from her collaboration, the

Urs Graf, *Witches' Sabbath* (drawing). 16th century. Graphische Sammlung Albertina, Vienna

two of them could profit handsomely from Rome's pedestrians.

In a sense it was the lucky ones who found their way to the bridge; the unlucky ones went to the Hospital of San Giacomo, which houses those suffering from venereal disease. This was a trip with no return. It was this terrible scourge, thought to have been brought by the troops of Charles VIII of France to Naples at the end of the fifteenth century, that made the courtesans as feared as they were worshiped by society. (For their part, the French maintained that the pope, conniving with the Spaniards, had plotted to spread the disease among their newly arrived garrisons.)

Sometimes courtesans were grouped with other marginal figures, such as witches, the distinction blurring as the century proceeded. As Zoppino relates, courtesans were thought to bind their lovers by the means of magic incantations and potions:

"Would you believe it? The other night I saw one of them coming from the Church of the Pace carrying a burning lamp she had stolen from the base of a cross." These holy objects were collected, says Zoppino, to cast secret spells enforced by invocations of the devil. "On hot ashes [they] design hearts," he continued, "which they pierce and inscribe with such lines as these:

> Before the fire goes out
> Make him come to my door
> May desire for me prickle him
> As I poke into this heart.
> (*Il ragionamento dello Zoppino*, p. 9)

The most powerful courtesan in Venice was herself brought before the Tribunal of the Inquisition, accused (falsely) of being both a heretic and a witch, but it is significant that she defended herself well and that the trial was suspended. In fact, throughout the sixteenth century, Venice was a city in which courtesans were celebrated and protected by the state. If courtesanry sprang up in the confines of the Roman curia, it came into full bloom in the Republic of Venice. Here they came from everywhere in order to enjoy the famous freedom Pietro Aretino himself had sought coming to the shores of the lagoon after the Sack of Rome.

· THE COURTESAN IN THE VENETIAN REPUBLIC ·

In Venice the courtesan population was divided, like the Roman one, into categories, an elite marching at the head of an army of mercenaries of love, who fought to win men's hearts and pocketbooks. Montaigne, visiting the city in the 1580s, commented that it harbored about 150 courtesans "living like princesses." However, according to the diarist Marin Sanudo and the Catholic-Reformist preacher Fra Bernardino da Siena, 10,000 to 12,000 courtesans lived in Venice in the early years of the century, more than one-tenth of the population. This sector grew rather than diminished in the late sixteenth and early seventeenth centuries, and the city fathers promulgated an increasing number of laws to regulate the great numbers of prostitutes flooding into the city from the *terra firma* and other places. Major government commissions were charged with the duty of controlling their activities and protecting them from abuse.

We should not imagine, however, that beautiful women began to be manufactured in Venice only in the early sixteenth century. Venetian women had always been known for their beauty. As early as the fifteenth century, tourists traveled long distances to Venice, just to catch a glimpse of the *raffinée* wives of the patricians, guarded—with almost oriental vigor—by their jealous husbands. Wives, economically powerful through a set of laws allowing matrilineal inheritances, were nevertheless kept out of

the public eye and, in most cases, left "uncontaminated" by culture. This arrangement suited the astute, often reckless, but outwardly decorous courtesans, who in every sense replaced wives on the social scene.

In sixteenth-century Venice, periods of relative political stability, increased emphasis on wealth and leisure, and the intensification of artistic and literary life under greater patronage combined with the psychological and physical openness of Venice to the people and products of other lands to create a new love of and need for sensual refinement. On the crest of this wave rode the courtesans, just as they perused the city—disguised—in gondolas, selecting their prey and rendering up to them unimaginable and expensive voluptuousness.

It suited the Venetian Republic at that time to have at its disposal innumerable beauties, both native and foreign-born. In the past Venice had imported its amorous material, thus satisfying the upper strata of the populace. Now Venice "merchandised" its own capital of goods, using beautiful women, who had always been in that society an ornament of and spur to marriage, as well as the pride of dynasties, to lure foreign merchants and diplomats to its shores. Once within Venetian precincts, the visitors spent exorbitantly on furniture, clothes, foodstuffs, and wine. By taxing and fining courtesans and prostitutes, the state also filled

Giacomo Franco, *Brides in Gondolas* from *Habiti delle donne venetiane*. Venice, 1628. Biblioteca del Civico Museo Correr, Venice

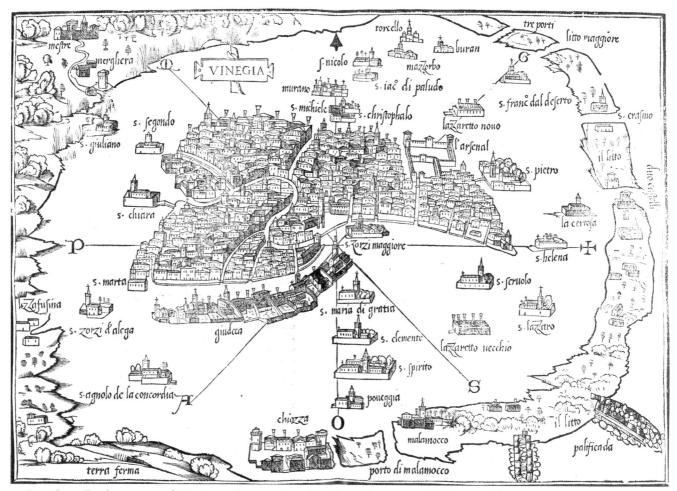

Benedetto Bordone, map of Venice and surrounding islands. 16th century. Biblioteca del Civico Museo Correr, Venice

chinks in its coffers. Regulation has always provided a source of income, and instances of courtesans buying their way out of legal requirements and chastisements were hardly rare.

Giuseppe Tassini, in his colorful compendium of prominent crimes in Venice through the centuries (crimes resulting in capital punishment), suggests yet another reason why the state looked benignly on the presence and activities of a large courtesan population: they could be politically useful. What better setting for a little espionage than these airy boudoirs painted and adorned in such a way as to put a man entirely at his ease and, one might add, off his guard? These boudoirs frequently make their appearance in paintings of the time as the backdrop for scenes of Venus disarming Mars as putti tumble on the floor or fly through the air using the god's halberd, helmet, and greaves as playthings.

A traitor to the Venetian Republic at the turn of the century learned too late just how armed with acuity and prudence courtesans could be. Antonio di Landi, secretary to the Senate at the end of the fifteenth century, was convinced that his mistress, Laura Troilo, was unable to understand the Latin he deliberately spoke at her house with a Venetian colleague in the pay of the duke of Mantua, whom he invited there for secret conversations. Laura, suspecting unsavory dealings, hid another lover behind the bed one day. Soon the Venetian Senate was apprised that its secret codes were being passed on to the enemy. On 26 March 1498, the traitor paid with his life, and his corpse was ignominiously displayed, the shame all the greater since he was a man well on in years.

Courtesans proved useful to the state in another, less direct way. Sodomy—a sign of homosexuality but also of an exhibitionistic manner of expressing violence or dissent in regard to authority—was an extremely widespread "vice" in the sixteenth century, more feared in Venice than syphilis and consequently punished by extreme means. Those found guilty could lose their heads to the ax and the rest of their bodies to the flames in a public place. In addition to keeping the Venetian family harmoniously together by providing an outlet for restless husbands, courtesans also represented a way to bring men back to a "healthy" heterosexuality. A curious treatise in defense of women written by the highest-ranking (nonnoble) citizen in the Republic expresses a "demographic" anxiety—the fear that, because of this problem, the race itself might face extinction. Thus, courtesans were encouraged to stand naked from the waist up on the Ponte delle Tette (Bridge of Tits) in Carampane to lure passersby.[4] That courtesans indulged in sodomy themselves, however, either because they were forced to or because they desired to, emerges from innumerable literary and other documents.

The most outstanding honest courtesans—Montaigne's "princesses"—must have had to work hard to maintain their status as first and best. Most of their time was spent conserving and enhancing their physical attractions, dressing in elaborate fashion, while sharpening their wits and creating a rarefied atmosphere around them.

Among the Venetian industries flourishing in that period, cosmetics must have been one of the most lucrative. Any woman who could afford them used immense quantities of creams, rinses, depilatory lotions, unguents, balsams to bleach their skin, and special tinctures for turning hair the exact brilliant shade of blond Venetian painters loved to render with their brushes. Courtesans even put make-up on their breasts. According to Tommaso Garzoni, who took universal folly as his theme, painters never equaled the colors women painted themselves. Their tools consisted of make-up brushes (such as those in Paris Bordone's *Courtesan at Her Toilet*) cloths, tiny soaps, pomades, tooth powder, oils, eau-de-cologne, Cyprus powder, aloes, civet, ambergris, and perfumes. No wonder Fra Bernardino da Siena preached in Venice against "distilled water, little pots, pointed sticks, musk, and all the rest." Why, the friar wondered, didn't these women

content themselves with the beauty God gave them? There were no limits to what Venetian courtesans would do in order to highlight their best features, meanwhile conforming to the current ideal of beauty, more than in any other age formulated by poets, writers, and artists.

Clothes naturally played a large part in the creation of their image. Cesare Vecellio's engravings of the clothing of Venetian men and women on various levels of society provide an excellent documentation of how they dressed. Among these are several significant examples of courtesan dress, revealing what these women wore on different occasions and how prostitutes' styles and habits differed from those of higher-class courtesans.

Here, for example, is what Vecellio—in the ample commentary that accompanies his engravings—writes about *Courtesans Outside of Their Houses*:

Courtesans who wish to get ahead in the world by feigning respectability go around dressed as widows or married women. Most courtesans dress as young virgins anyway. In fact, they button themselves up even more than virgins do. But a compromise must eventually be reached between the wearing of a mantle that hides their bodies and their need to be seen, at least to some extent. Finally, courtesans are forced to open up at the neck, and one recognizes at once who they are, for the lack of pearls speaks loud and clear. Courtesans are prohibited from wearing pearls. Indeed, in order to remedy this situation, some arrange to be accompanied by a lover-protector, borrowing his name as if the two of them were married. In this way courtesans feel free to wear things forbidden to them by law.

Aside from this limitation, however, they dress in the most lavish manner, their underwear including embroidered hosiery, petticoats, and undershirts, and garments of silk brocade. Inside their high clogs they wear Roman-style shoes. I am speaking, of course, of the high-class courtesans. Those, on the other hand who exercise their wicked profession in public places wear waistcoats of silk with gold braid or embroidery and skirts covered with overskirts or silk aprons. Light scarves on their heads, they go around the city flirting, their gestures and speech easily giving away their identity (*Habiti antichi e moderni di tutto il mondo*, Venice, 1590).

As for what the wealthy courtesans wore indoors in winter, Vecellio records that Venetian women who could afford them donned long Roman-style furs ample enough to let their limbs move freely.

Cesare Vecellio, scenes from *Habiti antichi et moderni di tutto il mondo*. Venice, 1590. Above left: *Cortigiane Moderne* (Modern Courtesans). Above right: *Meretriche Publiche* (Public Prostitutes). Left: *Venetian Woman Dyeing Her Hair Blond*.

Often these were covered outside with satin, *moiré ormesin* (a type of silk originally produced on the Persian Gulf but also made in Venice), and other similar materials, and lined with marten, weasel, and other furs. They wore colored, fur-lined slippers on their feet, closed with buttons or laces, and long, tight-sleeved dresses inside the fur mantles that reached down to the floor. Silk veils or silk nets called *poste* were arranged on their heads.

At the end of this description, Vecellio places the courtesan in her typical professional ambiance:

Courtesans especially favor these head veils fastened with buttons and bows. They also wear more elaborate skirts than other women. And even though they are forbidden to wear pearls at home, they wear them as well as other jewelry, including valuable earrings. Courtesans stand at their windows making amorous signs to whoever interests them, displaying an astute haughtiness. After frequenting a Venetian patrician, they grab onto his family name, using it as their own and thus fooling many foreign men who come to the city and mistake them for Venetian ladies. Procuresses lend a helping hand. When a foreigner expresses the desire to enjoy the favors of a highborn lady, a procuress dolls up some common prostitute, then leads her and him to a secret meeting-place with so much ceremony that he is taken in and believes she's a noblewoman. Not knowing what Venetian noblewomen are like—namely, that they care deeply about their respectability, the foreigners go around bragging that they have slept with them when this is as far from the truth as one could get!

Venetian courtesans disguised themselves as, and pretended to be, ladies, in order to effect their ends, but there was one fashion in which both categories could openly indulge: dyeing their hair blond. Vecellio's account of how they accomplished this renders his engraving of the scene even more fascinating:

VENETIAN WOMEN DYEING THEIR HAIR BLOND
It is customary, in Venice, to erect square, wooden, open loggias on top of houses, called *altane*. There, the greater part of the women of Venice devoted themselves intensely to the art of dyeing their hair blond, employing different kinds of washes and rinses especially devised for this purpose. They choose the hottest moment of the day to sit there, enduring great discomfort in order to achieve the desired result. Dressed in a particular sort of gown of silk or very thin cloth that is called a *schiavonetto* [a Dalmatian-style dress fashionable in Venice in the fifteenth

and sixteenth centuries], and wearing—to protect themselves from the sun—a lightweight straw hat called a *solana* with a hole on top, through which they pull the hair, the women wet their locks with a small sponge attached to a slender stick, while admiring themselves in a mirror.

Fortunately, a few beauty manuals of the Renaissance survive, one of them Giovanni Marinello's *Gli ornamenti delle donne* (*Ways for Women to Adorn Themselves*, Venice, 1562).[5] Volume II supplies various formulas for obtaining an effective Venetian bleach: for example, "You will obtain reddish-brown hair if you boil in pure water vine ashes together with barley shafts, twig-bark, peeled and chopped licorice wood, and a lime. Make a concoction of these ingredients; pour it off. Wash your hair, let it dry, then apply this liquid. Your hair will be shiny strands of gold."

A simple recipe involves some familiar food items: "Take the dried dregs of white wine and chop them up into olive oil. Comb this through your hair while sitting in the sun." A more exotic one counsels burning ivy bark, then sprinkling the ashes into boiling water, and pouring it off when it has reduced itself by half. "Boil in this liquid hayseeds and endive flowers, then strain."

A delightful parody of these recipes (some manuals give different ones for each major region of the peninsula) appears in one of Andrea Calmo's fictional letters to courtesans—in this case, to Signora Egidia. To keep her skin soft she is advised to make an absurd brew of such ingredients as ass's milk, sugared alum, and the yolks of twenty eggs.

Other texts describe the appearance of gentlewomen and—by extension—the courtesans who mimicked them. According to a traveler of the time,

Venetian ladies wear gowns padded in front and behind. Their blond hair is worn delicately braided and lifted up in front to form two tall horns almost half a foot high. These are kept in place by artful twisting alone. On their heads they wear only a veil of black crepe falling below their shoulders. However, they take care that this veil should not hide the beauty of their hair, their shoulders, and above all their breasts: in fact, they show themselves nude almost down to their stomachs! They seem a foot taller than their husbands because they wear wooden shoes at least a foot high covered in leather. Thus, they need one maidservant to help them walk and another to

HOW PROSTITUTES IN VENICE DRESSED

Public prostitutes operating in infamous places do not dress all alike. They may be all of a kind in another sense, but their various economic levels determine wide differences in the quality of their clothes. Nevertheless, most of them wear a somewhat masculine outfit: silk or cloth waistcoats adorned with conspicuous fringes and padded like young men's vests, especially those of Frenchmen. Next to their bodies they wear a man's shirt, more or less delicate according to what they can spend, that arrives below the knees, and over it they wrap an overskirt or a silk or cloth apron reaching to their feet, but in the winter season a gown lined in cotton or silk. Their clogs are ten inches high, decorated with fringes, their stockings embroidered silk or cotton, Roman slippers placed inside the clogs. Many of them wear men's breeches, often of ormesin [a kind of silk manufactured in Venice similar to that made in Ormuz in the Persian Gulf], and one instantly recognizes them for what they are because of these trousers and certain little round pieces of silver they use as ornaments. It is difficult to describe their hairdos, especially since one seldom sees them at the window; usually they stand in doorways and on the streets in order to draw passersby into their web. They try to be entertaining by singing little love songs, but most of them sound hoarse and off-key, as women of that low condition well might.

Cesare Vecellio, *Habiti antichi e moderni di tutto il mondo*, Venice, 1590

carry the train of their dress. You see them moving slowly, solemnly along, showing their breasts, whether they are young or old.[6]

In the case of Venetian wives whose jealous husbands hoarded them at home and brought them out only on official occasions, one can well understand the efficacy of such garb, especially the high clogs, which required that the women be accompanied and hence surveyed. But in the case of courtesans, it could only have been a fashion, for freedom of motion and inconspicuousness were necessary to most of their actions. A delicious contrast invests the image of the Venetian lady just now painted— her black veil oscillates in the breeze from the canal, revealing the silhouette of naked, round, firm breasts. In the "get-up" of the courtesan, the contrast is even more fascinating, for her long, formal skirt often concealed a pair of men's breeches. Evidently courtesans needed to switch, from one instant to the next, from simulacrum of respectable lady to enticing gamine free to move about the city

in disguise. The ambiguity must have been appealing to the men of that time, who enjoyed mingling the natural and "unnatural" ways of making love, often keeping male lovers and alternating them with their chosen courtesans.

Whatever the reason, the masculine mode was favored by both courtesans and prostitutes, as another descriptive passage from Vecellio attests. Masculine clothing was *à la mode* not only in Italy. Brantôme cites several examples in France, the most prominent person mentioned being Marguerite de Navarre. Brantôme himself seems captivated by the effect she creates: "Marguerite's masculine outfit suits her well, and her Adonis-like face bewilders you so you cannot tell whether she is male or female. She could just as well be a charming boy as the beautiful lady she is" (*La vie des dames galantes*, p. 67).

Of course, nothing abetted the use of disguises more than the practice of wearing masks at carnival time. Venetian courtesans took every advantage of

Anonymous, *Venetian Courtesan* (engraving). About 1590. The Elisha Whittelsey Fund, 1955,
The Metropolitan Museum of Art, New York. Top: Courtesan with raised skirt showing trousers.
Bottom: Courtesan with skirt lowered

Giacomo Franco, *Carnival Maskers* from *Habiti delle donne venetiane*. Venice, 1628. Early 17th century. Biblioteca del Civico Museo Correr, Venice

Giacomo Franco, *Maskers Throwing Rotten Eggs at Courtesans* from *Habiti delle donne venetiane*. Venice, 1628. Biblioteca del Civico Museo Correr, Venice

the opportunity to conceal their identities. They mingled with other maskers. Sometimes pranks were played on them. In an engraving by Giacomo Franco, maskers gather in Campo San Stefano at midnight for their traditional revels. In another, holiday makers throw rotten eggs at courtesans appearing at their windows.

Naturally, the Church did not look kindly on transvestitism and excessive masquerading, and the Venetian Republic also hastened to condemn these practices. But the main objection of the lawmakers and courts was the extraordinary amount of money spent on clothes in general at this time. In order to stem the tide of extravagance, officials instituted sumptuary laws throughout Italy in the sixteenth century. These documents make an important contribution to the history of customs, since they put every aspect of daily life under minute scrutiny: weddings and funerals, baptisms, banquets, balls,

theatrical events, domestic furnishings, men's and women's dress, jewelry, and gondolas.

The earliest of the Venetian laws—written in Latin at the end of the thirteenth century—regard, in incredible detail, patricians' marriage ceremonies. In 1512, the Venetian "Magistrato alle Pompe" (High Commission on Luxury) was established, headed by three Provveditori. Later, these commissioners collaborated with the "Provveditori alla Sanità" (High Commission on Public Health) in regulating prostitution.

Strange as it may seem today, the Venetian Senate often turned its attention to ladies' garments, issuing some quite harsh decrees against excessive luxury in clothes. The senators thought fit to prohibit both expensive materials and new fashions in general, which always mean the investment of ever more funds.

One of the precious materials outlawed by the

Venetian Senate was *restagno* (a delicate cloth woven with gold and silver, manufactured in Venice and exported to the Orient), together with certain rare types of silk. They judged particular dress styles ugly and immoral, noting that they had never been seen before in that city. These decrees are rich in curious details—for example, lawmakers inveighed against such seemingly innocuous innovations as "cut sleeves" (*maniche tajade*), especially "sleeves perforated and inset with ribbons of velvet or silk," a favorite style among gentlewomen and courtesans alike, seen in all its splendor in portraits such as Holbein's *Magdalena Offenburg as Lais Corinthiaca* and Titian's *La Bella.*

Another object of disparagement was the train, something Fra Bernardino da Siena called a diabolical "tail." Improbable as it seems, members of the Senate and the Provveditori alle Pompe earnestly debated the length of train that should legally be allowed. But even common whores wore trains held up by their servants.

There was more than an economic motive, however, for condemning the use of the high clogs often covered over with cloth of gold or silver and richly embroidered, that Venetian women favored. Although these kept the hems of elegant gowns from trailing on the ground and through the mud, they often caused falls, producing injuries and, worse, miscarriages in pregnant women. Hence the state, in prohibiting the high *pianelle*, was protecting its own—in this case, demographic—interests. Again, Venetian women were reluctant to sacrifice a fashion they loved, especially since many were somewhat short and longed to seem taller. An amusing print of the sixteenth century shows a rather heavyset, elaborately dressed Venetian courtesan on her

A COURTESAN DRESSED AS A MAN

In a letter from Pietro Aretino of March 1547 to La Zufolina, a courtesan from Pistoia known for her wit, the writer remarks on her hermaphroditic appearance:

Twice my good fortune has sent your fair person into that house which is mine and others—the first time as a woman dressed like a man and the next time, as a man dressed like a woman. You are a man when you are chanced on from behind and a woman when seen from in front. . . .

Certain it is that nature has so compounded you of both sexes that in one moment you show yourself a male and in the next a female. Indeed, Duke Alessandro [de Medici] did not wish to sleep with you for any other reason than to find out if you were a hermaphrodite in reality or merely in jest. For look you, you talk like a fair lady and act like a pageboy. Anybody who did [not] know you would think that you were now the rider and now the steed—i.e., now a nymph, and now a shepherd; that is, now active and now passive.

What more can I say? Even the clothes which you wear upon your back, and which you are always changing, leave it an open question whether my she-chatterbox is really a he-chatterbox, or whether my he-chatterbox is really a she-one. Meanwhile, even Dukes and Duchesses are diverted by the entertainment of that very salty, very spicy prattle of yours. Vaporishly it escapes from your lips. Your conversation is like pine-nut tartlets, like honey on the comb, like marchpane, to those who find it amusing. Neither Florence nor Ferrara would want you to be a housecat, who are a sly fox amid the hens and roosters.

Pietro Aretino, *Lettere*, VI, p. 249 (trans. Thomas Chubb)

Anonymous, *A Venetian Courtesan Assisted by Two Maidservants*. Bibliothèque Nationale, Paris

High clogs (*pianelle*) (modern photograph). Venetian, 16th century. Museo Correr, Venice

THE COURTESAN IN ROME AND VENICE

high clogs accompanied by two maidservants, one steadying her and the other holding her train. A rare brochure in the Biblioteca Nazionale Marciana in Venice rails against courtesans and their fancy dress, mostly—for dozens of lines—against the mode of the *pianelle*.

Perhaps the oddest corner of legal history anywhere in the world is the Venetian government's veritable obsession with pearls. The reason for this concern, responsible for a long section of the important ordinance against luxury of 1562, is that pearls age, in that era diminishing in value. Lawmakers were furious when they found Venetian women blithely ignoring the law or, rather, interpreting it in specious ways. "One strand" had been allowed, but now women wore chains of pearls all the way down to their waists. Since the 1533 law had been unfairly read by the female sector of the population, the wording now specified "no pearls on the hair or on the breast, and only a single strand around the neck and not going down to their skirts."

No limitations on exotic pets existed, although this was a quite visible and extravagant habit of Venetian women, particularly courtesans, who kept songbirds in cages on their windowsills. One of the best-known portraits of Venetian courtesans, and one of the earliest—Vittore Carpaccio's *Two Courtesans*—shows two bizarre figures seated on their well-furnished rooftop *altana*, surrounded by dogs, peacocks and exotic birds, idling away the time between clients.

Gondolas had become overly ornate and costly, and the government outlawed the use of gold and silver and precious materials here, too. Venetian gondolas had arched cabins where passengers could ride unseen: these were often draped with tapestries or silk. Carriages were similarly controlled.

Naturally, the lawmakers made a fuss about interior decoration. Indeed, as in the case of clothing, the proscriptions against excess disclose a great deal about how great houses were furnished in that period. The following ordinance, a compendium of objects courtesans were forbidden to wear or to own, gives a good idea of the irresistible temptations. The date is again 1562, year of major reform of the sumptuary law.

Prostitutes of this city are forbidden to wear gold, silver, or silk, except for caps made of pure silk. They are not to wear chains, rings set with precious stones, or any other kind of ring or earring. In addition, they are not to wear any jewels, real or false, and this applies both inside and outside their houses, even when they are outside the city. Furnishings must conform in every way to the law. There should not be anything of silk in the house. Forbidden are tapestries, fancy materials on the walls, elaborate headboards [*spalliere*], decorated chests, gilded leathers [*cuori d' oro*]. Instead, prostitutes are to use only Bergamasque or Brescian materials [rough materials manufactured on the mainland, mainly for export], fifty percent wool, plainly striped or colored as they are nowadays. They are not allowed to slash these materials [in order to insert, ribbon-style, more precious ones]; if they do, they will be fined 10 ducats the first time and banished the next time.[7]

In order to enforce these laws, which few took seriously, the authorities bribed informers, in a way that today seems unfair. They offered slaves their freedom, and free men a handsome portion of the fines collected as a reward. Nevertheless, noblewomen bought their exemption from similar laws, and courtesans usually chose to ignore the restrictions.

The setting in which she appeared was crucial to the courtesan—it was the jewel box in which the jewel of herself was radiantly displayed. Like the dwellings of patricians, the palaces of Venetian courtesans offered both an external and an internal splendor and majesty. Often these palaces had ceilings decorated in stucco, gold-stamped or arabesque-patterned leather along the lower portions of the walls, and tapestries or heavy silks covering the rest. In the pavements, semiprecious stones and mother-of-pearl might be inset in marble dust. There were paintings and small sculptures and various *objets d'art* scattered around the tables on which a small volume of Petrarch, together with other volumes, would be prominently displayed. The furniture was of rare wood, often gilded, and even the andirons were sometimes of finely worked silver.

Every material that came near the courtesan had to be of the highest quality. Her sheets were always of silk; her silk pillowcases were embroidered with gold and silver thread and decorated with pearls and jewels. Every empty surface was piled with brocade, velvet, and satin cushions. It was above all in the

Hans Holbein the Younger, *Magdalena Offenburg as Lais Corinthiaca.* 1526. Oeffentliche Kunstsammlung, Basel

Titian, *La Bella.* 16th century. Palazzo Pitti, Florence

Vittore Carpaccio, *Two Courtesans*. 16th century. Museo Correr, Venice

A WRITER'S FANTASY

Last night I was sleeping on my back on the mezzanine near a little orchard of mine. Just before dawn I thought I saw myself, blond, dressed in white, a purse full of silver at my side, walking along an alley with globes of pomegranates on one side and quinces on the other. Every four steps I came upon a laurel, a medlar, a peach tree, a sorb, a chestnut, a fig, a pear tree, an orange tree, and a cypress. On the ground there sprouted little twigs of jasmine and myrtle. Birds sang every variety of song.

Finally, I found a doorway fashioned entirely of damask roses, with a palm and an olive set like pilasters at each side, which led to a great courtyard filled with every variety of flower found in nature. In the middle was a fountain on a bronze pedestal made of porphyry, alabaster, and serpentine, with many figures done in ivory. Being tired, I sat down. Immediately two fairies came toward me. "Welcome," they said. "Welcome to you, too, sweet daughters," I replied. "Forgive me if I have dared to enter a place where I was not invited." They answered: "Dear Sir, it is of no matter. Indeed, you are desired by a gallant lady who wants everything good for you. If you stay, she will be gratified by your presence and adore you." I quickly bowed four times and said ten polite phrases.

Then we walked toward a high magnificent loggia paved with marble, where there were more than one hundred gilded doors with the lady's coat-of-arms painted on them. At one end was a tribunal covered with tin holding up a chair inscribed with these words: "The throne of Venus, daughter of Jove." Since it was time to eat, the fairies led me into a garden full of cedars where a group of winged youths naked except for a light blue veil across the most delicate parts greeted me, pouring mingled scented waters over my hands. I hardly need to tell you what a fine repast we had. After dinner we were served excellent sweets rivaling those of Cairo, while we listened to lutes, lyres, harpsichords, horns, fifes, organs and flutes.

When everything was cleared away, a mattress of crimson satin was placed on a little lawn and three coverlets of yellow, green and turquoise silk set on it one above the other, so that I might rest and digest my meal. In the blink of an eye, five maidens wearing the finest cambric worked in vertical ribbons began to sing suave melodies. Then the fairies led me to Madame Venus whose feet I kissed. She was sitting on the tribunal accompanied on one side by the nine muses and on the other by marine goddesses and woodland sylphs. Behind her were the Graces who came forward and embraced me like a brother.

Other appropriate ceremonies followed, whereupon the doors opened and women came forth. I saw Judith, Bathsheba, Esther, Semiramis, Olympia, Helen, Cassandra, Penelope, Dido, Phaedra, Lavinia, Lucretia, Faustina, Ortensia, Luciana, Angelica, Marphisa, Bradamante, Altabella, Thisbe, Fiordelise, Dama Roenza, and numerous others whose names I have forgotten. They all sat down and debated my coming there and the love I bear for you. They voted with little counters to give me three tiny receptacles, the first containing balsam to let you stay just the way that you are, and the third containing a powder for removing excessive hair on your body. Then I departed, bidding them farewell, kissing the hands of each of those lovely ladies. . . .

Lettere di A. Calmo, IV, 24

boudoir that the courtesan had the responsibility of exciting the senses and plunging her visitor into an irresistible atmosphere of luxury and sensual pleasure. Beds were inlaid or painted, sometimes with scenes from mythology and romances, and satin canopies billowed over them. The ceiling of the room could be decorated with appropriately lascivious depictions, and no boudoir would have been complete without an ample supply of the famous Venetian mirrors, examples of which appear in numerous paintings showing a young woman or Venus at her toilet and offering us intimate glimpses of beauties at work, studying their own images. Often it is the lover himself, rather than Cupid or a maid, who holds up the mirror. Other accouterments were combs and comb holders, pots for cosmetics, and brushes.

Dining well was surely one of the arts of the Italian Renaissance. Distinguished persons devoted large sections of their letters to descriptions of food and its presentation. Among the letters written to Aretino is one from a Neapolitan gentleman, Alessandro Andrea, apologizing for not having been able to send on certain olives from the south. He begs the writer "to ask Signora Angela Zaffetta, your neighbor and mistress over me to excuse me for not having sent her the cloves. I was not in Barletta [town near Bari in Puglia] long enough. Thank you so much for telling her this, as well as that I kiss her hand. Cloves from Ischia are just as good as those from Puglia, and I will see that she receives some of these" (*Lettere a Aretino*, pp. 180–81).

Angela del Moro ("La Zaffetta") was a Venetian courtesan who often found herself at table with Sansovino, Titian, and Aretino. She was noteworthy for her arts of dissimulation and also for an extraordinary punishment accorded her, to be discussed later.

It might have been Angela or any number of other Venetian courtesans about whom Niccolò Franco was thinking when, in a familiar letter entitled "Epistle to Whores," he credited courtesans with having reintroduced epicurean delights into the Italian social world: "Not only have you revived a lost age [i.e., a Golden Age], but you have brought it back in grand style, eliminating every-

Follower of Titian, *Allegory* (Alfonso d'Este and Laura Dianti?). 16th century. Samuel Kress Collection, 1939, National Gallery of Art, Washington, D.C.

thing rustic and coarse. Instead of acorns, blackberries, and strawberries, you propose sumptuous platters and set elaborate tables covered with richly woven cloths appropriate for such delicate foods" (*Le pistole vulgari*, f. 223v).

Such refinement was not confined to Venice. The Roman Imperia's gourmet tastes are enshrined in an amusing story that provides insight into the close-knit quality of the elite world around the Roman curia and the importance to Romans of even small pleasures. Paolo Giovio relates an anecdote about one of those polished parasites who frequented gentlemen's houses: he spotted a fine grayling at the fish market, and since by law a part of every fish over a certain size had to be offered to the Conservatori of the city, he took the prize to the Capitol hoping to be invited to sup. But from there the fish passed, as a gift, from cardinal to cardinal, arriving at Agostino Chigi's villa only to be sent on to Imperia. Rushing to her house along with the nomadic gift, the man was at last able to enjoy what he had been coveting all day.

Jan II van Grevenbroeck, *Courtesan* (watercolor).
18th century. Museo Correr, Venice

Jan II van Grevenbroeck, *Knight of Company of the
Hose* (watercolor). 18th century. Museo Correr,
Venice

Giovanni Bellini, *Young Woman at Her Toilet*. 16th century. Kunsthistorisches Museum, Vienna

AN ENGLISH WRITER VIEWS THE VENETIAN COURTESAN

Thomas Coryat journeyed from his native Somerset to Venice in 1608 when he was thirty years old. Among the sights he took in was the legendary Venetian courtesan:

For thou shalt see her decked with many chaines of gold and orient pearle like a second Cleopatra, (but they are very litle) divers gold rings beautified with diamonds and other costly stones, jewels in both her eares of great worth. A gowne of damaske (I speake this of the nobler Cortizans) either decked with a deep gold fringe (according as I have expressed it in the picture of the Cortizan that I have placed about the beginning of this discourse) or laced with five or sixe gold laces each two inches broade. Her petticoate of red chamlet edged with rich gold fringe, stockings of carnasion silke, her breath and her whole body, the more to enamour thee, most fragrantly perfumed. Though these things will at the first sight seeme unto thee most delectable allurements, yet if thou shalt rightly weigh them in the scales of a mature judgement, thou wilt say with the wise man, and that very truely, that they are like a golden ring in a swines snowt. Moreover shee will endevour to enchaunt thee partly with her melodious notes that she warbles out upon her lute, which shee fingers with as laudable a stroake as many men that are excellent professors in the noble science of Musicke; and partly with that heart-tempting harmony of her voice. Also thou wilt finde the Venetian Cortezan (if she be a selected woman indeede) a good Rhetorician, and a most elegant discourser, so that if she cannot move thee with all these foresaid delights, shee will assay thy constancy with her Rhetoricall tongue. And to the end shee may minister unto thee the stronger temptations to come to her lure, shee will shew thee her chamber of recreation, where thou shalt see all manner of pleasing objects, as many faire painted coffers wherewith it is garnished round about, a curious milke-white canopy of needle worke, a silke quilt embrodered with gold: and generally all her bedding sweetly perfumed. And amongst other amiable ornaments shee will shew thee one thing only in her chamber tending to mortification, a matter strange amongst so many irritamenta malorum; even the picture of our Lady by her bedde side, with Christ in her armes, placed within a cristall glasse. But beware notwithstanding all these illecebræ & lenocinia amoris, that thou enter not into termes of private conversation with her. For then thou shalt finde her such a one as Lipsius truly cals her, callidam & calidam Solis filiam, that is, the crafty and hot daughter of the Sunne.

Coryat's Crudities, I, pp. 404–5

Banquets, official and private ones as well, were always status symbols, visible extensions of the luxury of domestic surroundings and gardens. At a dinner in Ca'Lando in Venice in honor of the prince of San Severino, guests dined on twenty-two courses, including peacocks, pheasants, partridges and other game birds, some of which were forbidden at various times in the century by the sumptuary laws, as a kind of ecological consciousness exerted itself. Such strange delicacies as gilded bread and gilded ostriches also graced the table on that occasion and Marin Sanudo, the source of this information, claims that even the candles were gilded.

A courtesan could shine at balls, banquets, ex-

Benedetto Caliari, *Venetian Villa*. 16th century. Accademia Carrara di Belle Arti, Bergamo

Paris Bordone, *Portrait of a Woman as Cleopatra*. 16th century. Walters Art Gallery, Baltimore

cursions to islands of the lagoon, and theater parties, but it was at home that she triumphed and reigned supreme. There, in the combined coziness and grandeur of her own chambers she could leisurely introduce her ideals of a cultured and civilized life. In a suggestive portrait of a courtesan in the guise of Cleopatra, she is seated in an armchair, probably in her boudoir (where courtesans received important visitors), as poised and imperious as any queen.

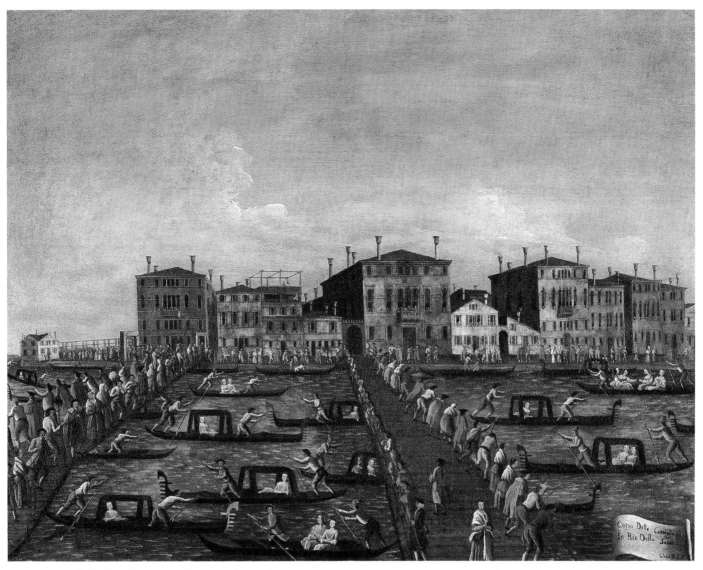

Gabriel Bella, *Courtesans Racing in Rio della Sensa.* 18th century. Galleria Querini-Stampalia, Venice

·Courtesans and Their Lovers·

Because courtesans had such an important function in Italian Renaissance society, their history incorporates the stories of the most influential men of their time—rulers, churchmen, and, inevitably, writers and artists, great numbers of whom strove for a niche in courtesans' hearts as well as for a place in their beds. It is interesting to note how the lovers rewarded their mistresses, in what settings they placed them, and, finally, how the men behaved.

Among the most celebrated of statesmen was Cesare Borgia. His mistress Fiammetta was the first Roman courtesan of the new age to rise to fame. She

was also apparently the first to have been a major property holder, as documented in her will of 19 February 1512, in which she leaves three large houses and an important garden—the *vigna* every courtesan coveted. Fiammetta also endowed a chapel in the courtesans' church, Sant'Agostino, leaving instructions for her own burial there.

Other courtesans of the turn of the century in Rome were Corsetta, La Grechetta, Albina, and Masina. Not unexpectedly, almost all of these were mistresses of great prelates. Masina was a favorite of Julius II before his accession to the papacy. At this

ORGIES AT A WEDDING

The festivities for Lucrezia Borgia's marriage to Alfonso d'Este in 1502 stretched on for weeks. Courtesan participation seems to have been quite marked.

On Sunday evening, October 30th, Don Cesare Borgia gave a supper in his apartment in the apostolic palace, with fifty decent prostitutes or courtesans in attendance, who after the meal danced with the servants and others there, first fully dressed and then naked. Following the supper too, lampstands holding lighted candles were placed on the floor and chestnuts strewn about, which the prostitutes, naked and on their hands and knees, had to pick up as they crawled in and out amongst the lampstands. The pope, Don Cesare and Donna Lucrezia were all present to watch. Finally, prizes were offered—silken doublets, pairs of shoes, hats and other garments—for those men who were most successful with the prostitutes. This performance was carried out in the Sala Reale and those who attended said that in fact prizes were presented to those who won the contest. . . .

. . . December 29th, a race between wild boars was arranged over a course from the Campo di Fiori to the Piazza di San Pietro. The boars were mounted, and those who sat on them used sticks to beat them and kept control of their heads by rings in their snouts, whilst other men guided them along and prevented their running into side alleys. There was also a contest between a great number of prostitutes, and they also ran from the pyramid in the Borgo into the Piazza di San Pietro. Further competitions were staged on the day after, but this time between horses. Races were successively held for the Barbary horses, the light Spanish mounts, and the ordinary cavalry chargers, from the Campo di Fiori to the Piazza di San Pietro, and in these contests there was a great deal of violence and injustice. . . .

The pope then withdrew to the adjoining Sala Paolina, and was followed by Lucrezia with her ladies and many others who all remained in the palace until five o'clock on the following morning.

At the Court of the Borgia, being an Account of the Reign of Pope Alexander VI written by his Master of Ceremonies, Johann Burchard, ed. and trans. Geoffrey Parker (London, 1963), pp. 194–95

---

time, the leading humanists of Rome gathered to discuss cultural matters in splendid settings, such as Angelo Colocci's formal garden outside the Porta del Popolo or another of his near where via Veneto begins to snake up toward Porta Pinciana today. Biagio Pallai, a secretary to popes, who became a bishop, held garden parties and gave suppers to which he invited courtesans, among them Imperia. When not promoting their careers, these men spent their time writing nostalgic Latin verses and ima-

gining that they were still living in the time of the Circus Maximus, the Forum, and the formidable hetaerae of old. The classicists Filippo Beroaldo and Giacomo Sadoleto (who may have been the father of Imperia's daughter, Lucrezia) attended the papal court by day and courted Imperia by night, with precious gifts (from shoes of gold to oysters) and their ardent but always academic verses.

The tone in Rome had already been greatly enhanced when Agostino Chigi, born in Siena in

School of Raphael, wedding banquet from the loggia of Cupid and Psyche. 16th century. Villa Farnesina, Rome

1466, came to Rome around 1487. Here was a banker to kings and popes who was also a patron of the arts and letters, as well as someone who adored beautiful courtesans. While managing business concerns spread through Europe, Africa, and the East (he was one of the richest men in Europe), Agostino indulged in the pleasures of sumptuous dinner parties held alfresco along the Tiber in the most splendid of all Roman villas created in imitation of ancient ones—his Farnesina in Trastevere, legendary for its gardens and loggias as well as the glittering life led there.

From Raphael, Agostino commissioned a chapel in Santa Maria del Popolo and requested the designs for the Loggia of Cupid and Psyche for the Farnesina, even supplying him with a mistress to keep him company as he worked. Since it was partly in honor of Imperia that he built the villa, Agostino arranged for himself and his beloved to be celebrated in the decorative schemes. Enshrined as *Galatea* driving a coach pulled by dolphins through the sea in a room that takes its name from this fresco, Imperia also appears sketchily in the illusionistic garden room in the various depictions of Psyche done by Raphael's disciples. Psyche, according to Ovid and Apuleius, aroused the wrath of Venus by being more beautiful than the goddess: a particularly appropriate theme for celebrating a courtesan.

Agostino's astrological ceiling referring to his birthday and illustrating how fortunate the man was is almost as well known as these other images. Generous and shrewd, called "the Magnificent" by those who admired the extraordinary combination of entrepreneurship and high living, Agostino had the good taste to have chosen the most outstanding mistress of the era, one who seems to have had every desirable quality.

One of the artists called upon to decorate Agostino's pleasure house was Giulio Romano, Raphael's foremost disciple and the painter who, south of Venice, offered the most explicit representations of courtesans. Courtesan life is reflected in his fresco cycle in the Hall of Psyche in the Palazzo del Te in Mantua, especially in the bold depictions of "loves of the gods" scenes such as *Jove and Olympia* amorously intermingling. Earlier, during the years in his native city, Giulio had ample opportunity to paint courtesans and to decorate the places where their lives unrolled. Villa Lante on the Janiculum was conceived as a literary-artistic *hortus* (a garden where philosophical discussions were held in classical times) commemorating the age of Leo X. Baldassare Turini commissioned the villa from Giulio Romano who imitated the style of the Vatican logge. Vincenzo Tamagni painted the two vaulted ceilings, which contain frescoes of eight female per-

LEFT: Raphael, detail from *Galatea*. 16th century. Villa Farnesina, Rome

ABOVE LEFT: Paris Bordone, *Portrait of Ottaviano Grimaldi*. 16th century. Palazzo Rosso, Genoa

ABOVE RIGHT: Paris Bordone, *Portrait of a Woman*. 16th century. The National Gallery, London

RIGHT: Veronese, *Mars Undressing Venus*. 16th century. National Galleries of Scotland, Edinburgh

School of Raphael. female portrait from ceiling of salon, first floor (fresco). 16th century. Villa Lante, Rome

School of Raphael, female portrait from ceiling of salon, first floor (fresco). 16th century. Villa Lante, Rome

sons popularly called "the loves of Raphael." The frescoes are ruined now, but the heavy make-up of some of the women and their decolleté dresses can still be made out.

In his major contributions to the Cupid and Psyche loggia in the Farnesina, Giulio's knowledge of, and identification with, the classical world came into play (the little portraits were supposed to be revivals of the antique and representations of contemporary beauty at the same time). But the most audacious example of Giulio's use of courtesans is in the experiment called *I modi*.

According to tradition, his designs showing sixteen Roman courtesans making love, each in a different way, with prelate and gentlemen lovers, were originally drawn on the walls of the Sala di Costantino in the Vatican in a moment of pique at the Medici Pope Clement VII. Subsequently they were made into prints by the greatest engraver of the Italian Renaissance, Marcantonio Raimondi, and further embellished, in a second edition, with sportive sonnets by Pietro Aretino. As a result of the ensuing scandal, Marcantonio was thrown into the Vatican prison while Giulio, already sought after by Federico di Gonzaga, duke of Mantua, prudently left Rome for his court.[8]

In a painting by Giulio in the Hermitage, there is a scene of a courtesan and her lover in bed with a procuress peeking in indiscreetly at the door that reminds one of an *I modi* illustration. The only difference is that in the latter, the lovers are copulating on the floor. In the work in the Hermitage, the courtesan wears the upper-arm bracelet, the *armilla*, that Venus and Flora often don in Renaissance painting, yet there is little to suggest that this is anything other than a realistic boudoir scene taking place in Cinquecento Rome.

Another painting by Giulio of a courtesan has a mysterious courtyard in the background. The woman portrayed is probably Beatrice of Ferrara who, as previously mentioned, seems to have posed for Raphael's *Fornarina* as well. In both portraits the sitter wears her dark hair in the same style parted in the middle. In the pair of anonymous poems called *Il vanto e il lamento della cortigiana ferrarese*, the first-person narrator, reputedly Beatrice of Ferrara, paints a self-portrait strikingly similar to the physical characteristics seen in the paintings:

> I have two eyes blacker than ravens...
> thin, finely drawn, arched eyebrows...
> coral lips and a sweet smile...
> a lovely forehead and clear features...
> the nose well-etched between roses...
> a neck of snow-white alabaster...
> breasts round and tight as unripe fruit.
> My secret parts are even more beautiful!

Pietro Aretino's sonnets appended to Marcantonio's engravings encourage us to believe it is again Beatrice of Ferrara shown in *I modi*, in an absurd but amusing posture, as she and her lover are pulled in a cart by Cupid.

Beatrice's most prestigious lover was Lorenzo de Medici. In was in honor of Lorenzo and his uncle Giuliano that Giulio constructed a theater in Campidoglio in 1514. At a banquet there, a "Triumph of the Medici Family" was presented onstage, and a long poem celebrating their genealogy recited, in the presence of the Medici pope, Leo X. Lorenzo de Medici, grandson of Lorenzo the Magnificent, son of Pietro II, and nephew of Giuliano, was appointed duke of Urbino by Leo X in 1516. He goes down in history as one of the most assiduous lovers of Renaissance courtesans. A dissipated person whose nocturnal appearances in the city of Florence had little to do with establishing law and order, he was guided in his excursions by the royal pimp named "Fora," a man of base origin who seems to have enjoyed official status. Pimps played the role of boon companions much as buffoons enlivened dinner parties at Pope Leo's court.

Lorenzo enjoyed a variety of dealings with courtesans. In the Archivio di Stato Fiorentino, among the documents dealing with war, diplomatic relations, and internal Medici family matters, is a letter

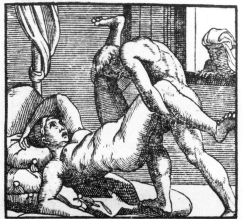

Copy of Marcantonio Raimondi (after Giulio Romano), *Lovers with Procuress* from *I modi*. About 1527. Private collection

Giulio Romano, *Lovers with Procuress*. 16th century. The Hermitage, Leningrad

Copy of Marcantonio Raimondi, (after Giulio Romano), *Lovers in Cart Pulled by Cupid* (Beatrice of Ferrara?) from *I modi*. About 1527. Private collection

Anonymous, *Portrait of Lorenzo de Medici, Duke of Urbino* (medal). 16th century

to Lorenzo from Nicolosa, a Jewish courtesan known for her mastery of the Hebrew psalms, asking for a present. Such letters are quite common in this period, so that we are fortunate to have a singularly uncommon letter to Lorenzo by Beatrice of Ferrara, composed just after she had moved from Florence, where, together with three other courtesans, she had been maintained in style by Lorenzo and some of his friends in a house at Pio outside of the city gates. When his mistress writes Lorenzo from Rome on 23 April 1517, she reveals more about herself than she does about him. At the same time the letter gives a rare glimpse of the intimate and friendly relations between the rulers of Florence and these women of obscure origins.

In this charming letter to the duke, who has just been wounded during the campaign of Urbino, Beatrice asks to be excused for not having written earlier. Unfortunately, her lovers "exhaust [her] with lovemaking night and day." Since it is now Holy Week, however, Beatrice has decided to devote herself to spiritual matters, putting off all her lovers until the following day. She has heard an extraordinary sermon in the church of Sant'Agostino:

All the whores in Rome came to hear that man preach. When he spotted the crowd, he tried to convert all of us. But that was really too hard. He would have had to talk for a hundred years to convince me. Nevertheless, he succeeded in convincing Gambiera to become a nun. . . . I might have been tempted to join the others, but each time it passed my mind I could not do "that thing" any more, I decided against it. In any case, I confessed and then gave the priest two ducats of solid gold. How sorry I am now! (*Lettere di cortigiane*, no. XXXIV).

Although she is "a sinner and a whore," Beatrice has prayed to the Lord for Lorenzo's recovery, and if Lorenzo recovers, she promises she will make a pilgrimage to Santa Maria di Loreto. She kisses his feet.

Three more Medici go down in history as lovers of Renaissance courtesans—Giuliano, Giovanni, and Ippolito. Giuliano de Medici, duke of Nemours, one of the three sons of Lorenzo the Magnificent, and Lorenzo's uncle, showed from the start little aptitude for political life. Gentle and humane, he hated violence and loved pleasure and luxury.

Giuliano was the cultured aristocrat, somewhat passive and self-pleasing but also quite amiable in society. In a copy of a portrait by Raphael (Raphael was attached to the duke's household in 1515), he is shown as a handsome, well-dressed chevalier. This captain of the church wears a large beret and gilded headdress, an overgarment with black silk damascened sleeves, and a large fur collar and cuffs. He is holding a billet. A green curtain behind him has been pulled aside to reveal a view of Castel Sant'Angelo.

Giuliano de Medici seems to have indulged like his nephew Lorenzo de Medici and his friends in the pleasures provided by mistresses. In 1511 he had an affair in Urbino with a widow, Pacifica Brandano, from which union Ippolito de Medici was born. Several letters by Lorenzo describe the veritable orgies in which the duke engaged in Florence. Yet as one of the interlocutors in Baldassare Castiglione's *Courtier*, Giuliano shows a nobler side of himself. We also know that he wrote love sonnets, some of them dedicated to a certain Luigia. It is possible that it is his mistress, a Florentine courtesan or wife, portrayed in the *Gioconda* (*Mona Lisa*) by Leonardo da Vinci and that she may have been present in Rome at a time when everything Florentine was in style and Beatrice and her group were coming from Florence to live there and to appear on the social scene. Giuliano brought Leonardo to Rome with him when he came to sojourn in the city for two years (1514–16). In 1515 he left for France to marry a princess of the Savoy line, then died the next year.

Giovanni de Medici (Giovanni delle Bande Nere) was a *condottiere* whose tragic early death on the battlefield in 1526 was greatly mourned. For Aretino, who loved him dearly, Giovanni was the "new Mars"; that is why the writer was chagrined, if amused, to note Giovanni's amorous escapades that placed him in a far less heroic light.

For example, one time the warrior stopped to visit a mistress in Reggio Emilia, tarrying too long since Aretino says that not only did the captain's "armor rust" but that he also found himself, quite like the ancient Hercules in the grip of Omphale, turning roasts on a spit and performing other household duties. Aretino's Mars must have resembled,

Church of Sant'Agostino, Rome (modern photograph). 16th century

Copy of Raphael, *Portrait of Giuliano de Medici, Duke of Nemours*. 16th century. The Jules Bache Collection, 1949, The Metropolitan Museum of Art, New York

Sodoma, bedroom scene from *Alexander and Roxanne* (fresco). 16th century. Villa Farnesina, Rome

for a moment, the protagonist of various Renaissance "Mars and Venus" configurations, where the gods are viewed in a boudoir caressing each other on a bed, as *amorini* play carelessly with helmet, greaves, breastplate, and sword. The situation recalls the many lascivious *Mars and Venus* scenes by Veronese, as well as *Alexander and Roxanne* by Il Sodoma in his Villa Farnesina fresco cycle. To show a man unmanned by love was not really to make fun of him; it was to reveal him conforming to one of the many roles of the time.

Giovanni's most formidable adventure along these lines was his abduction from Recanati of the Roman courtesan Matrema-non-vole; one of the charming scandals of the time, it proved a boon in the form of publicity for Madonna Matrema. Certainly, Giovanni must have been a dashing lover,

and he may well have been a *duro* with a heart. In his professional life, he was like the heroes of American Westerns—an outlaw for hire who obeys his own rules, instills fear in the enemy, and, when the camera is turned his way, displays a handsome profile and suave figure. The masculine figure in vogue then, however, could embrace culture without reducing his virility. Even in the act of kidnapping, carrying off, and "raping" his chosen courtesan, more or less subjecting her to a few days of erotic holiday on the battlefields, Giovanni delle Bande Nere never forgot the etiquette required of such situations. The letter to one of his officers ordering the abduction is written in a proper Latinate style. No doubt Giovanni smiled to himself when the episode was reported in gossip columns—that is to say, in letters and ambassadorial dispatches—since he knew it would only add luster to the reputation of his "victim."

Giovanni is usually portrayed in armor, such as in portraits by Bronzino and Titian that emphasize his fierce aspect as a *condottiere*. A fine medal portrait of Giovanni also exists by Francesco da Sangallo that has an appropriate winged thunderbolt on the reverse side, together with the inscription "Nihil Hoc Fortius" ("No One Stronger Than He"); one could hardly find a more convincing symbol of virility and power. In an ancient-style Roman toga, proudly showing his profile from the left, the bearded Giovanni, encouraged by flattering publicists like his friend Aretino, undoubtedly perceived himself to be a reincarnation of an elite warrior spirit from the past. His wife, Maria Salviati, shown heavily veiled in her corresponding medal, probably did not have any such illusions about herself.

Ippolito de Medici, illegitimate son of Giuliano and Pacifica Brandano, also had passionately wanted to be a soldier, but instead was made a cardinal by his uncle Leo X in 1529, when the young man was only eighteen years old. He rose to become one of the most influential personages at the pope's court. It was he, for example, who helped obtain the release of the engraver Marcantonio Raimondi from the papal prison after the episode of *I modi*.

In 1532, when Clement VII sent Ippolito as apostolic legate at the command of troops under Charles V in an expedition against the Turks threatening Vienna, Ippolito took his brilliant court with him onto the battlefield. Titian's portrait shows Ippolito just after this adventure, dressed as a Hungarian margrave and wearing a tricorn hat.

Ippolito was considered to have been the most fashionable man at Caterina de Medici's marriage in Marseilles a year later. Handsome, courteous, scintillating, liberal, his outward person and temperament corresponded to the highest Renaissance ideals. No wonder he appeared desirable in the eyes of courtesans.

On a visit to Venice, where he was honored by the Spanish ambassador, Ippolito was entertained by the courtesan Angela del Moro, assiduous habitué at the dinners of Aretino, Jacopo Sansovino, and Titian. To imagine the two together we have

Francesco da Sangallo, *Portrait of Giovanni delle Bande Nere* (medal). 16th century

Titian, *Portrait of Ippolito de Medici*. 16th century. Galleria degli Uffizi, Florence

only to glance at Paris Bordone's portrait of a woman that supposedly represents Angela and Titian's fine portrait alluding to the campaign in which the cardinal had recently taken part.

Ippolito was also driven to love an entirely different kind of woman—the great beauty Giulia Gonzaga, who was caught up in the fervent Catholic-Reformist activities around Renée of France, wife of Ercole d'Este. Ippolito was never able to break through Giulia's elegant reserve. It was during a visit to Giulia's villa in Fondi that Ippolito met his early death either from exhalations of the Pontine marshes or, as some believe, by poison at the instigation of his cousin, the tyrant of Florence, Alessandro de Medici.

In the early 1530s, Ippolito wrote a sonnet for the Roman courtesan Tullia d'Aragona, who had risen to become the epitome of the refined hetaera. This is not surprising since Ippolito was a devoté of mistresses and the muses, and, for her part, Tullia was used to receiving homages from men like Claudio Tolomei, Latino Giovenale, Ercole Bentivoglio, Bernardo Tasso, Benedetto Varchi, and Girolamo Muzio. The history of Italian *belles lettres* in this period seems to have been scribbled carelessly across her datebook.

So celebrated was Tullia by her contemporaries, that it is logical to leave both her physical and psychological description to the writers and artists who strove to portray them. Shortly, we shall see her painted both in words and in oils, the two widely contrasted portraits—one realistic and one idealistic—providing an *aperçu* into the complex nature of the courtesan.

Tullia distinguished herself by writing not only poetry but also a dialogue on love conforming to the abstract modes of the time. (As an interlocutor in another dialogue, by Sperone Speroni, one of her lovers, she was able to speak out more frankly in favor of sensual love.) Tullia was perhaps most exalted by the poet Girolamo Muzio who, among other epithets, gave her the name Tirrhenia, after the sea lapping the Western shore of Italy, and even recounted her biography.

Some verses by Muzio to Tullia were so ardent they risked being in bad taste, inviting the courtesan to receive her "fired-up lover" joyfully in her lap with wide-open arms. But when Cardinal Ippolito addressed lines to her, they spoke of her "enchanting eyes" and a particular way of laughing and, in general, were somewhat ethereal. "Beautiful spirit," he said to her, "you revolve within your own divine luminosity."

Ippolito's tribute to Tullia associates him with yet another Florentine lover, the only man whose attractiveness and elegance equalled his and one who, at that moment, was deeply infatuated with Tullia. The two men had other significant points of contact as well, for they were united by their sympathy for the Republican exiles from Florence and relied on each other in this at once political and spiritual commitment.

Filippo Strozzi, son of the founder of the banking family whose impressive palace still draws tourists and is the site of an annual antiquarian show, was the richest citizen of the city. His tragic life, beset with difficulties and punished with an early death, was one of the most romantic and adventurous of the Renaissance. As a prisoner of the Medici, he became immortalized for his heroism and ideological fervor. Even the often rigid Vittoria Colonna intervened in a vain effort to save his life.

At forty-three, when he became the lover of Tullia d'Aragona in Rome, Filippo was an accomplished politician, an experienced banker, a fighter for his beliefs, and a consummate lover, in addition to being an excellent musician who sang in the Florentine choirs during Holy Week. Given all these qualities and the worldliness he must have possessed, it is fascinating to see Filippo having to be wary of a courtesan's power and influence around the court. It was essential, in fact, not to reveal too much to Tullia.

Even though he had sided with the Republican cause at the time of the Sack of Rome, and had even been put on trial for treason shortly before his marriage to Clarice de Medici, Filippo never ceased abetting this struggle, whether publicly or secretly. Nevertheless, at this time, he was being drawn into a scheme engineered by Pope Clement VII for setting up the Medici once more in Florence. In the summer of 1530, Florence had capitulated to the combined forces of the newly allied pope and emperor. Now the pope was taking measures to concentrate power in the hands of Alessandro de Medici (supposedly the bastard son of Lorenzo, duke of Urbino) who, as despised tyrant of Florence, would be struck down in 1537 by his nephew Lorenzaccio. The assassin was fired not only by personal motives of rivalry, but also by the same Republican spirit that had initially moved Filippo Strozzi.

In 1531 Clement wanted Filippo to fund the construction of a fortress in Florence in which the imperial garrison would be stationed. The wealthy banker agreed, unaware that he would soon die tragically within those very stone walls. While arrangements were being made for the loan, Filippo dallied with Tullia, writing sonnets for her and possibly sharing knowledge of some of his secret affairs. In a letter from Francesco Vettori, the Florentine historian and diplomat, to Filippo in Rome, Vettori scolds his friend for not being more cautious in such a delicate moment:

I cannot understand why you must write to me with Tullia by your side. I must ask you not to read my letters when she is present. I know that you love her for her spirit (looks alone would not explain the attraction), but do not let the extent of your attachment put me in the position of being criticized by those whom I talk about in my letters.

Evidently, Tullia had the best connections at the papal court. In his cautionary letter Vettori goes on to beg Filippo not to fight in a collective duel in honor of Tullia that was presently being organized more for show than anything else, since "very few men like you are born in any one century."[9]

Filippo is necessarily tactful with Tullia, but fifteen years earlier, when he was the leader of the band of young men giving themselves over to pleasures of every kind in Florence, Filippo showed an unreasonably cruel disposition, as well as a propensity for debauchery, having—as his mistress of the time, Camilla of Pisa, puts it tartly in one of her confiding letters to their friend Francesco del Nero—"enough women and young men, both adolescents and little boys, that you might think he would be satisfied . . . and not look for more!"

Perhaps those exploits would have upset her less if Filippo had not tormented her with jests, among them an attempt, apparently unsuccessful, to turn Camilla and friends of hers over to a group of men for their pleasure. The most wicked trick that Filippo plays on Camilla, a woman who seems really to have loved him, is to pretend that she is infected and must go to the Hospital for the Incurables for an examination. The lovely courtesan, who devotes herself to poetry and music, is visibly upset.

By some miracle of preservation, we have a record of Camilla's reactions to the twists and turns of this love affair. Hers is a tremulous though sometimes adamant voice, one worth listening to, however, for what she has to say places in a curious perspective those men who juggled the future fortunes of Florence.

· CAMILLA OF PISA'S LETTERS ·

What must it have been like being the mistresses of such men? Did a woman feel free to "be herself"? Aretino was fond of contrasting the lives of the courtier and the courtesan, in order to point out that the latter enjoyed greater freedom. An emblematic passage in Francesco Pona's series of related novellas called *La lucerna* offers perhaps the most eloquent lines on this subject:

Freedom is the most precious gem a courtesan possesses and contains within itself everything she desires. Given this privilege, even infamy seems honorable to her. Since

she is not subject to the tyranny of husbands or parents, she can deliver herself to her lovers without fear of being killed for reasons of honor. In this way she is free to express natural appetites and feminine lasciviousness (*La lucerna*, p. 109).

Working on her own, the courtesan could elude some of the obligations and humiliations suffered by courtiers serving a master. But her daily life involved emotional difficulties that hampered this sense of freedom. Sensitive women called upon to love, courtesans naturally formed sentimental

Rosso Fiorentino, decorative ensemble. 16th century. Galerie de François I, Fontainebleau

bonds and took on obligations beyond their written or unwritten contracts, letting themselves be humiliated and punished "for love." Jealousy on the part of lovers, outrageous demands, absences and abandonments, cruel and irrational behavior had to be endured. Courtesans participated in an ongoing drama from which they may well have sometimes wished to escape. This drama has to some extent eluded the attention of historians and literary critics, since it was lived in private.

The court, where every action was observed, judged, and regulated was not the stage for courtesans, but rather the boudoir—a more intimate and hidden place, where lovers could vent all their passions and sometimes indulge in perverted behavior. When the curtains were drawn, lovers such as Lorenzo de Medici, duke of Urbino, and Filippo Strozzi psychologically undressed. A collection of letters by courtesans in the Archivio di Stato Fiorentino (*Lettere di cortigiane del XVI secolo*, a cura di Luigi Ferrai, Florence, 1884) reveals how difficult these men could be. To have been an official concubine must have been a demanding task requiring Machiavellian manipulative skills, as well as a self-controlled exterior.

The house at Pio outside the Porta San Gallo, where Camilla of Pisa, Beatrice of Ferrara, Alessandra of Florence, and a young woman named Brigida were installed around 1514 by a group of friends including Lorenzo de Medici, duke of Urbino; his brother-in-law Filippo Strozzi; Francesco del Nero, a relative of Machiavelli's; and Francesco degli Albizzi must have been extremely elegant if frescoes were painted for it by Rosso Fiorentino, the Italian painter who went on to fill the gallery of Francis I at Fontainebleau with erotic paintings and decorations. (Rosso also provided designs for Jacopo da Caraglio's licentious Loves of the Gods series). Unfortunately, no trace of the frescoes remains. This pleasure house functioned as a kind of private harem where the men went when they pleased to enjoy the company and charms of women who had groomed themselves for this purpose.

At times the correspondence between the powerful men of Florence and their honest courtesans suggests nothing other than the atmosphere of a college sorority house. Such a comparison is understandable: the women were young and at the very beginning of their careers. (By 1517 all of them are to be found firmly established in Rome, in private houses.) One courtesan writes to the lover of another to assure him that his sweetheart loves him; concern is expressed about recurrent illnesses. This collective spirit is touching, offering us yet another dimension of Renaissance life. Indeed, so domestic is the spirit of the arrangement that Camilla signs her letters to Francesco del Nero, Alessandra's lover, "Your sister-in-law":

If we wanted to thank you for all your courtesy toward us, gold, silver, and the greatest treasure in the world would hardly suffice. Let us not even discuss the matter, my sweet brother-in-law, since you and the others have beat us at this game. Indeed, even if we searched the whole world, we would never find two men so nice, so virtuous, so well-mannered, so gracious, and so free-spending as the two of you, merciful as Caesar, liberal as Alexander, and wise as Solomon. If we adore you and have elected to have you as our sole masters, we had an excellent reason for doing so. The only thing we beg of you is to call on your usual humanity reciprocating our devotion with your own precious and most desirable affection . . . .

Your sister-in-law [Camilla of Pisa][10]

This is Camilla of Pisa playing at being a wife but also, it seems, at being a courtesan. The high literary style she uses, with its Latinate syntax, is a naive yet not disastrous example of the vogue at that time in more or less formal correspondence. She and her friends were involved in more than a game, although the men teased the women in elaborate ways. Camilla tried to keep her dignity and not spoil the fun, even though already in the following brief letter, again to Francesco del Nero, an underlying anxiety emerges:

I am not going to say anything about Filippo's return. Now more than one of you is playing tricks on me. You men play so many deceitful games with us that we are going to stop caring about you. I hardly know how to convince myself that what you are saying is the truth. I called out to you so many times "hey, hey, hey" that I feel weak. Next time you can bleat like lambs, and I won't even give you the time of day. Tell Giovanni [Bandini] his pranks worked again, but I intend to get even with all of you some day. Well, that's enough. You are a cageful of crazy men. Alessandra sends her regards.

CP. [Camilla of Pisa] (*Lettere di cortigiane*, no. X)

The real danger lay elsewhere, in the realm of society today called "the establishment." The rigid customs of upper-class Florentine family life made its members sensitive to affronts and concerned to protect the purity of their lineage (although bastards born into noble families often rose to important positions). Clarice de Medici could intercept the precious missives sent between her husband, Filippo, and Camilla, although what the results might have been is incalculable—probably a mere distancing of the man from his mistress, since public scandals were out of the question. Camilla writes:

I was angry, that is true, but I am not sure whether I was right to take it that way. You say my beloved cannot have any sealing wax because you took all of it away last time; now you tell me he has three different kinds. Oh! What am I supposed to think? You must have given it to him! I begin to suspect that [Clarice de Medici] has got control

Jacopo da Caraglio. *Jove and Antiope* from the Loves of the Gods series. 16th century

IC
Giove in Satyro
Che non puo far di Cytherea il figlio
Che 'n mille guise mi trasforma il giorno
Et io cal suo uoler ratto m'appiglio
Spesso per forza a cotal gioco torno
Et ogni faccia mi ueste e piglio
Empiendo 'l ciel d'infamia alto et adorno
E tanto me dame questi rimoue
Che sono al piu del tempo altri che Gioue

School of Titian, *Portrait of Filippo Strozzi*. 16th century. Kunsthistorisches Museum, Vienna

of everything, and that is why I was furious! I wrote one or two lines for you, sending them to Messer Antonio [de Medici] who wrote back as though you had not written me any more letters. That is when I hit the ceiling and began to be convinced not that you were a traitor (as you claim I accused you of being), but rather that perhaps you had taken the easy way out, since it was much more in your interest to please her than to please me, because of the power she has and the fact that you have been a friend of hers for so long whereas you know me only a year (*Lettere di cortigiane*, no. XII).

In this same letter Camilla describes herself as "spontaneous" and someone who dislikes having to dissemble. The following letter gives us a taste of what she was like when she let her anger come to the surface.

Camilla of Pisa to Francesco del Nero:
May God bring misfortune on that woman who at this very moment possesses what is dearest to me in the world! I curse that night, even the moments that my lover spends embraced by arms other than mine. Cursed be the kisses and other acts meant to bring me pain and to injure me. Cursed be his faithlessness! It is unthinkable that a man who has someone who adores him and is ready to serve him rejects her so scornfully. For heaven's sake, I have noticed for two or three months that he was fancying something. Now that he has satisfied his desires, perhaps he will not wander so much. I bear it all as best I can, but if it were anyone other than Filippo I would avenge myself. His high station keeps me from effecting justice. Patience then; there is nothing I can do until he decides to come back (*Lettere di cortigiane*, no. V).

Camilla may have prided herself on being candid, but, given the circumstances, she had to do a certain amount of concealment. Secrecy was even part of the pleasure. In the same letter, Camilla reveals that she is mastering the arts of hermetic correspondence. An intermediary nicknamed "the demon" has given her an unsigned letter that she recognizes to be by Filippo; she has composed her lines so that if they fall into someone else's hands they cannot harm her. In the epistolary novel *Lettere amorose* (*Love Letters*) by Alvise Pasqualigo (Venice, 1581), this secrecy is inflated into a major enterprise, hundreds of pages dedicated to stratagems for hiding and conveying letters, making occult signs, and offering and withdrawing fetishistic gifts. Evidently the lovers' passion was fueled by such difficulties, many of which seem to have been deliberately constructed in order to make the affair that much more piquant.

The choice of each word and phrase in these letters is strategem as well, from Beatrice's queries about Lorenzo's health, Alessandra's "motherly" announcement to Francesco degli Albizzi that the handkerchiefs she is having made for him will soon be ready, or Camilla of Pisa's claim that she does not really need the 10 ducats Filippo has sent to her. The exhaustive parrying of their correspondence shows courtesans had to spend many hours defending themselves, whether from society as a whole or from their lovers.

For example, it emerges from certain complaints in Camilla's correspondence that Filippo amused himself by sending other men to the house at Pio to make love with her and Alessandra. Probably the men could be convinced to go away, but the situation was delicate if not humiliating. "Why does he try to trick me and give me in prey to others," Camilla asks. She was "born free" and does not consider herself anyone's slave. When Filippo threatens as a joke to have her sent to the infamous hospital, Camilla explodes, and for a moment contemplates sending back all of the gifts he has given her.

Despite their superior position, the powerful lovers of courtesans could sometimes be taken off guard. On the last sheet of the manuscript some scribbled notes for a letter from Francesco del Nero to Alessandra paint an embarrassing picture:

Filippo and I with some friends came at once to San Gallo Gate and for a long time, more than an hour, we walked up and down, but it was impossible to catch a glimpse of any of you. It seemed as if we would have to wait forever outside of those walls.

Perhaps there is no simple answer to the question of whether courtesans were truly free, but it is clear from these writings that their independence was precarious. Undoubtedly it is for this reason that some of them, like Angela Greca, turned to marriage.

Angela Greca, who took for herself the classicizing name of "Hortensia," came to Rome at the time of Leo X. According to Zoppino, she had been robbed by certain pimps at Lanciano and, arriving full of mange, was taken to a tavern in Campo di Fiore. Afterward she lived in a little house in Calabraga (Take-your-Pants-Down Street) maintained by a Spaniard, de Alborensis. Because she was attractive and loyal, a courtier of Leo's fell in love with her and elevated her in society. Her skill was to make lovers jealous. Il Coppetta dedicated romantic verses to her (and satirical ones when she left him). It is almost certain that she is the Greek courtesan Brantôme visited in Rome in 1555, considering her a touching reminder of the Golden Age of Leo X.

Satirical sonnets by Aretino tell us that Angela married Ercole Rangone, of the noble Modenese family, a soldier like his famous *condottiere* cousin Ludovico. In the late 1540s Ercole accompanied Anna d'Este to France for her marriage with the duc de Guise, then took up the post of ambassador at the imperial court. Evidently he was never much of a soldier, at least in Aretino's eyes, for the writer dares to poke fun at him in the sonnets, calling him a coward. Aretino's letters report that, in addition to writing Latin and Italian poetry and producing a translation of the Psalms, Ercole was also a fine musician. Perhaps that is why, in the *Sonetti lussoriosi* (*Lustful Sonnets*), Aretino, annoyed with how far Angela has risen in society, suggests that it would have been more appropriate for Ercole to serenade her with a rustic rebec than with lutes and other salon instruments. Again, according to Aretino, it is Angela Greca whom we see making love "frog-style" with Ercole Rangone in *I modi*.

Other courtesans could and did make brilliant matches as well. In the introduction to part IV, 8, of his *Novelle*, Matteo Bandello has Francesco Maria Molza, the poet, who was knifed by Spaniards because of his passion for Beatrice Spagnola, breathlessly relate a rumor:

My dear friends, I have to whisper into your ear if you have not heard it the greatest and most curious piece of gossip. Even if you do not believe it, it is true. The grand lord Gian Francesco Ghiringhello, a wealthy gentleman of Milan, has taken Caterina da San Celso as his wife!

Copy of Marcantonio Raimondi (after Giulio Romano), *Two Lovers in Frog Position* (Angela Greca and Ercole Rangone?) from *I modi*. About 1527. Private collection

Isn't this something? I certainly think so. Undoubtedly you all know this Caterina, since she is a famous courtesan. She has many good things about her since she plays musical instruments and sings extremely well and recites poetry perfectly with a practiced eloquence, and in addition cuts an imposing and handsome figure, and has been so blessed with beauty that she can vie with any in Milan, but at the same time she has continued the disgraceful habits of her mother who was a prostitute and has licentiously given her body over to many men. It would not matter so much if she had done this in private, but she has done it publicly. Otherwise I would not have said a word about it, for being the son of a woman and the husband of a woman, I do not like to say bad things about women. Recently she had another lover in addition to this Ghiringhello, but the latter seems not to have minded. Well, love knows no limits!

Caterina's arts, which won her a new position in society, together with the example of Camilla polishing her letters, suggest that courtesans armed themselves with much more than merely beautiful clothes and good manners.

· THE COURTESAN AND CULTURE ·

As Niccolò Franco suggests, in his "Epistle," courtesans evoked a Golden Age and brought the atmosphere of the ancient world into the modern one. Just as Machiavelli dressed in a toga to "converse" with Pliny and Cicero, courtesans, often wearing classicizing garb, persuaded their admirers that they were not only manifestations of an ancient phenomenon—the hetaera—but also the goddesses and nymphs those women, too, had fantasized being. An alchemy of the imagination took place. Courtesans worked themselves up into states of autoexaltation, using a kind of natural sorcery to become, if only for a moment, what lovers, artists, and they themselves thought they were: priestesses of Venus, sometimes even Venus herself.

Had their relationship to culture, history, and myth been only tenuous—mere pretension—courtesans would have been figures of ridicule for everyone, not only satirical writers and disadvantaged rivals. But something earnest lay behind this striving. Idealizing painters and sculptors handsomely pay homage to it, while writers offer sonnets in the Petrarchan and Bembist modes as well as flowery dedications and letters.

Many passages in literary works in the sixteenth century discuss courtesans' cultural aspirations and achievements. Culture formed an essential aspect of the appeal of these women; without it, they were naked, uncosmeticized, impotent to captivate men of quality. If Imperia learned to write poetry under the tutelage of Niccolò Campano, known as "lo Strascino," Matrema-non-vole was celebrated for enforcing strict rules of good linguistic usage among those in her circle. The "language question" was for a long time a major issue for Renaissance intellectuals; thus Matrema-non-vole's concern for purity and decorum of speech was as fashionable as it was pedantic. The character Ludovico, in *Il ragionamento dello Zoppino*, makes this wry comment about her: "She's just like Cicero and knows by heart the works of Petrarch, Boccaccio, Virgil, Horace, Ovid, and thousands of others."

Similarly, Lucrezia Squarcia is depicted in *La tariffa delle puttane principali di Venezia* (*Price-List of the principal Venetian Whores*) as

carrying around her little volume of Petrarch
and the poems of Virgil and Homer,
often debating the merits of the Tuscan tongue.
(*La tariffa*, p. 24)

The little volume of Petrarch was an indispensable accessory for both ladies and courtesans. A fine example of a *petrarchetto* appears in the remarkable portrait by Bronzino of the Renaissance poet Laura Battiferri, wife of the sculptor Bartolommeo Ammannati.

Whether they read them or not, courtesans also carried prayer books, elegantly bound volumes given to them by their lovers. Even their appearances on sacred occasions had a theatrical atmosphere. What better place to be seen than in the most frequented churches? In *Il ragionamento dello Zoppino*, Lorenzina is pictured as the center of attention when she attends Mass: everyone bows to her and gathers around. Ten men would accompany her, ten follow behind, and two wait for her outside. Matrema, trailed by ten maidservants and ten pages, went to church accompanied by marquis, ambassadors, and dukes; Beatrice of Spain by Spanish noblemen ("Don this" and "Don that"), Angela Greca by counts and lords; Beatrice of Ferrara by prelates, abbots and poets; Tullia d'Aragona by adolescents. A veritable curiosity, Madonna Nicolosa, an elaborately groomed Jewish courtesan, strode through the churches of Rome carrying huge fans, followed by several maidservants as she recited aloud the Psalms in Hebrew. In Venice, another Jewish courtesan—Bellina Hebrea (Beautiful Jewess)—made everyone marvel by singing the Psalms in her superb voice.

Touchingly, a few courtesans are known to us today only as the possessors of sweet singing voices and players of stringed instruments, faculties that seemed to have something divine about them at the time. Take, for example, the Florentine courtesan Nannina Zinzera about whom Antonfrancesco Grazzini (Il Lasca), the poet and *novelliere*, remarks:

> Not even in heaven, among the happy souls,
> is such sweet harmony to be found
> able to move mountains and still winds.
> (*Rime burlesche*, p. 571)

Many courtesans were called "Sirens" for their practiced and alluring voices. In Francesco Pona's *La lucerna* (*The Lamp*), a lamp, having passed through many metempsychoses and finding itself reincarnated as a courtesan from Padua, says of this new self:

I sang like a Siren. Whenever I touched a harp, a lute, or a guitar, and sang along with the melody, I was so vivacious and performed with such feeling that even Senocrates or Anti-Love himself would have swooned with love (*La lucerna*, p. 121).

One of the most praised of all courtesans for her fluid singing voice and ability on the lute was Gaspara Stampa. So admired was Gaspara along these lines that Perissone Cambio, a foremost composer of the time, composed madrigals in her honor and dedicated a book of them to her.

Bronzino, *Portrait of Laura Battiferri*. 16th century. Loesser Collection, Palazzo Vecchio, Florence

Giacomo Franco, *Courtesan with a Lute*. Early 17th century. Biblioteca del Civico Museo Correr, Venice

GASPARA STAMPA'S
"RHETORIC OF SUBMISSION"

Who could recount my present state,
the happiness I feel, the intense delight?—
one of the elect angels who reside in heaven?
perhaps a lover who experienced the same thing?

I always stay close beside my lord,
taking pleasure in his brilliant eyes, his words;
indeed, the lofty thoughts, the divine concepts
formed in that precious intellect sustain me.

Often I gaze upon his lovely face
and, as I contemplate it, seem to see there
all of the glory and well-being of Paradise.

Only one thing threatens the hopes I have—
the fear that he may be separated from me,
for I would have him with me till the last hour.

Gaspara Stampa, *Rime*, CX

Gaspara was one of two major poets of the Italian Renaissance who were courtesans; the other was Veronica Franco. Tullia d'Aragona produced, with the help of Sperone Speroni and other lovers, a volume of verse that, presented to the Medici duke of Florence, obtained her exoneration from the obligation of wearing the yellow veil courtesans customarily donned in that city.

France contributed yet another courtesan poet to the roster, the fervid Louise Labé, glory of her native Lyons, whose personality left its mark on both literature and customs.

Gaspara Stampa was a jeweler's daughter born in Padua around 1525. At her father's death when she was still quite young, she went with her mother, brother, and sister to live in Venice. There she was educated in literature and music by such men as the humanist Fortunio Spira and the composer Perissone Cambio. Her brother, Baldassare, died tragically young, having established a reputation as a lyric poet, and her sister, Cassandra, also a courtesan, became like Gaspara renowned for her musical

talents. Around 1548 Gaspara became the lover of Collaltino del Collalto of Treviso, who left her three years later. Gaspara died shortly thereafter, and he went on to marry a woman of his own rank. The romantic legends that inspired many writers, such as d'Annunzio and Rilke, have fed on the myth that Gaspara committed suicide in despair over her lover's defection. It is now known that she died of a female ailment from which she would probably have recovered today.

From 1548 to 1551, when her lover went twice to France to fight for Henry II and also served in the Po Valley and at the siege of Parma, Gaspara suffered, loved, and wrote. Unlike the defiant courtesans who defended themselves and lashed out at the abuses of their lovers, Gaspara submitted endlessly. Her *canzoniere* recount her long enslavement to the whims of Collaltino, whose sole fault, she says, is "ruthlessness in love." Yet she also admits that she derives creative energy from fierce agitation, and has chosen a cult of suffering as a means of fueling her literary efforts.[11]

Whatever the cost of Gaspara's masochism in her own life, it produced a balance of pleasure and pain that functioned well as a literary topic and as a description of the continual dualism of courtesanry—at once free and bound, exhilarating and humiliating:

> Love made me such that I live in fire
> like a new salamander on earth
> or like that other rare creature, the Phoenix,
> who expires and rises at the same time.
>
> All the joys there are are mine, my game's
> to live burning but not to feel the pain
> and not to care if he who causes this
> has any compassion for me or not.
>
> As soon as the first flame went out,
> Love kindled another, as far as I can tell
> a much stronger and more vital one.
>
> As long as he who stole my heart this time
> stays satisfied with my burning,
> I'll not repent of burning as I love.
>
> _(Rime,_ CXXXIV)

Gaspara's cult of liberty could probably not have existed anywhere but Venice. It was life in the Republic that permitted courtesans the freedom and creative possibilities they needed to function in their careers. Here is Gaspara describing her adopted city:

> These shores I have loved so ardently
> most hallowed and blessed shores in the world,
> dear dwelling place of precious liberty,
> nest of illustrious, tranquil people.
>
> _(Rime,_ CCVIII)

Another courtesan who enjoyed the benefits of the Republic was Veronica Franco, who demonstrated, in addition to her considerable literary talents, a political consciousness, or at least there was an ideological convergence between herself and the state. As long as she identified with Venice, her survival was assured. "Great Dominator from on high of the sea," she apostrophizes, "royal pure, unviolated Virgin/Unparalled, unequaled in the whole world!" Venice is also, for her, the "Earthly Venus." No courtesan loved her city more.

RIME DI MA·
DONNA GASPARA
STAMPA.

CON GRATIA ET
PRIVILEGIO.

In Venetia, per Plinio Pietrasanta.
M. D. LIIII.

Anonymous, frontispiece to Gaspara Stampa's _Rime_ (engraving). 1554. Biblioteca Angelica, Rome

Veronica was born in Venice in 1546. She had three brothers. Her mother, a former courtesan, became her daughter's procuress. When quite young, Veronica married a doctor, Paolo Panizza. She separated from him when she was eighteen, by which time she had given birth to a child by a lover.

Before she was thirty-four Veronica had had six children, not all of whom survived. One who did seems to have been fathered by Andrea Tron of a great patrician family, one by a man named Pizzomano who was tried by the Inquisition for having kept a runaway nun in his house as a concubine, and one by Lodovico Ramberti, the son of an apothecary shop owner at the Rialto. Lodovico passed poison to his brother who was in prison for having murdered their aunt, so that the brother could commit suicide. Despite his own dramatic family life, he had time to occupy himself with Veronica's, for he drew

VERONICA FRANCO'S CHALLENGE

No more words! To the field, to arms!
I intend to rid myself of pain
even if I end up dying for it.

Should my complaints be read out?—
after all, it is you who provoked me.
But why quarrel about precedence?

I can consider myself challenged,
or I can challenge you–it's all the same;
I'm grateful for any chance to get even!

You choose the site or choose the weapons,
and leave the other choice to me
or, if you want to, you decide everything.

I'm certain that you'll soon perceive
how ungrateful and faithless you were
and what a mistake it was to betray me.

For unless love holds me back
I'll extract the live heart from your breast
bravely with my own hands

just as I'll rip out from its roots
the falsely lying tongue that wounds me—
you'll already have bitten it!

If none of all this saves me,
in desperation I'll attempt
to avenge myself through bloody murder;

then satisfied with having killed you
yet filled with regret, I'll turn and plunge
the knife into my very own heart.

Now that my mind is bent upon revenge,
my disrespectful, my rebellious lover,
step up and arm yourself with what you will.

What battlefield do you prefer? this place?
this secret hideaway where I have sampled—
unwarily–so many bitter sweets?

Let my bed be set up here before us!—
this is where I took you to my bosom,
the traces are still there of our mingled bodies.

Past is the time when I would sleep there,
past is the time when I enjoyed,
now weeping night and day I flood it with tears.

Nevertheless, elect this very space
once-precious nest of joy where I endure—
alone–all sorts of torture and distress

to be the site of our encounter,
so that the news of cruelty, deceit
will die out here, not spread to others' ears.

. . .

But what if you should sue for peace,
lay down your weapons, choose to use the bed
for love's own purposes and love's own wars?—

should I go on fighting you?
I hear that he's considered vile
who, begged forgiveness, fails to grant it.

If ever it should come to this,
I know that I would never swerve
from the course of honest and just behavior.

Probably I'd follow you to bed,
then lying stretched out there and skirmishing,
I'd not give in to you even an inch;

instead, to punish you for your rotten ways,
I'd get on top and in the heat of battle,
as you grow hotter still defending yourself,

we'd die together shot down by one shot.

Veronica Franco, *Rime*,
Cap. XIII

up wills to enable her son Achiletto (possibly his son as well) to inherit most of his worldly goods.

Veronica's practical sense came to her aid throughout her life, most noticeably when she was summoned by the Inquisition in 1580 to answer to charges—apparently false—that she had been employing spells to exercise power over her lovers, had neglected to fast and to attend Mass, and had let Germans frequent her house. Trial records, recently recovered, report Veronica's speech on this occasion. It seems she spoke in a colorful, earthy Venetian dialect when she was not posing as Diotima.

Certainly it must have been a quite different tone of voice she used when attending Domenico Venier's salons. Domenico was a poet suffering from gout and confined to a chair, who gathered around him the literary luminaries of the time, including men such as Giorgio Gradenigo (who exchanged amorous verses with the talented noblewoman Irene di Spilimburgo), Celio Magno, Bernardo Tasso, and Sperone Speroni (these last two had been firmly caught in Tullia d'Aragona's net). Familiarity invests the relationship between Veronica and Domenico, evidenced in the letters between the two, and Domenico contributes a sonnet to an anthology Veronica puts together in honor of a poet of the nobility.

The most remarkable quality of Veronica's letters—published in 1580 and republished in our time by Benedetto Croce (1949)—is Veronica's awareness of precisely who she is, the limits of that and also its advantages. To someone who accuses her of being a courtesan she replies: "I may not be virtuous, but I recognize and appreciate virtue in others." In fact, the letters demonstrate that she is virtuous insofar as she asks favors for people who need them, expresses gratitude for gifts, and consoles friends who are desperate, drawing to their attention the values of family tradition and the high ideals of Venice itself. To those who seek her love in vain she is gentle but direct. With those who seek to harm her, she is necessarily patient, striving to effect with logic and persuasion what she cannot by means of force.

For every occasion, she has an appropriate response. In a letter to a mother who plans to make

Anonymous, *Portrait of Veronica Franco* (engraving). 16th century. Biblioteca Marciana, Venice

her daughter a courtesan, Veronica frankly paints the worst picture she can of that profession. Since the daughter, who has bleached her hair and awkwardly exposed her breasts, is unattractive, only disaster can lie ahead.

The arts and culture in general have a high place in her system of values. She tells Tintoretto that no painter of the past can compare with him, and confesses: "If my destiny had allowed it, I would have spent all of my time agreeably in the circles of talented persons. . . . Surely you know that among all of those who try to win my affection the dearest ones to me are those who practice arts and letters . . . . " And she busies herself arranging musicales and inviting her admirers to come favor her with their "harmonious discourses". On a more familiar note she urges them to join her around the fire for a little supper. Perhaps an old friend will do her the favor of bringing along a flask or two of malmsey.

Follower of Tintoretto, *Portrait of a Lady* (Veronica Franco?). 16th century. Worcester Art Museum, Worcester, Massachusetts

School of Tintoretto, *Portrait of a Woman* (Courtesan). 16th century. Museo del Prado, Madrid. Note the similarity of the likeness to *Portrait of a Lady* (Veronica Franco?) above.

Veronica's poems—long odes in the *terza rima* style Dante perfected, display her classical education and command of the Italian language as well as her negotiating skills. A courteous poem thanking Marco Antonio dalla Torre of Verona for having had her as a guest in his country villa, Fumane, becomes a hymn of praise to architecture and a mode of living modeled after the antique. Her love poems are conventional, but fresh. She can be jealous, ashamed, tormented, pained, and often arrogant about her powers: "Such a priestess of Venus am I/ that whoever experiences me this way/ quickly forgets my singing and rhyming" (*Rime*, Cap. II, 154–55).

The greatest coup of Veronica's career as a courtesan occurred in the summer of 1574, when Henry of Valois arrived in Venice for eleven days of festivities on his way home from Poland to be crowned King Henry III of France. In addition to banquets and ceremonies, Henry indulged in a visit to Veronica at her home near San Giovanni Crisostomo. Among the events planned were concerts and balls; for the official arrival of Henry III at the Lido an arch designed by Palladio with panels painted by Veronese and Tintoretto was set up. The scene of Henry III's arrival has been imaginatively reconstructed by the painter Andrea Michiel (Il Vicentino). Among the crowd greeting the new French sovereign at the shore is a blond woman accompanied by a small page, whose heart-shaped face, delicate features, and elaborate blue gown suggest that she is probably Veronica.

Some say that it was the patrician Andrea Tron, father of one of Veronica's children, who introduced Veronica to Henry; others say that the new king chose her from an album of portraits of courtesans provided him by the government. (The latter suggestion is unlikely, although such albums did exist. A startlingly frank nude bust of a woman, whose features do not at all resemble the courtesan's watercolor in the album *Mors italiae*, significantly has the name "Veronica Franco" in script above. The inscription is probably not contemporary with the artwork, but may be sixteenth century.)[12] However it came about, the royal visit to Veronica became the talk of Venice, and Veronica used the ensuing publicity to her advantage. To insure that Henry never forgot his trip to Venice, the courtesan sent him poems along with her portrait. In an accompanying letter, she reminded him of a kind offer he had made in regard to a book of poems she was preparing, and declared that she would dedicate it to him. If Henry had indeed volunteered to cover the printing costs, he never followed through on his promise. The next year, when the book appeared, it was dedicated to the duke of Mantua.

In her final will and testament, Veronica left, among other things, a dress of pale yellow satin with silver inserts and gold and crimson embroidery, a silver salver with her coats of arms, and exactly fifty-one pearls. Not mentioned in her bequest, but more important for posterity, she left her volumes of poetry and familiar letters.

Louise Labe, muse and mistress of some of the best French poets of her time, was herself an outstanding poet. Born in April 1522 in the city of Lyons to a fairly prosperous rope maker, she married Ennemond Perrier, who practiced the same trade. The couple moved to a handsome house with a fine garden, where she held an indoor or outdoor salon, depending on the season. Her social status was never entirely clear, although it cannot be debated that she and another poet who was her dear friend, Pernette du Guillet, enjoyed a remarkable sexual liberty unavailable to respectable women in that era.

In one of her poems Louise went so far as to deny that she had ever taken money; nevertheless, her lifestyle invited such speculation. Her great love, Olivier de Magny, wrote a vicious satire in which he pictured Ennemond attending to his business with the full knowledge that his wife was practicing her profession at home. Another poem, the anonymous "Chanson de la Belle Cordière" ("Song of the Rope Maker's Pretty Wife"), describes Louise receiving men from different walks of life including lawyers, millers, and Florentine gentlemen (an unkind allusion to her good friend and supporter Tommaso Fortini). Not least of all, the reformer John Calvin, disturbed by a scandal in which Louise's cousin was involved, railed against this young woman who went to visit the prelates of her city inappropriately

garbed, calling her, in a pamphlet, a "meretrix."

When Eleanor of Austria, second wife of Francis I, made her official entry into Lyons in 1533, Louise took part in the festivities, and it is possible she delivered an oration in Latin before the king. Some years later she added an original note to the visit of Henry II and his mistress, Diane de Poitiers, to Lyons by conspicuously planting symbols of the lovers in her garden and writing a poem about the intertwined "crescent" and "ivy."

On these happy occasions, Louise made the acquaintance of men of culture, such as Clément Marot, Pontus de Tyard, and Olivier de Magny. Since the learned poet Maurice Scève had tutored her in classical languages and lent her his precious volumes of Dante, Petrarch, Boccaccio, and Castiglione, Louise was fully prepared to hold her own. In fact, she wrote her first sonnets in Italian.

Undoubtedly, Louise cut a striking figure in society. She loved to dress as a young man, a chevalier, wearing a costume that had its own ironic severity—a brightly colored doublet of a high color and a velvet beret with a plumed feather. Probably she did not, as legend would have it, participate in the siege of Perpignan (1542) against the forces of Charles V (a battle that ended badly for the French) but rather in the ceremonial tournament that preceded it.

De Magny's description of her in an ode is conventional: her forehead is like crystal, her eyebrows little ebony arches, her cheeks roses, her hair golden sands, her eyes joyful torches in the night. A considerably more charming self-portrait leavened by a salutary note of humor appears in a long poetic work, *Le Débat entre la raison et la folie* (*The Debate between Folly and Reason*); in effect she describes the ideal fashionable woman of that time.

Consciously identified with Sappho, in her poetry Louise is alternately tender and passionate. In an oft-quoted sonnet, she imitates Catullus, in almost every line begging her lover to kiss her ("Kiss me, kiss me once again . . . "). In another, she rejoices at an imaginary union with her lover during her sleep. Elsewhere she is more abstract, calling her lover "the soul" that has been separated from "the body"—i.e., herself. Drawn to contemplate her own mortality, she begs from heaven only a little time to celebrate her lover with her "pretty lute."

Often Louise addresses herself to the women of Lyons or to women in general, as if there existed at her back a whole chorus of female sympathizers for whom she spoke:

> Fair women, do not blame my having loved,
> Or having felt a thousand flames so ardent,
> A thousand pains, the gnawings of torment,
> And weeping found my life away consumed.
>
> Let not my name by you be abused,
> If I have erred there's present punishment.
> Sharpen not its point already violent,
> But know that Love, at the time he has appointed,
>
> Without a Vulcan's talents to descry
> Or laying blame on beautiful Adonis,
> Can if he wishes fan a greater fire,
>
> And leaving little of a winning chance,
> Awaken in you a stronger, stranger desire.
> Watch out, or you'll be unhappier than I!

In his *Dialogues*, Pietro Aretino writes at a bemused distance from the phenomenon of the cultured courtesan, focusing rather on the uses to which an astute courtesan put the knowledge at her fingertips and the talents society was led to imagine she possessed. Through his witty female mouthpieces—the robust courtesan-mother Nanna, the godmother, and the wet nurse Antonia, Aretino points out the advantages of having at least a rudimentary knowledge of literature and music. Young Pippa is told to "sing as best you can some doggerel you learned as a joke, thrum the monochord, beat the lute, appear to be reading Ariosto's *Orlando furioso*, Petrarch's poetry, Boccaccio's stories, which should always be in your desk."[13]

Aretino can afford to be offhand about courtesan culture—he was not actively threatened by it—but minor writers devote considerable time to debunking the courtesans' claims and fiercely satirizing them. In *La tariffa* the courtesan Tullia d'Aragona, who bruited it about that she was the daughter of the cardinal of Aragon, is described as washing tripe in the waters of Helicon. However, Maffio Venier's attacks on Veronica Franco, which include the remark that her breasts hang so low she could paddle a gondola with them, are slightly tempered by a momentary homage to how well she practices the "*solfeggio*." Clearly, the prowess of courtesans in the cultural sphere provoked a deep ambivalence in gentlemen, prelates (Maffio was an archbishop), and writers of the time.

T W O

THE COURTESAN IMAGE IN LITERATURE

· THE COURTESAN SPOKEN TO AND SPEAKING ·

Naturally, as a centrally important figure in Renaissance culture, the courtesan received attention in literature from practitioners of both the high and low styles. The most delightful and balanced response to the newly prestigious figure of the courtesan is a series of imaginary letters to sixty courtesans by the Venetian writer Andrea Calmo. Forming the fourth volume of his collected letters, these virtuoso pieces constitute a collective compliment to the caste while offering readers a picture of life among the courtesans. With his theatrical skills, Calmo makes us extremely curious to know (but we never shall know) what the replies to his letters might have been.

Calmo was an important playwright and comic actor, one of the founders of the commedia dell'arte. These letters have great importance for the history of Italian theater, since they offered material for some of the first *canovacci* (sketches of plot situations), evolving into the monologues of Pantaloon, the old Venetian merchant foolishly in love with young girls. The letters relate courtesans' lifestyles, speech, dress, amusements, and methods of

manipulating their lovers, and reveal as well Calmo's emotions as he pleads, protests, explodes with anger, and persuades, pretending to be enamored of all of the women whom he addresses.

In the following letter, Calmo tries to persuade a Roman courtesan to come to Venice, as many of her colleagues have already done in response to a recent senatorial edict against this caste in Rome: "I was surprised . . . you didn't have the courage to come graze in our lagoon." When Calmo was there visiting a prelate friend at the time of the Jubilee, he was shown much courtesy. Now he would like to repay in kind by showing "Romana" the splendors of Venice. The list of places the two will visit resembles a modern touristic itinerary. Calmo suggests that by living in Venice, "Romana" will also enjoy some unusual pleasures, such as being serenaded below her balcony while being entertained by buffoons and being taken for excursions on the water: "The Honorable So-and-So and crowds of young men will sing morning songs, while you hold sway over them, laughing, tricking, getting gifts and money out of them, and making them behave according to your

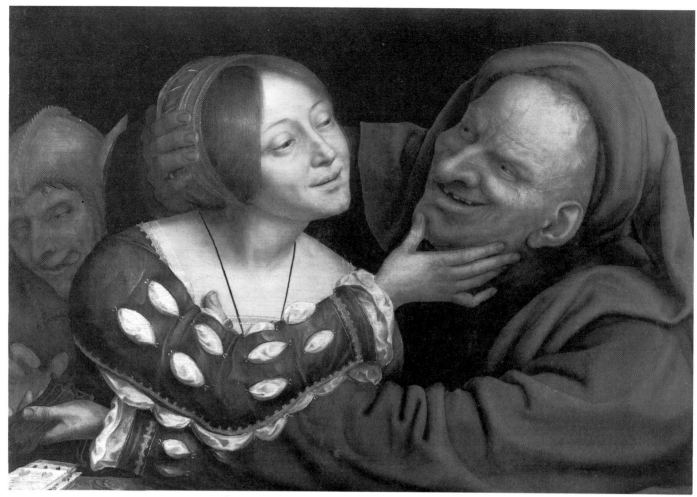

Quentin Massys, *Ill-Matched Lovers*. About 1515–25. Ailsa Mellon Bruce Fund, National Gallery of Art, Washington, D.C.

whims. Before long you'll be one of the most famous courtesans in Venice, a member of the inner circle . . . . So while the fountain's still flowing, let them drink" (*Lettere di A. Calmo*, IV, 13).

Toward the end of this letter, Andrea Calmo flaunts his acquaintanceship with Roman courtesans of the moment by sending his regards to "La Bruneta" (Brunette), "La Hebrea" (the Jewess), "La Todeschina" (the German), "La Checa" (short for Francesca), "La Padoana" (the Paduan), "Belfronte" (Beautiful Visage), and others. If Rome were not so far away, he says, he would send "La Romana" a box of civet.

While Calmo makes a courteous gesture to La Romana, he shows himself resentful, then revealingly servile with Brunela. Clearly, the two have lived out a certain history together. The writer—in his own mind the ideal lover—has maintained Brunela in grand style.

Dear Madame Brunela,

Now that I have thrown away a fortune on you, skilled as you are in tricks, deceptions, and traps, you have told everyone you do not love me any longer. I will be curious to see whether that new lover of yours lets himself be worn to the bone and runs to do your bidding as I did. Just keeping you in pets cost me the sale of two pieces of land. . . . Doesn't it seem to you now that you were in paradise, with your parrots, jays, larks, cardinals, pheasants, doves, Persian cats, squirrels, martens, guinea pigs, and monkeys? The whole thing bankrupted and exhausted me. I bet my rival will not maintain you with gondolas, a Moor, a houseboy, and two housekeepers as I did, idiotic as it seems now. If being an Indian-giver weren't so odious, I'd ask for half of it back.

How could you have afforded all those delicacies if I hadn't satisfied you every moment? . . . Peacocks, guinea-hens, capons, partridges, thrushes, quails, oysters, pastries before dinner, dressed squash, plum tart and green ginger, desserts such as quince or marchpane with sugared cinnamon, as well as bread, wine, and cheese. I had to play the astrologer to divine your appetites. As a reward, I got locked outside, bade farewell, with nary a glance in my direction. I haven't even mentioned the furnishings—tapestries and rugs, damask draperies, gilded footstools, painted chests, Brescian curtains, pewter-ware. One item of clothing after another was the least of it. Pearls and rings seemed trifles. To complete the picture, you emasculated my purse every night that I slept with your Excellency . . . . How audacious you were, always one step ahead in the game, forever blaming me. I had to apologize every time I felt happy. Poor fellows!—taken in by dragons, bitches, serpents of your kind who devour, suck, bite, poison, and mutilate . . . (*Lettere di A. Calmo*, IV, 16).

Calmo's "persona" spends the rest of this letter wallowing in self-pity. He is not only bankrupt, but he also cannot earn a living because the citizen class to which he belongs frowns on manual labor. Therefore, nothing is left for him but to float along like a butterfly, living parasitically off others. In short, the author of this letter has fallen so low he now offers to be his ex-mistress's servant, pimp, or both: "I guess I will have to counterfeit madmen, pimps, buffoons, and courtiers. However, since I supported you when things were going well, you ought to maintain me in my old age. . . . All I need is a bit of space. I don't eat very much or wear special clothes. In return I will do any job you order me to do" (*Lettere di A. Calmo*, IV, 16).

In the comic letter to Madame Celestina, easily imagined as a mime, embryonic material appears for what we have already signaled as Andrea Calmo's most significant stage role—that of Pantaloon. In Renaissance art there are many examples of the "old man and young girl" configuration—Quentin Massys's *Ill-Matched Lovers* or the jesting *A Woman between Men of Two Ages* by a painter of the School of Fontainebleau, the theme of which, as in these letters, is mercenary love.

Some of the preceding letters lead one to imagine that a precarious balance of power existed between Calmo and his mistresses; the writer's status seems to be no higher or lower than theirs. But in the following letter to the humorously-named Madame Vitruvia, Calmo grovels, albeit in a wry, subtle, and mocking fashion. The detailed description of the ideal physique contained in this letter is extremely interesting, although we can never be sure when Calmo is joking and when he is serious. What is sin-

cere is the author's admiration for the bold phenomenon of the courtesan. The letters form the shrine he imagines should exist so that "the whole world would come to marvel and pay homage."

Dear Madame Vitruvia,
Well-designed artifact, paragon of a woman, may my tongue, my expression, my very words not disturb or scandalize you. I swear by Hercules, Alexander, and Caesar that as long as I have lived and surveyed the world, I have never seen such an attractive creature, such a well put-together lass, such a gallant woman as you. If I were a painter, I would introduce your figure in every canvas, on every ceiling, and on every wall, in order to bring honor to myself among those who gaze upon that image. O benign, favorable, courteous heaven who created such a stupendous *mulieribus* rosy as crimson satin, white as mountain snow, soft as ravioli, incisive in her walk, gracious in speech, and amiable in practical transactions.

No matter from what angle one looks at you, you are neat and lovely: your form is majestic straight-on, sideways or in profile, even in the shade. Your constancy is papal, your excellence imperial. If I were a sculptor, I could find no better subject, outdoing Vitruvius, Phidias, and Danti [a sixteenth-century Italian sculptor]. By simply observing you and trying to carve your form, one notes your suave gaze, the mild expression, the perfect waist. What folds of the throat, what muscular jaws, what miraculous flesh! Oh, dear, what a delicately rounded body, what wide flanks, what a curved chest, what quick legs, what solid breasts, what rounded arms, what long fingers, what a narrow waist and broad shoulders, what small feet! I am convinced that Nature made you at the height of her powers . . . (*Lettere di A. Calmo*, IV, 26)

In a letter to Madame Lucida, Calmo boasts about his looks, his artful conversation, and his musical talents. Here and in many other letters he paints himself as a deliberately deformed version of the ideal courtier-lover-intellectual. Naively, ostentatiously, the writer lists his possessions, exaggerating his financial possibilities in order to lure Lucida and offering such irrelevant details as the fact that his dressing gown is of such fine cotton that it could fit in a nutshell. "Even though these things are only transitory objects, earthly dust," he writes, "I will give them to you if you promise to make me your husband," politely adding "as soon as your current marriage is over . . ." (*Lettere di A. Calmo*, IV, 4).

Again pretending to be rich, Calmo sends Madame Orsolina (Little Bear) an elaborate list of Christmas presents he plans to give her. The descriptions are replete with details of the lavish materials then in use in women's finery, including the embroidery and lacework for which Venice and the islands of the lagoon were known. The list contains a plethora of allegorical subjects Calmo absurdly imagines will be woven into the shifts, scarves, caps, and veils he is preparing for her:

I am sending you, first of all, two shifts of Rheims cloth fashioned by a Jewess in Candia. One is in the Apulian style in crimson silk. Across the front you will see figured the wedding of Cupid and Psyche celebrated in the clouds; below the waist, the infatuation of Priapus with the Fairy Lotus within a cypress grove; over the shoulder blades Mars and Venus caught in Vulcan's net; on the left sleeve the triumph of Neptune and Thetis, with Glaucus, Triton, and Galatea in the middle of the sea; on the right sleeve Orpheus seated atop a hill playing the lute and singing, while being courted by different animals.

When his multiple offers of gifts, money and the delights of his own company are rejected, Calmo turns to vituperation and invective, sometimes uttering the rhetorical commonplaces of the satires against the courtesans, but usually striking an individual note through his odd, humorous metaphors and comparisons drawn from daily life or invented on the spot. Madame Aquilana ("High-and-mighty Eagle") gives herself airs, believing she is of a different social class from him, but Calmo knows better. It is all dissimulation:

Proud, vainglorious lady, how demanding you are! You hold yourself off. You make fun of my appearance, claiming I'm not on your level. By heaven, I know what makes a man a man. I have polish enough. Isn't it about time we admit that everyone in the world has the same mother and father? What is the point in puffing oneself up? Perhaps you intend to imply that I am a bastard rather than well-born? How wrong you are. As for intelligence, I would not trade places with a sultan, even if you offered me a fortune. . . .

How many arrogant women who criticize gentlemen pull down servants, peasants, and bakers over their bodies? History is full of queens made pregnant by dwarfs, empresses seeking their pleasure in lavatories, countesses carrying on with Saracens, learned ladies sleeping with stableboys. Away with your idle gossip! You think you can fool me, offering cabbage for lettuce and beans for grain. For my part, I never deal in lies and falsities. I behave well, speak sincerely, and wear my heart on my sleeve. But you—you are as layered as an onion, as secretive as a mole, and as stealthy as a fox.

Now that you have grown more refined, no one can approach you. Still, you remind me of people who stripe their gray cloth with velvet and line rough wool with silver, or decorate leather with precious metallic threads. Are you so sure that you are the phoenix of our world, ruling the heavens, while earth trembles beneath you? If you believe this you are crazy. Remember that ships in the harbor can still sink into the waves, squash at the tip of the plant withers, and horses can fall down in the *palio* [the racecourse] and break their ambitious necks . . . (*Lettere di A. Calmo*, IV, 48).

One of the most fascinating of Calmo's letters contains a dream fantasy that is an apotheosis of the courtesan viewed in the midst of ceremonies connected with her cultural image. Pretending to have dreamed it, Calmo takes us by the hand in an ascent to a paradisiacal realm that is also the classical Parnassus. It is all a compliment to one woman, Madame Oliveta, whom Calmo wants to put on a pedestal, but it is also an exquisite parody of medieval allegorical dream visions. Calmo is particularly skilled at depicting in words idealized erotic scenes similar to those created by contemporary artists—for example, Tintoretto's *Concert* in Dresden and Palma Giovane's *Parnassus*.

Many species of trees adorn the approach to this *locus amoenus*. The architecture of the palace, the courtyard, the garden, the fountain, the loggia, and the throne are all envisioned in great detail, and the place is peopled with nymphlike presences. After a banquet, a nap, and a concert, the gods appear, first of all Venus. The muses and Three Graces necessarily make their appearance, as do a horde of celebrated heroines of history and romances, including Ariosto's. Gifts are ritually offered to the writer and the vision ends, but not before Calmo redimensions the event by listing the gifts, which will be for his lady. These are cosmetics—indeed, depilatories! The illusion and the reality both depend on fictive elements: it is all "cosmetics." Even Calmo's talent for juggling words and phrases, while inspiring so many shifting emotions, is a prestidigitation that

Tintoretto, *Concert*. 16th century. Staatliche Kunstsammlungen, Dresden

leaves behind a faintly bitter taste; the marginal class of intellectuals to which Calmo belonged had to scramble to keep pace with the profit-minded, socially mobile courtesans they desired.

Andrea Calmo's fantastic letters delicately woven through with threads of mockery and self-mockery differ dramatically from Pietro Aretino's realistic and sometimes heavy-handed treatment of the courtesans in his justly celebrated *Dialogues*. Nevertheless, Aretino is no more the courtesans' "antagonist" than Andrea Calmo. He, too, lives in symbiosis with them and even goes so far as to speak through them.

With the breezy familiarity of a sonnet by Dante describing a merry band of maidens and poets departing on an imaginary boat ride, Aretino chronicles dinner parties held in Venice in the 1530s that were attended by famous writers, artists and courtesans. Angela del Moro is often present, as is an-

other woman known for her musical talents, Franceschina Bellamano.

In his own household, Aretino ruled like a sovereign. He retained a staff of attractive and compliant women whose status was vague. In one of his letters he refers to them cynically as "women . . . called 'Aretine' [Aretino's women] who were governesses of mine and now are ladies. . . . " The relationships may have changed, but Aretino's life remained entangled with those of his women. Darker chapters of his erotic life are hinted at in the *Priapea* of Niccolò Franco (ninety-nine sonnets written to defame Aretino as a pederast and sodomite) and in other sources. Whatever the truth of his relations with men, Aretino's friendships with courtesans and concubines, notwithstanding some unsavory episodes with the husbands, have a consistently luminous quality.

Passages about Perina Riccio in Aretino's *Letters*

provide insight into the joyous, somewhat irregular life lived in the Aretino household on Riva del Carbon along the Grand Canal, where the scourge of princes turned out his fierce pieces with the fervor of a journalist, between frolics with the "Aretine." Perina was the wife of a Venetian named Polo Bartolini. Perina, Perina's husband, and Caterina Sandella, who married a certain Bartolo, lived together with Aretino in his house. In thanking a publisher for a lavish gift of flowers and fruits, Aretino sensuously describes each object, then adds, apropos of some limes, "You should have seen Perina and Caterina jump up and down at the sight of them!"

This was not a life of orgies, though characterized by erotic freedom and lightheartedness; rather something more like what today is called, for lack of a better term, "the extended family." In that sense, the atmosphere in Aretino's household resembled that of the house at Pio where Camilla of Pisa and other courtesans lived in more or less domestic style with frequent visits from their Florentine lovers.

Aretino describes Perina and Caterina's frequent embraces and the pleasure he takes in watching Polo, "her husband and my disciple" (words that well indicate who wields the power) caressing and making a fuss over his wife. Like a feudal lord, Aretino arranged the marriages and continued to possess the people as well as the pleasure they experienced even among themselves. Aretino also boasts about his devotion to the financial well-being of Caterina and Perina, once going so far as to call it "charity." It was an odd harem but Venice is after all a city turned toward the East, and in any case a good dose of Tuscan rusticity probably brought the sophisticated setting down to earth.

All around Aretino were art and artists. This writer prided himself on his critical faculties and received many gifts, commissioning some paintings himself (e.g., the *Apollo and Marsyas* fresco by Tintoretto on his ceiling). Above all, Aretino served as an art dealer, procuring important paintings, sculptures, and other art objects—ancient and modern—for the rulers of Europe, while promoting the careers especially of Titian and Sansovino but also of others. His friendships with painters are well known, and he can be credited with creating an ambiance in which they could operate. Titian's portraits of him are among the painter's best, and Marcantonio Raimondi produced a magnificent engraving of his head. His theories of and judgments on art may have influenced Vasari in his revision of the *Lives of the Artists*.

Aretino's own *Stanze in lode di Angela Sirena* (*Stanzas in Honor of Angela Sirena*) in a conventional Petrarchan style were embellished by miniatures by the artist Jacopo del Giallo. Aretino uses the pretext of a thank-you note to Jacopo to tell the world exactly how excellently these love poems to Angela Sirena were illustrated:

Sweet fellow, I remained speechless when I saw the miniatures that your talent, industry, and affection for me have produced. I am not blind; indeed, many is the time Raphael, Sebastiano, and Titian have followed my advice, since I am familiar with both ancient and modern art. Miniaturists usually paint like stained-glass makers, coloring parts with ultramarine, blue-greens, grain lacquers, and ground gold, configuring a strawberry or a snail. But your work is a total design, and you also work in relief. Everything is softened and nuanced as if you were painting in oils (*Lettere*, I, 33).

The dedicatory page to Empress Isabella seems to have been particularly beautiful (it earned Aretino a stunning necklace of gold) and in the same letter Aretino praises a prayer book covered with gold and precious gems made in memory of Ippolito de Medici, but it is those words "softened and nuanced as if you were painting in oils" that offer the most revealing insight. Herein lies the Venetian taste for vague definition through large color zones of broad brushwork, indeed the kind of thing we find an extreme version of in Tintoretto's portrait of Caterina Sandella, the mistress of Aretino who bore him his much-beloved daughter Adria. (Caterina is also portrayed on three medals, two of them by Alessandro Vittoria.)[14]

This portrait, unlike any other of a courtesan, shows a woman with a wild, imperious quality about her. She is neither young nor particularly attractive, and she is certainly not well dressed, but she is vigorous, one might even say willful. The look in her eyes is challenging, the visual equivalent of Veronica Franco's remark about whoredom. She is real, but this is a reality in motion—caught in the act; what the act consists of besides self-assertion and presence of mind, is obscure. No saint, no lady, this figure hardly fits into our category of "honest courtesan." She is anomalous on canvas as she must have been in life—a woman exercising her freedom, enjoying her affair with an important man of culture as she received considerable remuneration, and in other ways profited from the venture.

A wide gulf seems to separate Aretino's personal relations with mistresses and personalities such as Angela del Moro from his exposé of the professional life of the courtesan; however, it is only a thin line, the threshold one passes over when moving from the individual to the collective, from the relative to the absolute, from the lived experience to the literary "exemplum." There is evidence that Aretino considers himself a kind of *puttana di lusso* (an upper-class prostitute) who uses a phallic pen. Identifying so intensely with the figure of the courtesan, his depiction of her in the *Dialogues* is necessarily highly charged and dramatic.

In the sixteenth century, literary dialogues could be set in various places—the castle at Asolo, where Pietro Bembo's discourses on Platonic love are imagined to have taken place; the ducal palace in Urbino (background of Castiglione's *The Courtier*); or gardens like the Florentine Orti Oricellari, where humanists, including Niccolò Machiavelli, met to ponder history. For these scabrous anecdotes, Aretino chooses a vineyard under a fig tree, a symbol of fertility as well as of the "low" literary style the writer deliberately employs.

As in Boccaccio's *Decameron*, the structure of the *Dialogues* is a series of tales. As the various women talk, life in the bedroom and life on the streets unrolls vividly before our eyes, and the anatomy of a psyche—that of a shrewd courtesan grown old, now procuress for her daughter—unveils a world scarcely visible from the perspective of traditional literature and, for that matter, of Italian art of the time. In Italian art, the courtesan is most often idealized, even exalted, rather than shown in compromising situations or as old and decrepit. Naturally, the realistic version, which errs on the side of caricature, may be just as insidiously distorting as the idealizing

Titian, *Portrait of Pietro Aretino*. 16th century. Palazzo Pitti, Florence

Tintoretto, *Portrait of a Woman* (Caterina Sandella). 16th century. Private collection

Anonymous, *Newlywed Venetian Bride, Noble Venetian Matron, Venetian Courtesan* (engraving). Bibliothèque Nationale, Paris

one. Only by merging the two contrasting conceptions can one form a true picture of the life of the Renaissance courtesan.

Aretino had several motives for overplaying his hand. Almost certainly, he is describing Venetian society under the mask of the Roman setting. In Rome, where he lived until he fled to the Republic after the Sack of Rome in 1527, Aretino's life had been turbulent, to say the least (he had even been knifed for his writings). Now, as an honored guest of the Republic, Aretino could take every license as long as he did not point an accusing finger. In addition, he seems to be inventing a new kind of naturalistic style suited to talking about erotic matters, a "phallic poetics." In general, Aretino employs what might be called a mimetic hyperrealism, as he offers up "things that are alive" from daily existence,

things actually seen as opposed to what he calls Boccaccio's "painted pictures."

When the *Dialogues* begin, Nanna and Antonia, two mature courtesans, are chatting. These characters were almost surely real persons; their names appear in the census of 1527. Nanna, daughter of a courtesan who lived on via dei Banchi Nuovi and a police informer, whose house was always "packed like an egg" while all Rome danced around her, has decided to make her daughter a courtesan instead of a nun or wife since she—the mother—has tried all three roles and has found courtesanry to be the most satisfying. This categorization reflects the roles women played in the sixteenth century. For example, wife, widow, and courtesan are placed side by side in an anonymous engraving of the time.

At least one generation has preceded Nanna in

THE COURTESAN IMAGE IN LITERATURE

her profession: Nanna's mother was once known as "the beautiful Tina." Nanna is moved to describe for Antonia her early life, in which she recapitulates all the roles open to a woman of the time, even that of widow. Nanna, among other things, coldbloodedly murdered her husband.

When Nanna enters a convent as a fashionably dressed girl, her clothes (borrowed from a well-known courtesan of the time, Madame Pagnina) consist of a pearl necklace, a silk gown girdled with gray amber beads, a cap of gold cloth, perfumed gloves and, amusingly, "a virgin's crown interwoven with roses and violets." This last gesture is apparently unnecessary, since no one in this paradise of the flesh seems to have been a virgin. The novitiate uncovers the debauchery of the place and is herself initiated into its mysteries. She takes part in banquets attended by abbots, abbesses, priests, and nuns; views scenes of "official" copulation, is herself deflowered, and participates in orgies.

The convent has rooms that are decorated with amorous "positions," such as those painted over the brothel door in Pompeii, not yet discovered in Renaissance times. Aretino describes each of the four walls of frescoes at length. The first wall contains the "Life of Saint Nafissa," an invented comic personage considered the patron saint of courtesans (Mary Magdalene was their actual saint, and Saint Mary the Egyptian a figure related to their plight). Having given away her worldly goods as saints are wont to do, Nafissa has gone to ply the trade of prostitute in Rome. She is shown sitting on a stool on—where else?—the Ponte Sisto in Rome, chasing away flies with a rather primitive fan; nearby is her straw mat and a little dog. It is a sad vision. In subsequent scenes Nafissa solicits a customer, taking him to her cell, undressing him, letting him take her "as a stallion would a mare." Then Jews rob her of the coins she has earned after they have made use of her body. Finally, the beleaguered Nafissa dies, and all of the men who have ever possessed her attend the burial.

After this conversation, Nanna and Antonia leave the vineyard and return to Nanna's house on via della Scrofa near Piazza Navona. During the next two days they return to the vineyard to sit un-

Anonymous, *Courtesan and Suitor* (watercolor) from *Mors italiae.* 16th century. Beinecke Library, Yale University, New Haven

der the fig tree and discuss the misdeeds of wives and then life as a courtesan.

At the opening of her narration of life as a courtesan, Nanna offers a monumental account of her arrival in Rome. It seems that nothing was more prized then than a fresh, lovely young girl whose status was somewhat in doubt. Nanna's experienced mother takes rooms for them in Tor di Nona in the *rione* Parione where Nanna is instructed to appear at the window, letting men have glimpses of her charming features. Soon she becomes the talk of the town, and a veritable procession rushes to get a look at her. Men boldly knock on her door. While the mother fends them off, the daughter catches sight of what is in store for her. If no other source provided a description of the lovers of Roman courtesans, the following passage would fill that lacuna:

I almost went blind . . . staring at the elegant spectacle of all those noblemen in their velvet and satin capes, gold chains around their necks, some mounted on horses that glistened like mirrors, gliding by as soft as silk with their servants at the stirrups, in which they put only the tips of their boots, holding their pocket Petrarchs and reciting verses with the affected nods and grimaces (*Dialogues*, I, 3).

An image of seductiveness, Nanna on the second floor peeks through the blinds, occasionally letting the men see her "purple satin gown neat and simple without sleeves" (to show off her beautiful arms), and her hair "braided in a circle" around her head, seemingly "a silken skein laced with threads of gold." Unashamedly, the mature courtesan recounts how the men dropped the reins of their horses and gazed in rapture "as prisoners gaze at a ray of sunlight." She felt, she says, "impregnated by their stares." Intense looking is possession in a literal sense, and as paintings of lascivious women can sexually excite the beholder, Nanna's account of how she stimulated the men who came to gaze upon her is meant to stimulate the reader.

Men admired Nanna's face and body, but the reader is encouraged to admire her cunning and professional finesse. Faced with the specter of the predictable end of courtesans—"selling candles" and/or "the French pox," Nanna resolves to avoid that fate:

Ah yes, it is really a fine sight to see one of those whores when she is no longer able to hide her age behind paint and make-up, pungent toilet waters, ceruse, fine gowns, and broad fans and must start pawning her necklaces, rings, silken gowns, and headdresses, as well as all her other trappings, and has to enter one of the four minor orders, just like young boys who want to become priests (*Dialogues*, I, 3).

Rather than risk the possibility of the "four orders"—innkeepers, procuresses, washerwomen, and beggars on church steps—as well as being branded on her forehead, as Nanna eventually was, or oth-

Anonymous, *Franceschina at Eighteen* (wax medal). 16th century. Victoria and Albert Museum, London

Anonymous, *Franceschina at Eighty* (wax medal). 16th century. Victoria and Albert Museum, London

Crispin de Passe, scene from Prodigal Son series. 17th century. Folger Shakespeare Library, Washington, D.C.

erwise scarred by angry lovers, Nanna works toward secure goals. First, she sells her virginity over and over, torturing lovers with infinite delays. Next, she schemes to steal their belongings along with their hearts, engaging in her service some pimps whom she reimburses with favors instead of cash. Quite in the manner of Andreuccio of Perugia in Boccaccio's tale of courtesanry in Naples, her lovers are frightened into fleeing, leaving behind in their haste their rich mantles and doublets.

Given her practical bent, Nanna knows that it is wiser to choose "tavern keepers, cooks, chicken pluckers, water carriers, middlemen, and Jews" rather than flashy courtiers who are usually in debt. It seems she has the law on her side, as well, whether legitimately or not, for men whom she has robbed and who complain about it are soon "sent packing like nitwits" by the judges of the nearby Savella court. Another technique for swindling involves organized cheating at cards. Many times courtesans' living rooms functioned as casinos.

Nanna plants a hustler at her gaming table to "do in" a series of lovers:

Oh, how much money I have earned by swindling this man or that! Many men often used to dine in my house, and after dinner the cards would appear on the table. "Come on," I would say, "let's play for two julios' worth of candy. The man who gets the King of Cups will have to pay." When the candy was lost and paid for, those who had cards in their hands could no more stop playing than a whore can stop being a whore. So they pulled out their money and began gambling in earnest. Then two of my shills walked in, men who looked like simpletons, and they let themselves be coaxed for a while and finally picked up cards that were phonier than doubloons minted with lead; and then, still acting like dullards, they pocketed all the guests' money. All the while I was telling them by dumb show what cards the others held in their hands, for I didn't put much faith in the fake cards. (*Dialogues*, I, 3).

A suggestive scene at a gaming table appears in a fresco on a vault in the library of the University of Bologna. In this painting, by Niccolò dell'Abbate, well-dressed courtesans with plumed hats play cards

Jan Sanders van Hemessen, *Prodigal Son*. 16th century. Musées Royaux des Beaux-Arts de Belgique, Brussels

with gentlemen. Tavern scenes featuring profligates and prostitutes engaged in gambling and other vices are frequent in the north. The painter van Hemessen in his *Prodigal Son* (Brussels) shows us some extremely well-dressed women (one with *tajade* sleeves) cavorting in a place well supplied with dice and tankards.

Some of the strategems Nanna employs are highly naive, such as feigning illness in order to receive expensive medicines which are returned for cash the following day, or pretending to undergo abortions, or faking a disappearance to a nunnery. Other more elaborate ones are similar to the intrigues of novellas by Aretino's contemporaries. Often a few precious brushstrokes compose a lively scene from real life, as for example when Nanna, dressed like a boy, snatches a cape from the back of her manservant and jumps up to sit behind a mon-

signor on a mule, while a lover she has just tricked into giving her ten crowns goes inside the house, furious, to slash a portrait of the courtesan hanging on the wall.

In Rome in the early 1530s, Tullia d'Aragona—daughter of the courtesan Giulia Campana (Giulia of Ferrara) and, according to the family myth, Cardinal Luigi d'Aragona—literally towered over other courtesans, being very tall. Evidently hers was an intellectual rather than a physical kind of beauty; at least Giraldi Cinthio's description of her is not flattering:

This man was so crazy about her that he did not really notice what she looked like—for example, that she was overly tall, not at all noble in her bearing, with a homely face that in addition to a large mouth and thin lips was spoiled by a long nose with a hump in it . . . (*Hecatommiti* I, intro., 3).

He is forced to add, however, that

although the rest of her face was not attractive, she possessed two devilish eyes that as they skipped about inflamed men's hearts.

Celebrated *salonnière* and, as already mentioned, author of poems and a philosophical dialogue about love, Tullia was the culmination of everything the cultured courtesan was supposed to be.

Naturally, Tullia felt free to choose her own lovers. Freedom was the most precious treasure a courtesan could possess. She might relinquish her freedom temporarily, but once a courtesan had surrendered her freedom and pledged her love to one or perhaps several persons, she could not arbitrarily attempt to get it back. Such an act would be nearly criminal, or so it is judged to be in the impressive novella by Giraldi Cinthio in which a real episode in the life of Tullia d'Aragona is narrated.

It seems that although she was rich and pampered, adored, and spoiled by her lovers, one day Tullia allowed herself to be persuaded by her mother (who was, according to custom, her daughter's procuress) to accept the advances of a German merchant who promised to pay 100 ducats each night if Tullia would sleep with him for one week. According to Giraldi Cinthio's account (where Tullia is called Nanna and Paolo Orsini, a devoted young lover of Tullia's, is called Sauli) Nanna, after the experience of one night, was revolted by the vulgarity and filth of the merchant and refused to proceed with the arrangement. Unfortunately, her wellborn admirers had already learned of this outrage to their honor perpetrated by their idol, and it was too late to save face. Vituperated by Sauli, Nanna was forced to leave Rome together with her mother. In fact, Tullia d'Aragona and her mother did have to leave Rome because of such a scandal. After returning to her native town in the Po Valley, then moving on to Venice, Ferrara, and Florence, meeting with success everywhere she went, Tullia eventually went back to Rome.

The most interesting aspect of this tale is how intense her lover's anger becomes when he discovers that Tullia has soiled—indeed, desecrated—the honest courtesan image. The honest courtesan was

already surrounded by a special radiance reserved for the most exclusive of that caste; and Tullia had the added luster of cultural accomplishments. As he loads the dice, Giraldi Cinthio takes pleasure in describing the dramatic contrast between the manners of the refined courtesan and those of the beastly foreigner:

This is how the German Johann, wealthy as he was, took care of his own person: his clothes no matter how expensive were always full of filth, whether grease spots or snot and other ugly things, so much so that you could smell it all a mile away.

Giraldi goes on to describe the man at board and in bed, yet the effect is grotesque rather than ridiculous. At the dinner table, he "belches and cleans his nose with the tablecloth." He squats by the bedside to relieve himself before climbing in beside his mistress. Falling onto the floor when he tries to remove his trousers, he ends by getting into bed still wearing the filthy clothes. As the man's long toenails cut her, his unkempt fingernails "tear at the delicate flesh of the courtesan's breasts." In that exquisite boudoir designed for the transports of divine love, the abyss between the two figures is almost sadistically delineated. Giraldi slyly allows that, mercifully, the merchant did not even desire to lie with the courtesan a second time. But meanwhile the damage is done, and Sauli—speaking for Giraldi himself—immediately directs his anger at the transgressing courtesan.

"You buried yourself alive when you slept with that filthy German," her lover tells her. "Now let him bury you when you're dead!" Curses follow one after the other: "May birds of prey digest you in their entrails!" "May you get a good case of syphilis!" And so forth. The more vigorous Sauli's wrath, the firmer the impression that the courtesan's cultural image was sacred and inviolable.

The disappointment lovers felt when women failed to live up to their images could be overwhelming. This was because the patrician class itself had devised the courtesan as an idealizing mirror of its own image. "I regret that you have me sculpted in your heart," Sauli tells Nanna, "for it is sculpted in an abominable place where all criminal acts and deceits dwell." Now "the veils have been ripped away," and he sees clearly for the first time.

The courtesan represented an "honest," if artificial pleasure. The "conversation" (which Montaigne complained cost as much as the sexual transaction) offered an alternative to sexual experience *tout court*, covering over voluptuousness with ethical imperatives and giving a new dimension to intimate relations, now seen as an amorous servitude, an expanded courtship. In a sense, the courtesan was the "other" self of the patricians, an ideal, hypothetical self, an imagined dream, a projection, a sublimation of commerce, war, and government administration in a gratuitous activity that nevertheless had meaning.

Courtesans were often portrayed admiring themselves in mirrors. By incarnating art, culture, femininity, ease, and Platonic spirituality, courtesans seemed to possess exactly the qualities lacking in men who were rich in every other way. The discovery that a superior realm lay beyond their usual sphere led men to view themselves as impotent although potent, and poor although rich. The process was circular since the noble class created what it needed while courtesans astutely made themselves into precisely what the nobles lacked.

This complex process had a built-in contradiction, since courtesans could function both as an extension and as a negation of patrician power. Sometimes circumstances or caprice led a courtesan to rebel against the role that had been created for her, thus making her seem for a moment to have a split personality. Always she ran the risk of not perfectly embodying the fiction she and her lovers had invented, of not offering the consecrating experience that was like an ancient "mystery." If she tried to produce the experience artificially, however, she laid herself open to accusations of witchcraft.

When, from time to time, the patrician became aware that the courtesan was not his other, ideal self but rather something quite different, he was tempted to amputate—symbolically or materially—the part of himself that threatened to undermine the perfect integration of his personality. In other words, the patrician could be tempted to execrate instead of to adore his mistress, to violate her in-

stead of to protect her, to associate her with evil and mortality instead of good and divinity. If a woman failed to keep the pact between them, if she indulged exhibitionistically in promiscuous loves, if she gratuitously encouraged her *bravi* to wound or assassinate someone or ruin his reputation, or if she showed an excess of avarice or lust, she automatically renounced her privilege of existing in a social continuum with the nobility.

Having been for a man the most precious object in his universe, the courtesan now seemed the opposite. His desire for retribution could take various forms, the most logical being a sexual one. To take by force a woman who has proclaimed herself free, to possess her rapidly and brutally—this was a possible solution, even if in choosing it one ran the risk of committing the same kind of crime the courtesan had committed—that is to say, reducing the spiritual to the material. There was a further possibility: in the same way that a courtesan subverted a code of behavior, one or more men could "subvert" her, perversely making her sexual part a "seat" of abomination. Thus, the offended lover transformed the natural sex act into a sodomitic one.

Of course all of this could be done with words rather than acts. In the Renaissance, nothing was more dangerous for a courtesan than a literary lover, no matter of what social class:

Praise musicians and singers even if you take no delight in them and do not understand what they are doing. If there is a scholar present, approach him with a happy countenance, showing him that you esteem him. . . . Why, all you need is for one of these fellows to write a book against you, and everywhere the talk will be about the slanders they are so good at inventing about us women. You would be in a nice fix if someone were to print your life as a certain idler has printed mine!
(Aretino, *Dialogues*, II, 1)

This is the sound advice Aretino's Nanna offers her daughter Pippa. Aretino's disciple, Lorenzo Venier, wrote a long satire about a mass rape that may or may not have taken place. Whether or not this literary *tour-de-force* was a spoof, "thirty-ones" (as they were called) were part of the life of Renaissance courtesans, even the most elite among them.

Aside from scarring or otherwise mutilating a

courtesan, the thirty-one was the most terrible punishment a lover could wreak upon her. The lover lured the unsuspecting victim to an isolated spot, such as a vineyard or an island, and then subjected her to the lust of thirty-one lower-class men in order to degrade her. A "royal" thirty-one meant rape by eighty men. One imagines that the experience was never pleasant, but in at least one of his three accounts of thirty-ones in the *Dialogues*, Aretino claims that a woman chose it freely in order to satisfy a natural appetite.

Lorenzo's *Il trentuno della Zaffetta* (*The Zaffetta's Thirty-One*), a lively poem of more than 900 lines, tells of an adventurous boat ride on the lagoon in Venice ending in the "friendly" mass rape by eighty men of the haughty courtesan and friend of Aretino Angela del Moro (known as "La Zaffetta" because her stepfather was a "zaffo," a policeman). Since Venetian laws prohibited violence, abductions, and rape, it is the story of a crime—a crime that goes unpunished because of the high social status of its instigator, a patrician of the illustrious Venier family inscribed in the *Golden Book* (the registry of aristocratic names) and soon after counting even a doge in its ranks.

The rape of Angela del Moro is supposed to have taken place on 6 April 1531, the year 1531 being the presumed publication date of Lorenzo's poem. The pretext for the punishment seems to have been quite flimsy. One day at the appointed hour reserved for him, Angela refused to open her door to her lover. The disgruntled lover, whom I assume to be the author of the poem, although it is not entirely clear, feigns nonchalance, but secretly nourishes a terrible grudge.

Then one day Lorenzo invites Angela to travel to Malamocco, a village on an island in the lagoon, and to Chioggia, where a banquet in her honor will take place. The courtesan lightheartedly accepts, and the couple, along with some friends, merrily set out over the water. The beginning of the trip and the subsequent developments are all narrated in a sarcastic, incisive style, and there are many colorful vignettes of Angela herself, rapid portraits in words of a courtesan dangerously off guard.

A gondola is "solemnly prepared" appropriate for a fiancée about to be married; two strokes of the paddle make it shoot half a mile out. The talkative Angela insists on sitting up high in the midst of the gondola the way wives do. But as soon as the group debarks at Malamocco, she shows her true colors, abandoning finesse and good manners:

> As soon as this whore arrived
> in grand style at Malamocco,
> coyly sighing she produced these words,
> "Well, dear one, shall we eat?"
> Then spying before her a steaming partridge,
> she seized it and downed it in one gulp
> and faster than you can say Ave Maria
> guzzled six goblets of malmsey.
>
> (ll. 201–16)

Angela's comportment during the banquet is deliciously described. A charming if silly and reckless woman emerges, conveyed to us mostly by what the poet says about her, what she says, and the sounds of her speech—to use Lorenzo's own word, a *cicaleccio* (cicadalike chirping or buzzing).

Chattering while she tugs on the men's beards, Angela begins to recount her grand origins—in other words, the history of her family and how she acquired her name. Then, inspired by delusions of grandeur she makes the outrageous proposal that her lovers should rent for her Ca' Loredan, one of the fanciest palaces in Venice. In that house she will have luxurious furnishings, including the Venetian *spalliere*, engage six servants and a page, enjoy the use of a boat, and feast from private stores of wine and grain. "This country bumpkin wants to set herself up with more good things than ever a queen had," Lorenzo drily remarks.

But when the company arrives at the next stop, the town of Chioggia, Angela grows alarmed. Proudly she announces: "A person like me hardly intends to spend the night here." She is furious that the boatman does not obey her and turn back, yet soon resigns herself and cheerily goes ashore. In this interim she continues to describe the presents she expects Lorenzo to give her—"I want a gold cap [*scuffia*]!" she exclaims. As soon as she is on the landing, however, she finds herself surrounded by a band of Lorenzo's accomplices. The courtesan still does not understand. The description of her arrival at the tavern in Chioggia is worthy of Alexander Pope, although not half so gentle (after all, the eighteenth-century gentleman was only describing the rape of a lock of hair):

The famous Zaffetta giving herself airs
and wearing half a perfume shop on her person
adorns her speech as if she were a nymph,
proceeding slowly, leaning on one man then another.
Here in Chioggia she wants to seem an empress.
(ll. 277–82)

She is "leaning" presumably because of her high clogs. After a dinner of oysters (considered an aphrodisiac—in Dutch paintings they appear as sexual symbols) and abundant wine, the lovers go to bed. Angela with one eye open and one eye closed does not know whether it is day or night, but Lorenzo is wide awake, determined to avenge himself on a *facchina* (a porteress; porters, most of them from Bergamo, were considered by Venetians humble, awkward, and gullible).

Not even contemplation of Angela's beautiful buttocks dissuades the lover from his intent, for, as Lorenzo succinctly puts it, speaking of himself in the third person, "The man craves vengeance not lovemaking." In fact, throughout the poem, sex is a question of honor, not of lust. Sexuality is taken for granted and presented in a comic light.

When it is announced to Angela that she is about to undergo a "royal" rape, she is furious and begins to curse, as indeed the daughter of a policeman should. The first assailant is a squalid sodomite who knows her father. Although she offers him permanent sexual rights if he will have pity on her, the man does not relent. "He sodomizes her on a whim," Lorenzo clarifies, "not out of desire."

In the following episodes, Angela is subject to the will of a procession of peasants and laborers—fishermen, gondoliers, servants, porters, priests, and sacristans. The taste for grotesque, misogynistic descriptions recalls the infamous *Puttana errante* (*The Wandering Whore*) attributed variously to Lorenzo Venier and to Pietro Aretino (but probably a pastiche assembled by both of them together with others).

After the fishermen, boatmen, and porters, follow priests and sacristans, and there are parodies of orations and confessions with Angela given a mock absolution together with a sermon about practicing the right rather than the wrong kind of courtesan love. Having come to know her character, we are not surprised to find the woman furious rather than repentant, but she has the sense to try to save her reputation. Pretending to be moved by her tears and sighs, Lorenzo promises Angela that the public will hear of only eight men, but when the band returns to Venice from Chioggia they write on the walls that Angela Zaffetta has satisfied no fewer than thirty-one on 6 April (the total, as we know, was eighty). Meanwhile, the courtesan in disgrace is ferried back home on a cargo boat used for transporting melons.

Another fine vignette is drawn when Lorenzo comes to describe Angela's godfather, the "furious, bestial, wrathful Borrin" who "with clenched teeth" and a pistol in hand, marches up and down in front of the portico, swearing in a loud voice. Nothing Borrin says or does influences the forces of order in that district of the city. The Five Wisemen [a regulatory commission] and the Captains of the Quarter blithely ignore the matter. What could a mere policeman do, in any case, faced with the power of the great Venier? Angela, however, demonstrates her own kind of power.

Although she has to have recourse to doctors and all of the courtesans in the neighborhood lock themselves indoors out of fear, only six days pass before Angela lords it over her admirers again:

Even more outrageous than before,
that thief plays Queen Isolde on her balcony.
(ll. 703–4)

Having failed to reduce her verticality to a horizonality, Lorenzo bitterly observes that Angela thinks of herself as mighty and tall as the belltower in Piazza di San Marco, emblem of Venice itself and, as Lorenzo was perfectly aware, a phallic symbol.

Finally, the author writes, it is natural desire—the erotic drive in men—that makes the balance between the sexes unequal in favor of women. Since she is so powerful and such a necessity (the moral goes), the courtesan must be courteous, or society will fall apart; at least it will see its fondest images reversed.

Angela survives the attack, but her future is in question, for one of the purposes of the thirty-one was to expose a courtesan to syphilis, thus ruining her career. For centuries prostitutes were blamed for its origin and spread and in this respect likened to devils.

No vituperation is spared, on the part of satirists, primarily in Italy, in regard to courtesans, their wicked habits and misdeeds. Long poems by anonymous authors range from processions through Hell (where throngs of courtesans and procuresses are named) to fake prognostications, unpleasantly descriptive catalogues (including one rare Florentine manuscript that was conceived as a competition for the most illustrious whore of the city), and the epic Rabelaisian fable of *La puttana errante*, the intention of which was to mock Elena Ballerini, a noted Venetian courtesan. In Venice, a whole genre sprang up of popular compositions devoted to the *bravi* and their vicissitudes in relation to the courtesans who employed them. Perfectly divided between the good and the evil visions is the French poet du Bellay, who allows a joyous courtesan and a sourly repentant one to narrate their equally convincing stories.

At the opposite extreme of the spectrum were virtuous and benevolent courtesans, those who could truly love. A generous act on the part of a Venetian courtesan kindles magnificent instincts in two Ferrarese gentlemen, in a tale by Giraldi Cinthio, aimed at presenting the Ferrarese court as the seat of liberality and courtesy. Ardelia in Sforza Oddi's play *L'erofilomachia* (1572) is a kind of courtesan saint, the first example after Terence of the sentimentalized prostitute who became so popular in eighteenth- and nineteenth-century literature. More courteous than her courtier lover, Ardelia exhibits an amazing eloquence both when couching her passion in Platonic terms and when arguing as a jurist might, in order to set the plot straight.

It is in fact through their speech that courtesans redeem themselves, defend themselves, and even—sometimes—come to exist at all, in fiction and in life.

· THE COURTESAN DEFENDS HERSELF ·

Sometimes courtesans responded to abuse with grace and at other times with effrontery. Isabella da Luna, at least as she is evoked in two of Bandello's liveliest stories, seems to have protected her interests using both methods. Still living in Rome when Brantôme came there in 1555, Isabella da Luna had been born in Granada. According to Zoppino, early in her life Isabella da Luna had followed various armies through Europe, in the role of what the Germans, using a bastardized French term, called the *marketenderin* (marcher-into-the-tent). The camp follower became in fact a stereotyped figure in northern art. A striking example of one of these is the prostitute in a tent in a drawing by Urs Graf entitled *Soldier Visiting the Harlot Fortuna*.

In the mid-1530s, after having followed the imperial army through the Netherlands and Germany and even on to Tunisia, Isabella came to Rome to "retire," but many adventures were still ahead of her. Some of these were real escapades and some were forays into the realm of wittiness and skilled repartee. Like many courtesans, Isabella da Luna was known for her sharp tongue and her willingness to use it.

One night Isabella saved her reputation and self-esteem through the use of that tongue. In part II, novella 51, Bandello relates the story of a clever trick Isabella paid on an ungenerous dinner guest. The setting of this tale is of particular interest suggesting the ambiance in which women like Isabella spent so much time.

Isabella's principal lover at this time was Umberto Strozzi, a Mantuan relative of the Florentine banking family to which Filippo Strozzi, great lover of courtesans belonged. Umberto willingly advised the lovely courtesan about finance and real estate, negotiating for her the sale of an expensive building in Rome. At the time of the dinner party in question,

Urs Graf, *Soldier Visiting the Harlot Fortuna* (drawing).
16th century. Städelsches Kunstinstitut and Stätdische
Galerie, Frankfurt am Main

Isabella was already well established as a landlady
collecting her rents.

Isabella often entertained in her own establishment, but she also enjoyed coming to dinner at Umberto's in the house where he lived along with
friends, two brothers also from Mantua. Another
person who frequented this household was the envoy of the cardinal of Mantua, Rocco Biancalena, a
man unusually well-acquainted with the facts of Isabella's existence.

To enliven these evenings, the hosts devised entertaining pretexts, although they stopped short of
making the banquets into "symposia," with the formal or informal telling of tales, as in classical times.
One night Rocco confessed that he was dying to tell
the truth about Isabella. If allowed to do so, he
would offer a splendid dinner for the group. It was
typical of Isabella that she enthusiastically accepted
the invitation to attend this event, remarking,
"What can you say about me other than I am a

whore? Everyone knows it already. There is no need
to blush about it!" These words foreshadow a similar
if more eloquent defense on the part of Veronica
Franco, who, decades later in Venice, smoothed her
greatly ruffled feathers by saying to her lover Maffio
Venier, who had verbally abused her:

> If you insist on calling me a whore
> that is all right, for if I am one
> there must be praiseworthy whores in the world!
> (*Rime*, XVI, 178–80)

(Veronica has been analyzing word-by-word the
cruel pun Maffio made of her name: Ver Unica Puttana (True Unique Whore).

Fortunately for Isabella, Rocco had character
traits far more serious in the eyes of Renaissance society than her trade of venal love, for he was given
to *maldicenza* (saying spiteful things about people)
especially behind their backs. Rocco had been in-
dulging in this vice particularly in regard to a superior of his, a certain Romeo, envoy of the cardinal's
who had recently arrived in Rome and naturally had
been welcomed at the Strozzi home. Perhaps it was
true that Romeo was as stingy as Rocco painted him
to be; still, it was not kind to describe the watered-
down wine and meager meat served at his table, especially when Romeo was out of the room.

When everyone including Romeo gathered for
the supper on the appointed evening, Rocco first
handed Isabella a three-page account of her life that
she was to read aloud. Isabella, graciously taking it,
read a few lines, then pretended to be reading from
the piece of paper but, instead, went on to recite—
as in a litany—all the terrible things Rocco had said
about Romeo, adding at the end, "Is not the behavior of this rascal Rocco outrageous? I think he
should be hanged! I never met Romeo, but people
say he is very pleasant." Romeo, recognizing the
truth of what had been said, promptly left, and
Rocco, in danger for his career (he was presently living in the same house as his superior), followed soon
after. The others went on to enjoy the fine dinner
and to celebrate Isabella's triumph.

There are other instances in Renaissance literature when it is the courtesan's role to mete out justice; often it is she who gives a sense of measure and

Ludovico Pozzoserrato (Ludwig Toeput), *Courtesans and Gentlemen*. 16th century. Private collection

balance to intercourse of every kind. Although not quite ready to accept the figure of the honest courtesan triumphing brilliantly on the social scene and feeling that he must call even Isabella *sfacciata* (disgraceful) and *meretrice publica* (public prostitute), Bandello cannot help wondering at her image and painting the "humanistic" atmosphere appropriate to her and in which she flourished:

What other women frequent so many different kinds of brains as the courtesans of the Roman [i.e., papal] court? Since Rome is their natural meeting place, the most outstanding and noblest minds of the world go there to compete with one another. There, every species of literary genre flourishes, whether Latin and Greek or Italian. There one finds great experts in law, philosophy and natural and moral sciences; there miraculous painters come . . . .

The courtesans' stage viewed on a large scale was the papal court, on a small one the individual salon. Thus Bandello pictures the Strozzi household in

Rome as an ongoing salon: "In their dwelling, there is continuously singing and playing, as well as discussions about Latin and Italian literature and many other noble subjects." Finally, Bandello focuses on Isabella herself, making it clear why she, above all, was invited to appear there:

Isabella provides superb entertainment in every social ambiance for the reason that she knows how to comport herself with men of every kind and answer them back. She is extremely agreeable and pleasing, quick and concise with words, and she knows how to give a retort on any subject. She speaks Italian well [remember that Isabella was Spanish] and, if someone stings her, she flashes back with a quick retort.

Does even Bandello fear Isabella's sharp tongue, or the sharp tongue in general of the courtesan? As an agent of justice, Isabella has punished Rocco for more than slandering his superior in the diplomatic world. The crime about to be perpetrated before her skillful intervention could be called, in terms of the

Bartolommeo Veneto, *Flora*. 16th century. Städelsches Kunstinstitut und Städtische Galerie, Frankfurt am Main

courtesan's role in culture, a "crime against dissimulation." The courtesan's other nature (what she is as opposed to what she seems to be) must always remain hidden, and she must always function as an illusion. When he exposes courtesans in an unflattering light, Bandello reveals an uneasiness about what he is doing, as if it were a kind of *lèse-courtisanerie*, something that simply is not done and that risks injuring society's own image of itself.

In another Bandello novella (IV, 16) Isabella da Luna fails to pay her bills and tries to fend off a creditor by offering her charms instead of money. When the governor of Rome, a bishop from Pavia, hears about her bribe, he sends a sergeant-at-arms with a summons to the courtesan, presenting it to her in front of her house. Cursing him, Isabella rips it up. She lands in jail for a while, until she pays her debt. At that point, the governor decides to make her an example to others of her kind and sentences her to

a public whipping. Isabella is hoisted over the shoulders of one man while another applies fifty whiplashes to her naked buttocks. All Rome gathers to watch this "noble spectacle," the red blood colorfully splashed over the pure white. As if shaking himself reluctantly out of the stupor that such a sight provokes in him, Bandello closes with the description of Isabella, her feet upon the earth once more, shaking herself as a dog might and marching off with as proud a demeanor "as if she were going to a wedding."

A dog going to a wedding?—all of Bandello's ambivalence is captured in this comic story in which the courtesan is diminished and degraded, but paradoxically aggrandized at the same time.

The same dual vision of the courtesan's nature invests novellas by many Italian authors of the time, constituting an irregular series of palinodes offering two sides of the same story and showing the courtesan as both high and low, responsible and irresponsible, socially corrective on the one hand and capable of abusing her power on the other. It is understandable that writers were perplexed. Bandello tells us, in one place, that one could never get to the end of describing what courtesans do and are.

The "honest courtesan" is an ambiguous concept, and this duplicity inevitably affects her depiction in literature and the visual arts. Since courtesans always had to seem something other than they were, the contradiction between appearance and reality was one of the prime characteristics of their profession. A courtesan's successs depended on her ability to produce a continual optical and psychological illusion.

The courtesan appears in literature and in art both dressed and undressed, but neither mode is guileless. She is half-dressed in her role as Flora, with one or both breasts skillfully exposed, as portrayed by Palma, Titian, Bartolommeo Veneto, Jan Massys, and others. Dressed, courtesans were simulacrum and lure. As they appear in repertoires of dress such as Cesare Vecellio's and Giacomo Franco's, and as they are described indirectly in sumptuary laws, courtesans imitate the aristocratic class of women.

If her outward appearance resembled that of a re-

LETTERS FROM A LOVER TO COURTESANS

Can you imagine, you who are life itself to me, how much I suffer, envying this fortunate sheet of paper that in a short while will be worthy of touching those extremely white hands and of being looked at by those graceful eyes that are the reason Love is feared, indeed revered? I swear that I am so troubled by this fact of writing that I write thousands of letters, then burn them all. I am almost tempted to disobey you, not writing any more, but then I get a hold of myself and realize that this object does not have sensation or intellect and therefore cannot know how blessed it is. Oh dear, those ruses the gods used to employ in order to enjoy the women they loved suddenly comes to mind, and I am in a cold sweat thinking that perhaps Jove has transformed himself into that very sheet in order to touch those lovely hands of yours, those suave breasts between which sometimes you used to offer, for a few precious moments, a nook for my written words to lie in. I am right to worry, for neither Leda, nor Europa, nor Danae, for whom he turned himself into a swan, a bull, and a golden rain could compare with you. . . .

Ah, noblest of mistresses, don't you realize that the more you call yourself noble and me ignoble, the more the opposite emerges as the truth? If you are noble, isn't he who loves you noble as well?—if you don't know that, then you're ignoble. If you weren't low-class you wouldn't have found excuses to send away someone who, thinking you, a gentle soul, loved you as much as his own life. In other words, you are not noble; how can you dare—lowest of the low— announce to the world my lack of nobility? All that you can say about me is that I loved. . . . If women like you had any recognition of your own worthlessness and squalor, you would consider yourselves blessed if low-class men took you on to serve them—I mean those men who, . . . loving as they do that sole part of you they have a taste for, are the reason that you boast precisely of what you should be ashamed of. You and your peers judge as worthy only that man who has worldly goods, not the one who lives virtuously. Well, go on wallowing in mud, you painted toads. Sell your fake beauty to whoever can pay a high price for it, but please do not be so arrogant as to compare your merchandise with the kind that those women offer who love honesty more than any other thing and who sell the true and divine beauty of their spirit to whoever is willing to pay for it with the sweat of his virtuous qualities: these buyers alone are noble.

Girolamo Parabosco, *Lettere amorose*, 26, I, 11

spectable woman, a courtesan's actions were different. The courtesan dissembled not only in her clothes and physical trappings, but also in her gestures, speech, and behavior. What she said and did often had a second meaning, and finesse could be merely a way of instrumenting codes of etiquette in order to attain specific material ends.

A letter of Aretino's, admiring and ironical by turns, painting a psychological portrait of Angela del Moro, reveals a great deal about the techniques of dissimulation:

You do not use astuteness, soul of the courtesan's art, in order to betray, as others do, but in such a clever fashion that whoever spends his money on you is sure to gain rather than to lose. . . . Moderate in whatever you do, you take for yourself only that which is given, never plundering the stores of that which has not been offered. Deceit is not part of your make-up. Your womanly cunning has a noble turn to it. You abstain from the usual feminine chatter and keep away from silly people and pompous asses. Only those who honor you properly are allowed to enjoy your loveliness and the rare splendor of your person . . . . Lies, envy, malice—staff of courtesan life—are not what motivates your heart and tongue. You cultivate virtue and honor those who are virtuous—a quality rare among those people who do what others want, for a price. For all these reasons, you are worthy of having me call myself yours. . . .

(Flora, *Lettere*, I, 291)

Not only did courtesans wear disguises and practice the arts of deception, but they also were always meant to be undressed and "read"—seized beneath the veils thrown so casually over their bodies. Much about them was deliberately artificial and transparent at the same time, starting with their names and genealogies, which satirists, who were often rejected suitors, brutally demystified. This was especially true of the poetic constructs they wove around their persons and those of their lovers. These were never to be taken at face value, but as imitations of life that almost became the thing itself.

Gaspara Stampa, making love with Collaltino, fancies she is Alcmena in the arms of Jove as "dawn delays so much longer than usual in coming." Veronica Franco becomes Leda and Danae when Henry III of France comes to her bed to enjoy her as a god might. Culture encouraged courtesans to dramatize, and they enriched the repertory with their self-images.

Veronica is perhaps the most skillful of all in the art of composing her image for the public. Her words are an extension of her self, and through them she becomes an Amazon, Venus, and finally Venice. When she gives herself to Henry, she does so as a representation of the goddess, then precipitates the experience into the actual gift of her portrait (not the lost one by Tintoretto, but a small enameled one in relief, probably shut into a case). She also sends him poems, one describing the portrait, extending and qualifying the image.

In the sonnets to Henry, Veronica fuses imagery of Mars and Jove, stating that the king has been tested by a thousand battles. Coming to her "poor house" without his usual regal adornments, he has made her "an Alcmena, a Leda, a Europa, a Danae," and himself Anfitrione, a swan, a bull, a shower of gold. Being like Jove, he has elevated her to divine stature, but the implication is that she has transmitted a sacred *eros* to him as he appeared in earthly form. Even kings have to frequent courtesans. He has gone to her for sacramental reasons (the cult of pleasure); she now makes the experience permanently available to him through images:

> Take, King, perfect, paragon of virtue,
> that which my hand stretches to give you—
> this sculpted and colored configuration,
> sign and metaphor of my real self.
>
> (*Rime*, II, 1–4)

This portrait is being exchanged, as Veronica explains in an accompanying letter, for the one of himself that the king has left in her heart. A particular pride invests this triple gift in the form of her physical person and intellect, her poems, and a living image of her face. The portrait mirrors her, the poem mirrors the portrait mirroring her, and she herself is originally an artificial image such as Flora mirroring a mythological concept or ideal of beauty. In each manifestation, she is herself and not herself, an individual (a noble soul in a noble body), and also the very symbol of what is most desired.

Ultimately, Veronica's image, or one like hers, is the one Venice itself projects, and thus we find this image diffused across walls, ceilings, and canvases, always in a new form. Perhaps this is because the courtesan is a multiplication of images, but it is also because a portrait is a contradiction in itself, since it is the fixed image of something alive and in motion. Veronica sends Henry III her portrait as a sublime memento of one night's eros, but the woman herself cannot be transferred or preserved, cannot be given once and for all. What the image contains is the conception that the woman had of herself, and that is the gift she and Renaissance culture give to the individual lover and to the world.

THREE

The Courtesan Image in Art: The First Phase

· The Genesis of the Mistress Portrait ·

When Renaissance artists began to portray courtesans, developing this into a major genre, where did they look first for precedents? In the ancient world courtesans figured greatly in the visual arts. Especially beautiful ones modeled for paintings and sculptures. In addition, monuments were set up, sometimes in temples, to illustrious courtesans. These seem to have been of two types—civic examples, in which the courtesan appears as herself or as a symbol to illustrate a virtue or a good deed, and religious examples, in which the courtesan represents a goddess, most often Venus.

An example of the first type is a courtesan dear to Boccaccio's heart—Leaena, who defended her lover by mutilating herself. Pliny, Plutarch, and Polyaenus all relate the tale of Leaena, a Greek courtesan, mistress of Aristogeiton, one of the men who slew the tyrant Hipparchus in 514 B.C. Even extreme torture could not make Leaena confess who had carried out the deed. Finally, unable to bear the pain, she bit off her tongue. The Athenians, desiring to honor this courtesan's heroism, set up a statue of a bronze, tongueless lioness in the Propylae on the Acropolis. Lactantius, writing from the Christian point of view about the episode, insists that the reason an image of the animal whose name she bore was used instead of a bronze of the heroine herself was that "it was unlawful to set up a statue of a courtesan in a temple." But the presence in temples of the many Venuses modeled on courtesans and intended for ritualistic use gives the lie to this argument, as does the fact that a painting of Pompey's Flora also found its way into one of these sanctuaries.

In the spirit of humanism, Renaissance artists eagerly plucked heroines of the ancient world from the shadows of legend, releasing them from the suffocating confines of the compendia to which "illustrious women" had been relegated and setting them up as examples of boldness and exceptionalness. Hans Holbein the Younger, in designing a frieze of ancient historical scenes for the top floor of the facade of Hertenstein House in Lucerne, included, among five scenes of ancient history showing high ethical qualities, *Leaena before the Judges*.

The tradition of raising up statues of courtesans in

Hans Holbein the Younger, *Leaena before the Judges.* 1517–18. Oeffentliche Kunstsammlung, Basel

Anonymous artist, *Portrait of Empress Theodora* (mosaic). 6th century. Church of San Vitale, Ravenna

the ancient world derived from an impulse to honor women whose benevolent actions toward the state deserved commemoration. Physical beauty was also considered a positive influence on the onlooker, as though the aesthetic had taken on a "civic" function.

Theodora's statue was raised at Constantinople on a porphyry column, but what did people see when they looked at her—the lascivious, comic stage actress of the early years, the cunning mercenary, the concubine of Justinian inflaming the emperor's heart and loins, or the sanctified legal wife endowed with authority and thought to be the transmitter of divine influence? In a mosaic portrait in San Vitale, Ravenna, Theodora is shown heavily laden with jewels and pearls, her image wavering at that fragile dividing line between earthly and heavenly power.

It is well known that Praxiteles immortalized the courtesan Phryne as Aphrodite of Cnidus, and that Apelles painted her in the guise of Aphrodite Anadyomene (Aphrodite at her bath). In both instances the implication must have been that the courtesan was not only like a goddess, but that the goddess herself, had she descended to earth, would have chosen to be portrayed in this form. In other words, her mortal woman's beauty already radiated the divine.

But it is one thing to raise up an image of an actual woman; it is quite another to give her the attributes of a deity.

In Praxiteles's statue of Aphrodite of Cnidus, the two natures are subtly intermingled. A handsome woman, aware of and self-confident about her nudity, is about to bathe, revealing her beauty naturally. As she does so, the natural, realistic act weds a contemporary concept of the ideal physical manifestations of a goddess. The real becomes ideal, and the ideal real. Lucian speaks of "the beautiful line of her forehead and brow, and her melting eye full of joy and pleasure." The narrow eyes of the gaze seem to look beyond us or perhaps—which is the same thing in Platonic terms—within, finding there a spiritual beauty akin to the external one.

The Aphrodite of Cnidus was important, both as a cult image and as a portrait of a beautiful woman who had actually existed. Physical beauty was literally adored in ancient Greece, and mythology offers many examples of gods and goddesses falling in love with mortals. Venus and Adonis is the most obvious example, although Paris must have offered something unique if he was called upon to judge the goddesses' own beauty contest. As for the goddesslike, beautiful woman, she was, if not actually worshiped, at least keenly sought after as though she were one of them.

Attracted to beauty, the highest of the gods [Jove] goes through roof tiles in the form of gold or turns into a bull, or as an eagle frequently sprouts feathers, as when he went to get Aegina (Ath. XIII. 566, amended in Ovid *Met* VI. 113).

Not only gods but the highest ranks and most intelligent of men were similarly beguiled. A legend gleefully adopted by Renaissance artists has Aristotle so vanquished by the beauty of the courtesan Phyllis that he let her ride him as a horse.

Beauty provoked conflict as well as adoration, however, raising the unresolvable issue of whether love is rational or irrational. The satellite courtesans of Aspasia, a number of whom she imported from Asia, were blamed for being the cause of Pericles' stepping up of the Persian wars. But, viewed in the right light, even the fierce conflicts of man against man could be seen as justified by the great prize of beauty. " 'Tis no cause for anger that Trojans and well-greaved Achaeans should suffer woes a long time for such a woman as Helen," lament the elders of the people in the *Iliad*, "for she is marvelously like the deathless goddesses in countenance" (III. 154–58).

Beauty inevitably aroused lust; nevertheless, the Greeks were convinced that the sheer contemplation of beauty could have socially beneficial effects. Although their interest was more in her material, cosmically regenerative powers than her strictly amorous ones, it is noteworthy that the Romans claimed to be descended directly from Venus.

Since it was thought that beauty could move a man to civic virtue, portraits of courtesans had a clear function as long as they were conceived for and displayed to the public. It is only when they

Praxiteles, *Aphrodite*. 5th century B.C. Vatican Museum, Rome

Master of the Housebook, *Aristotle and Phyllis*. 16th century. Ashmolean Museum, Oxford

Francesco Morandini (Il Poppi), *Apelles and Campsaspe*. Late 16th century. Palazzo Vecchio, Florence

came to fulfill private desires that their function became ambiguous and their actual physical destinies hazardous.

In the fourth century B.C., Lais was a renowned model for artists. Noticing her when still quite young as she was coming from the fountain of Pyrene, the painter Apelles expressed astonishment at her beauty. When he invited Lais to a banquet he was planning for friends, the latter criticized him for having invited a girl instead of a courtesan. "Wait three years," he flung back at them, "and you will see before you a beautiful woman ripe for pleasure." Lais was reputed to have such beautiful breasts that painters came especially to copy them. In this respect and in others she was a bitter rival of Phryne's.

Funeral monuments were set up to courtesans in ancient times, and it is significant that Lais's burial place was long disputed, Polemon claiming that the tomb lay on the banks of the Peneus River where a stone urn bore the inscription:

> Proud, unconquered Greece was slave to
> Lais, Love's incarnate deity
> Whom Corinth bred. Now she lies in her grave
> Among famous Thessaly's fields . . . .
> (Ath. XIII. 589b)

while others such as Pausanius insisted that Lais's grave was in Corinth near the Cranion, in a grove of cypresses before the city gates. "Here one finds, in the precinct of Bellerophon, the temple of Black Aphrodite and the grave of Lais surmounted by a lioness holding a ram." Epigrams in the *Greek Anthology* also speak of the courtesan's dying at Corinth, and supposedly a Corinthian coin, showing Lais on one side and the lioness with a ram on the other, remained a tribute to her existence.

The seemingly divine wisdom of Aspasia lifted her above ordinary mortals; similarly, Phryne's beauty gave her a status that exempted her, at least in one instance, from the rigor of the law. Phyrne, the living Aphrodite of Praxiteles and Apelles, was on trial for heresy in Athens. A device either of her own invention or of her lawyer's (the sources are in disagreement, and it would be useful to know) enabled her to save herself by putting her beauty on display. According to Athenaeus,

Euthias brought a capital charge against Phryne who had come to Athens from Thespia. When she was acquitted he was extremely mortified. . . . Hyperides appeared for her, and when he saw that his defense of her was proving ineffective and that the judges would surely find her guilty, he led her out, tore open her tunic, and laid bare her bosom, concluding his speech with an appeal to the indulgence people should feel at that sight. By invoking this priestess and prophetess of Aphrodite, he filled the judges with fear, and she was saved from being put to death and was acquitted (Ath. XIII. 590).

Statues, paintings, funerary monuments, coins, and literary tableaux vivants all attest to the power of the beautiful courtesan to be represented in cultural life. In Alexandrian times, the mistress portrait seems securely to have come into its own, as testified by the example of the Greek Campsaspe. A story connected with the painting Apelles did of her for Alexander intrigued the imagination of Renaissance artists, posing as it did a problem they were grappling with regarding the private courtesan portrait, something new on the cultural scene in 1500 as well.

Apelles painting Campsaspe in the nude became a commonplace for Renaissance art and art theory. In late Mannerist painting, there is a striking representation of it taking place in the central square of a city that is an architectural fantasy: *Apelles and Campsaspe* by Francesco Morandini (Il Poppi). Engravers particularly enjoyed this theme and the opportunity it lent to show the artist together with his model. The School of Fontainebleau produced several engraved examples, one of which—by Leon Davent—is reproduced here.

The legend concerning this painting is a simple one: evidently Apelles, having been commissioned by Alexander, with whom he was on friendly terms, to do a portrait of the king's mistress, fell in love with her, and so great was his desire and so lovely the painting, that Alexander literally gave her to him.

One way to interpret this story, emphasizing the lifelikeness of the painting itself, is as a parable about naturalism in the arts. The painting was so true to nature that it could substitute for the actual person. But there is a troubling message concerning the model herself, whose wishes seem never to have been consulted. This spontaneous discarding of famous courtesans is puzzling. It is said that Pompey (108–148 B.C.) conceded his mistress Flora to his good friend Germinius, who had fallen in love with her.

It is reported also that when Flora the courtesan waxed old, she most delighted to talk of the familiarity which she had with Pompey, being a young man: telling that after she had lain with him, she could not possibly rise from him, but she must need [bear the sign of his teeth on her body]. She would tell also how one of Pompey's familiars and companions called Germinius, fell in love with her, and was a marvelously earnest suitor to obtain her goodwill: and that she answered him flatly, she would not, for the love she bore to Pompey. Germinius thereupon broke the matter to Pompey himself. Pompey, desirous to pleasure him, granted the request: howbeit Germinius after that, would not come near Flora nor speak

Leon Davent, *Apelles and Campsaspe* (engraving). 16th century. The British Museum, London

unto her, albeit it appeared that he yet loved her. But Flora took this not courtesanlike, for she was sick a long time for very grief of mind, and the thought she took upon it (*Lives*, V, 1.3).[15]

If Flora was "sick for a long time with grief and longing," there is no reason to think that Campsaspe was any less sensitive.

Perhaps the deeper meaning of the Apelles–Campsaspe–Alexander story is that, by painting a portrait of a woman or writing a poem about her, one could possess her. This is, of course, the opposite of the truth that modern artists, above all Picasso, discovered. His model and muse, viewed in so many bewildering ways, finally and humorously eludes him.

If by the time the Greek painter has finished making a portrait of the king's mistress she is his, there is no reason why her very person should not be his reward for having created such a beautiful painting. The story is somewhat related to the legend of Pygmalion, for in a sense the artist creates the woman of his desire. The woman and the painted image become interchangeable—one is the equivalent of the other, and both are "real." The portrait can in fact seem more lifelike than the person, who is more evanescent than the absolute that is attained by art. Since both art and nature are necessary for enjoyment, it is precisely in order to offer his friend and official painter as complete an enjoyment as possible that Alexander, treating Campsaspe as though she were an extension or mirror image of the figure on the canvas, releases her to Apelles. If the courtesan, in this instance, was conceived of to start with as an object, in art she becomes further "objectified."

Yet it is precisely when the object of desire becomes a work of art that a reversal occurs. Men begin to revere and fall in love with the images created after these beautiful women, as if the naturalistic representations contained a power, a life force of their own. Plutarch goes on to tell us how, even after Pompey had abandoned Flora herself, Flora's image played an important role:

All this notwithstanding, it is said that this Flora had then such fame for her passing grace and beauty, that Cecilius Metellus setting forth and beautifying the temple of Castor and Pollux, with goodly tables and pictures: among the rest, he caused her picture to be lively drawn for her excellent beauty (*Lives*, V, 2.4).

Falling in love with statues and paintings, even making love to them is an ancient fantasy, one of which the Renaissance was keenly aware. Giorgio Vasari, writing in the introductory section of the *Lives* about art in antiquity, tells how men violated the laws, going into the temples at night and making love with statues of Venus. In the morning, priests would enter the sanctuaries to find stains on the marble figures.

To be located in an inner sanctum was one of the destinies of Renaissance courtesan portraits as well, although now it was a question of palace boudoirs and baths rather than temples. In ancient times, one kind of Venus was placed in Pompeiian broth-

els, and another in temples. In the Renaissance, the functions are merged in a single figure, but some of the sacred quality still clung to these objects, and men still made love to them with their eyes.

One of the questions that continues to emerge as one contemplates courtesans in Renaissance art is whether these representations, like certain ancient ones, wielded, or were thought to wield, a magical power. Some were kept as private icons in intimate places, along with emblematic specimens of antique art.

Cardinal Bibbiena, for whose bath in the Vatican Raphael made lascivious designs that were transferred to fresco by Giulio Romano, decided to keep in this lush setting a beautiful statue of Venus from ancient times. Pietro Bembo, the poet who became a cardinal, attempted to dissuade him from doing this, in order to appropriate for himself the image Bibbiena had wanted to exalt by placing it in his private shrine, but failed to succeed. To console him for the loss of it, Bembo had added: "You may come and gaze at the statue whenever you like, even if it is in my possession" (*Lettere*, Milan, 1809, I, 49–52, 25 April 1516).

The thought of the cardinal and cardinal-to-be standing rapt together before the nude Venus is mildly outrageous considered by today's standards, but the papal court in this period was notorious for licentiousness, and the two men figured as interlocutors on the subject of love in Castiglione's *Courtier*. Bembo's *Asolani* (prose discourses) argue the case for so-called Platonic love, but sensuality is never very far away, and Bembo's own long-term relationship with a concubine was well known and publicized. Many grieved her death, and poets of the time composed poems to her memory.

If ancient statues of Venus were hoarded, worshiped, and made love to as "mental" concubines—visual hostages—it was only a small step to place portraits of contemporary Venuses in the same context. Even today it is legitimate to wonder whether Raphael's *Fornarina* is a kind of garden deity meant to be worshiped and to see Leonardo, who craved to create an image of a woman "all of a man's senses could possess," having produced in the *Gioconda* an object capable of seducing the men who looked at it. The singular dangers of humanistic imitation in this instance were patently clear to some critics.

In his *Dieci libri di pensieri diversi* (*Ten Books of Various Thoughts*), Alessandro Tassoni, taking his clue from Pliny, expresses his discontent that contemporary artists have taken up the habit of the ancient Greek painter Arellius of portraying his mistresses as divinities.[16] But artists had been doing this for well over a century and continued to do so into the next age.

By coming at a later time, there was an advantage, since it was possible to compliment a woman by posing her as a classical goddess or heroine, or even as a courtesan of classical times posing as goddesses and heroines. Hans Holbein the Younger, whose curiosity about antiquity has already been noted, created a pair of paintings—one mythological and one historical—in order to pay homage to a Swiss woman whom one art historian calls "a highborn but frivolous young lady of Basel" but who seems to have been a courtesan. The sitter of the painting, Magdalena Offenburg, daughter of a wholesale merchant and widow of the son of the mayor of Basel, lived licentiously and let her own daughters do likewise. The painting was probably painted for a rich lover. Although it has been speculated that the Cupid in the *Venus* pendant was Holbein's own son Phillip, we do not know whether the artist was ever Magdalena's lover or not. A unique humanistic experiment, Holbein's double portrait of Magdalena as Venus and Lais of Corinth opens itself to all kinds of interpretation.

Ostensibly the subject is a mistress presenting herself in the best light by taking on the garb of two prestigious figures. So-called "fanciful" or allegorical portraiture was fashionable in this period, notably in France, where mistresses of kings and kings themselves took on the guise of such mythical figures as Diana and Actaeon. For a portrait by Bronzino, the Genoese admiral and statesman Andrea Doria posed in the nude as Neptune. Holbein planned, but never carried out, a monumental wall painting showing the Queen of Sheba coming to Solomon, in which Solomon would have had the features of Henry VIII of England. The artist and theoretician Lomazzo posed himself in a self-por-

Marco Dente (Marco di Ravenna) after Raphael's design for fresco decoration in the bath of Cardinal Bibbiena, Vatican, Rome. 16th century. Bibliothèque Nationale, Paris

trait as Bacchus holding a thyrsus in his hand; and in the eighteenth century Angelica Kauffmann painted herself as a bacchante. Hence, although she might have been portrayed as a Magdalene as her name suggested, Magdalena must have been flattered to pose as Venus and a votary of Venus of ancient times.

It has been suggested that the painting of Magdalena as Lais has, if not an outright satirical, an ironic intent of exposing the woman's greedy mercenary habits by showing her with an outstretched arm over a ledge scattered with golden coins. Although it is unlikely that the pose could have been managed without the sitter's cooperation, the painter was certainly free to make observations about Magdalena as a courtesan, and in a sense *Lais*

Anonymous, *Mars and Venus* (fresco from Pompeii). 1st century B.C.
Museo Archeologico Nazionale, Naples

Gilles Congnet, *Mars and Venus*. 16th century. Ex collection Hans
Kisters, Kreuzlingen

School of Fontainebleau, *Sabina Poppaea.* 16th century. Musée d'Art et d'Histoire, Geneva

can be seen to qualify *Venus*, if only for the reason that it is closer to the reality of the sitter.

Lais is a finer painting than *Venus*: Magdalena is shown in a more flattering pose; the features of her face are at once clearer and more idealized; her name is carved classical style in relief on the edge of the parapet behind which she is seated—all reinforcing the impression that Holbein is exalting rather than denigrating her.

A clue to the meaning of the painting may lie in the outstretched right hand, which is copied from Christ's left hand in Leonardo's *Last Supper* in the refectory of Santa Maria delle Grazie in Milan.[17] Lais holds her palm up toward the spectator in Christ's gesture, "Here is my body." This gesture may be a crude reference to the courtesans' profession—namely, the offering of their bodies for sale. If so, then the intent may well be humorous, but possibly something slightly different.

Lais of Corinth, the courtesan who posed for sculptors and painters, rivaled the great Phryne. Like many renowned personages, Lais was in her time criticized and calumnied. For example, it was said that since she was jealous of Phryne, Lais threw open her house to many lovers, making no distinction between wealthy and poor ones, turning no one away. Surely this alone would have constituted a basis for the analogy with Christ, even if a "democratic" generosity was in one case charitable, in the other lascivious and mercenary to boot. But a specific description of Lais coincides perfectly with the portrayal in Holbein's portrait. Epicrates comments about Lais when she is past her prime:

When Lais was young, she was wealthy and scornful; one could have had an audience with Pharnabazus [a satrap of Persia known for his inaccessability] more easily than with her. But now the years have carried her to the end of her professional life and her beautiful body is ruined. It is as easy to have access to her as to spit. Truly she is always going around prepared to drink with anyone. A stater or three-obol piece is a prize for her. Young or old, she welcomes them all. She is so humbled that she holds out her hand for anything that is offered to her (Kock ii.282).

The quotation fits, although it is troubling that the handsome and still-young Magdalena is posed as a courtesan available to all.

There is a further possibility of interpretation. Although it is nowhere made explicit, the Renaissance courtesan seems to have had a "sacramental" function for her lover. As the representative and embodiment of love, a courtesan offered her lover the possibility to participate in a divine eros by conjoining with her. The circumstances of courtship leading up to the act of love were intended to intensify and ennoble the experience. In a painting of *Mars and Venus* attributed to Gilles Congnet, Mars, his armor removed, sits at a clavichord looking back over his shoulder at a reclining nude Venus. Prominently placed between the two are a large loaf of bread on a plate and a conspicuous glass of wine. What could have been meant here if not that the courtesan offers a "consubstantiation," if not the spirit becoming flesh, at least a symbolic and real means for an ascension to true knowledge?

Certainly, it would be carrying things too far to suggest such a complex meaning for the Holbein portrait, which is a witty, worldly, and possibly ambiguous compliment to an enterprising, desirable woman. On the other hand, either consciously or not, the reference to Christ's gesture is present and has a meaning. If Lais offered herself to everyone in order to spite rivals and earn a living, the modern—that is, the Renaissance—courtesan, charged with the duty of representing Venus to her contemporaries, may do so because she is generous and aware of the transforming powers she possesses and can transmit. Like Christ, she may not be entirely understood.

Another example of a portrait of a Renaissance courtesan posed as a mistress of the ancient world is *Sabina Poppaea*, Nero's concubine who eventually became his wife. In this provocative painting by an artist of the School of Fontainebleau, an interesting feature is the elaborately transparent veil that, far from concealing, makes a show of its impossibility to conceal, thus taking on the role of theatrical prop, drawing attention to the beautiful breasts and milky flesh of the sitter.

Breasts are foremost in Lucretia portraits as well; in northern Italy there is a flurry of them. This particular historical personage symbolizing chastity seems an inappropriate guise for the courtesan, but the paradox only gave the painters a chance to reveal the possibilities of contiguity and disparity. Lorenzo Lotto's buxom *Lucretia* in her slightly decolleté, extremely elegant gown seems to be holding her name up to challenge more than to inform.

One of Girolamo Parabosco's mistresses was also named Lucrezia. She willingly posed for Micheli Parrhasio as her namesake, the virtuous, suicidal Roman princess. The writer's description of his emotions gazing at this portrait reveals a great deal about the complex feelings such works were meant to create in the viewer:

Sweet Parrhasio, I have just now seen your *Lucretia*: this is no painted image, indeed it is quite alive, and will make you immortal. This Lucretia is so wondrously beautiful and so fantastically executed according to such a wise design . . . that there is not a man on earth who would dare to confess than he remained continent gazing at such a lovely figure . . . . You have instilled a marvelous beauty in the eyes and the face . . . . We see her dying in the most vivid imaginable way, and one almost hears her heartrending moaning for her lost chastity (*Il primo libro delle lettere famigliari*, 29).

Courtesans also posed as heroines of romances and as real-life muses of poets of the past. In the late sixteenth and early seventeenth centuries, there are many depictions of female figures from poems by Ariosto and Tasso. Ruggiero and Angelica are sometimes shown in the poses of Mars and Venus, the painter taking advantage of the contrast between dressed and undressed bodies. An example of a muse is Giorgione's *Laura*, but this may be more than a courtesan named Laura; she is perhaps herself a poetess, creative subject as well as object.

Reviewing the various classical and romance poses in which the gesture of exposing the breasts bears a special significance, one is led to reflect once more on how the idea that beauty, particularly the sight of beauty, as a civilizing force reasserted itself in the Renaissance. Much of Renaissance art could be termed a "defense of Phryne" in the sense that the display of physical beauty becomes one of man's highest purposes.

The tale of how Phryne saved herself by baring her breasts to the judges impressed writers as well as artists. In a novella by Giraldi Cinthio, a courtesan accused by her lover of unfaithfulness, who fakes a suicide by pretending to stab herself, is compared by the author, in luscious terms, to Lucretia. At the sight of her breasts, her lover relents and forgives her. As the scene begins, Philene begs Africano to have mercy on her. When she hands Africano a sword and asks him to kill her with it, he thrusts it aside angrily, saying, "Why don't you try out those tears on the man whom you really love?" The courtesan replies:

"You gave me this sword, Africano, in order that I kill myself, and so that you can feel proud about it, I intend to kill myself. I would rather delight you by dying than annoy you by staying alive. . . . " Having said this, she tore open her clothes and aimed the sword into her left breast. Again it seemed as though she would leap upon the sword and let it thrust her through. This woman had the softest, the most beautiful, and the most lascivious breasts ever seen in the world, and Africano in the past had kissed them thousands and thousands of times. Therefore, as soon as he saw the sword point aimed toward the part of her that had been his greatest delight, he could not stand it any longer. Believing she really meant to kill herself, he moved the sword aside and, out of his mind and weeping, cried, "Sweetheart, what are you trying to do?" The cunning woman pretending to faint away let herself fall over into his arms and, with her breasts uncovered and tears rolling down her cheeks, sought to infatuate the young man more than ever (*Hecatomitti* I, intro., 3).

As in the case of the Parrhasio painting that so stirred Parabosco, a properly lascivious image can move the heart, almost morally uplift, at the same time as it incites sexual desire in the onlooker.

In these examples of breasts being exposed, there is at play a dialectical relationship between the concealed and the revealed. A passage in Athenaeus recounts Phryne's skill in employing techniques of concealment and revelation.

Phryne's beauty resided more particularly in that which is not seen. For which reason it was not easy to get a sight of her naked. She wore her clothing wrapped closely about her and did not frequent the public baths. But at the Eleusinian gathering, on the festival of Poseidon, before all the Greek world, she stripped, let down her hair, and bathed in the sea. And this inspired Apelles to paint Aphrodite Anadyomene . . . (Ath. XIII. 590–91).

We have seen how laying Phryne's bosom bare at her trial produced a religious awe in the judges. The Fer-

Lorenzo Lotto, *Lucretia*. 16th century. The National Gallery, London

rarese courtesan in the poem of that name, after describing in eloquent terms her other features, consonant with the canons of feminine beauty of that time, brags that her "secret parts" are the most beautiful of all. A curious poem of the early seventeenth century in the dialect of Friuli (Venetia Giulia) offers an elaborate, lush description of a mistress's genitalia, each part—clitoris, lips of the vagina, and so forth—presented with suitable metaphors. Aretino's Nanna gives an equally startling

description of her own body, but the effect is meant to be comical.

The hand on the breast in Renaissance painting reveals what is usually concealed. A tradition had grown up whereby the hand on the heart signified a pledge of faithfulness to a loved one or to an authority. In our period it also signifies devotion, but above all appears to be a symbolic gesture of display.[18] On the most obvious level the breast is a sign of fertility and regeneration. Ironically so, for the

Giorgione, *Laura* (Portrait of a Young Woman). 16th century. Kunsthistorisches Museum, Vienna

Paris Bordone, *Courtesan*. 16th century. Earl of Wemyss Collection, courtesy the National Galleries of Scotland, Edinburgh

Palma Vecchio, *Portrait of a Woman*. 16th century. Gemäldegalerie, Staatliche Museen Preussischer Kulturbesitz, Berlin

courtesan wanted no children. Yet to the extent that her iconography absorbs attributes of ancient goddess figures, she too comes to represent "the source," the milky beginning of all life, as well as the nourishing of the mind, the filling of a psychic space. The breast not only pointed to but also actively raised and offered, seemingly caressed by the hand of she who displays it, was a kind of plenum, a sphere signifying satiation. In addition, it was in itself a rounded, full form—eminently tangible yet held at that baffling and intriguing distance at which art holds things.

The gracefully curved arm and reposing hand had a semisacred function, then, the gesture somewhere mysteriously between pointing, offering, and withholding. This is the double act of concealing and revealing in the Fornarina's delicate grasp of her "insufficient" veiling or the suggestive potential of the Gioconda's hands held demurely but explosively before her waist, a kind of threshold or sill the viewer must pass over in order to approach the essence of her femininity.

Over and over the painters represent this gesture, as in Paris Bordone's *Courtesan* in the Earl of Wemyss collection or Palma Vecchio's two portraits of courtesans in Berlin, one of which, destroyed during the war, showed the courtesan against a backdrop of vine leaves, possibly signifying a connection to the cult of Bacchus, and also suggesting that these women are nymphs as well as goddesses and real women. There is a connection to Christian iconography, as well, through the motif popular in northern art of the Madonna Lactans (the Madonna suckling the Christ Child).

The symbolism of the breast in courtesan portraiture still retains a general social meaning, but now adds a new element to it. The paintings of Renaissance courtesans add a psychological dimension to ancient functions, fusing cult motifs with the particularized conceptions of individual women. Drawing on earlier traditions, striving to endow their creations with the magical qualities possessed by images that once were worshiped and propitiated, the artists gave their work a universal power by their ability to individualize.

The primary scope seems to have been to produce

an image so lifelike and at the same time so attractive that it could literally seduce, both spiritually and physically. Pietro Aretino, writing to Federico di Gonzaga, duke of Mantua, announces the imminent arrival of a statue of Venus by Sansovino in these terms: "It is so true to life, so animated, that it fills the mind of whoever looks at it with lascivious desire" (*Lettere*, I, 8).

Two other female figures from mythology were taken up by artists to induce these reactions.

·THE MYTHOLOGICAL GUISE: FLORA AND LEDA·

In a sense, it is fortunate that no ancient statue, mosaic, or painting of Flora, the goddess who presided over springtime and flowers and who became fused with Flora the courtesan, was known to the Renaissance.[19] This very absence of iconographical reference, together with rich literary sources and the explosive, new phenomenon of the Renaissance courtesan stimulated artists to create Flora, conjuring up the colors of her flesh and hair, the garments she willingly undresses from, her pose, and her meaning.

The ancient Roman Floralie, the festival dedicated to Flora, had a Greek precedent, for courtesans were celebrated there too for their virtuous deeds. Athenaeus points out that the Hetaerideai Festival in Magnesia had in common with these women only the name, but he goes on to relate the origins of the foundation of a temple to "Aphrodite the Companion/Courtesan" in Abydos. The prostitutes of Abydos managed through their wiles to gain possession from enemy guards of the keys to a fortress where their oppressors' arms lay. Having slain the guards and brought the weapons to their countrymen, they were afterward honored for their heroic actions with a temple. In Ephesus another sanctuary was dedicated to "Aphrodite the Companion/Courtesan." In a milder act of social commitment, Athenian courtesans raised funds for Pericles's army at the siege of Samos. One ancient writer mused, "No wonder there is a shrine to the Companion/Courtesan everywhere, but nowhere in all Greece is there one to the Wife!"[20]

At the Roman Floralie dedicated to Flora, goddess of Love, provocative games were played and courtesans were paraded out before the public as in a Miss Universe contest today. Scantily dressed, they performed a ritual striptease for the spectators.

The Christian moralist Tertullian, scandalized by such display, commented, "It is exactly as if these women were up for sale and someone were reading aloud their addresses and prices!" But Ovid in the *Fasti* praises Flora "whose gifts match human desires" and advises everyone to pay tribute to her: "This goddess is not terrifying or proud. She wishes the games played in her honor to be accessible to crowds of simple folk and invites us to enjoy youthful beauty as long as it is in flower since once roses fade men scorn the thorns" (V. 11).

Writers, embarrassed by the excesses of this public celebration, invented the legend that the immensely prosperous courtesan Flora had donated at her death all her money to Rome, and it was to honor her that the festivities were devised. The same story is told of Acca Laurentia, the shepherd's wife who was supposed to have nursed Romulus and Remus, the founders of Rome, and who later became a famous prostitute and married a wealthy man.[21] Like the Vinalie celebrated in the spring, the winter Laurentalie was another festival in which the courtesans played an important role.

Two legends contribute to the Renaissance notion of Flora. In Greek mythology, Flora, a nymph violated by and subsequently wedded to Zephyr, was the embodiment of springtime. For the Romans, Flora was also a real Roman courtesan for whom the holiday was established. It is difficult to determine exactly when Flora, the goddess of flowers in Greece and Rome, became crossed with Flora Meretrix, but as a votary of Venus, the latter was naturally associated with springtime, fertility, and renewal.[22] A chapter of Boccaccio's *De claris mulieribus* (*Concerning Famous Women*, 1359) is entitled "Flora the Prostitute, Goddess of Flowers and Wife of Zephyr"; actually, the images had merged much earlier. In the

Palma Vecchio, *Portrait of a Woman*. 16th century. Gemäldegalerie, Staatliche Museen Preussischer Kulturbesitz, Berlin

THE COURTESAN IMAGE IN ART: THE FIRST PHASE

School of Fontainebleau, *Woman with the Red Lily*. 16th century. Gift of anonymous foundation of New York, High Museum of Art, Atlanta

School of Leonardo, *Flora*. 16th century. Galleria Borghese, Rome

fourth century A.D., Lactantius had accused the Roman Senate of drawing a mythological cover over the fact that they were honoring a public prostitute.

Although there are suggestive precedents in a Verrocchio sculpture and in Botticelli's *Primavera*, Leonardo da Vinci is generally credited with being the first to introduce into Renaissance painting the theme of Flora as courtesan. Leonardo himself may never have produced a painting of Flora, but several paintings by followers of his, such as Francesco Melzi, Giampietrino, and Bernardino Luini, show Flora in what is recognizably a Leonardesque pose, and scholars are convinced that the master himself did at least an important study of this figure.[23]

A cartoon in Chantilly close to the master's style and pricked for transfer shows a nude bust of a woman. Carlo Pedretti sees in the face "turned to front view, framed as it is by curly and braided hair, . . . a deliberately Classical mask suitable to the subject of Flora."[24] An anonymous seventeenth-century portrait in the Accademia Carrara, Bergamo—like the preceding, one of ten nude female half-figures in Leonardesque style called the Nude Gioconda—is also extremely suggestive. Since everything in the painting not occupied by the woman's head and body is covered with flowers, there can be no doubt that the half-nude figure is meant to be Flora Meretrix. The versions of Flora dressed are rather more nuanced. Despite the demurely lowered eyelids of Francesco Melzi's *Flora* in the Hermitage, Leningrad, sometimes called *Columbine*, the alluring pose tells us that this could well be a goddess of love incarnated in an attractive woman. In a *Flora* attributed to Giampietrino, Flora, frontally placed, holds a bunch of flowers. As many Floras do, she seems to be offering her charms along with the flowers she holds in her hand.

This female half-figure of Flora, life-size and in direct contact with the viewer is picked up by various currents of sixteenth-century art, becoming ultimately transformed by Venetian painters; but the impressive production of Flora images in the sixteenth century is not limited to Italy. The School of Fontainebleau artists created several outstanding examples; one anonymous painter has even been given the name Maître de Flore.

When the Maître de Flore depicts Flora in the classicizing, nude royal-mistress style that became popular at the French court, he is quite attentive to the matter of botanical variety, offering his flowers in great profusion and also making a sexual allusion by placing them on the goddess's hips. His *Triumph of Flora* is a fantasy on the Flora theme, a kind of Renaissance pageant in which Flora is attended by nymphs (as Venus, in turn, is adorned by the Three Graces). *Woman with the Red Lily*, a painting by an artist of the School of Fontainebleau, draws notably on the *Fornarina* for its inspiration, thus shedding light on the meaning of Raphael's masterpiece as well.

The Dutch painter Frans Floris seats his *Flora* in a magnificent Renaissance villa garden. The flowers in her lap have a sexual symbolism (she is herself a flower opening to the world for its pleasure), but there is also a great horticultural interest. Flora risks becoming absorbed into a still life in such instances.

Jan Massys's *Flora* offers a "reclining Venus" figure with an idealized portrait head, a suggestive combination that recalls how empresses and aristocratic ladies of ancient Rome sometimes had representations of their heads placed on statues of goddesses. The same woman in a similarly voluptuous pose returns in this artist's *Susannah*. Clouet and others of the French school influenced Massys, who studied painting during his years in exile in their country.

Much less idealizing and rather surprising in their mundaneness are the several Floras by Tintoretto and his school (presently in the Museo del Prado, Madrid). One holding three rosebuds is especially impudent. She wears leaves, possibly laurel, tucked into her bodice which were often an ornament, particularly for courtesans. Another exposes one breast. The interest in these works lies in the fact that they have been produced in series as commodity items and according to convention. The rendition by Palma Vecchio, however, seems to have been conceived in an entirely different spirit.

Palma Vecchio's *Flora* holds a nosegay of buttercups and roses in her hand. There is a ring on the third finger of that hand. A dark ribbon has loosened almost of its own power and, on the sitter's right sleeve shoulder, turned lining-side out. The chemise hangs emphatically, calling attention to itself, underlining with its down-curved arc the delicate, pale rose nipple. Indeed, the candid border of the chemise grazes the underside of the small, round point that, becoming an object of our contemplation, takes on an almost metaphysical quality.

The hair seems to drip like liquid gold over the woman's left shoulder, darkening in the hollow between neck and shoulder and then brightening to a transparent, platinum sheen over the sitter's flesh, disappearing into a featheriness as strands approach the slightly, subtly shaded left armpit. It is all almost not mortal, but there are those dark, but not too dark, brown eyes of a real woman.

The dipped chemise and green ribbon are a theater curtain, parted to reveal the staged presence of a courtesan. The left hand seems to open up a scene of beauty, to unwrap a package at the same time as it rests on the lowered gown as on the arm of a chair. Perfectly poised, the woman is not surprised to be

Francesco Melzi, *Flora* (Columbine). 16th century. The Hermitage, Leningrad

caught in the act of undressing; in this she is not unlike Salome unveiling herself.

The long face, the classical nose, the gaze, the fine eyebrows, and other features of this human goddess seem to be brushed in by nature itself. The artist shows Flora conscious of the miracle of her being but also aware of the devastations time could wreak on her carnal manifestation, her own person. In order to represent this, Palma uses a beautiful woman who impersonates the goddess while illustrating the maxim *carpe diem*. The artist goes one step further by showing a woman presenting herself and at the same time meditating on that very offering. There is a splendid veiled melancholy inherent in the gesture, contrasting with if not actually created by the steady, lucid gaze. This is a figure of beauty who presents herself for serious contemplation knowing that only as an image will she endure, and only as an image will we be able to continue enjoying her. And yet she is a courtesan, a woman who sells herself for money, who can be "had." Her offer, then, is ambig-

Tintoretto, *Flora*, 16th century. Museo del Prado, Madrid

Palma Vecchio, *Flora*. 16th century. The National Gallery, London

uous, for she cannot be "had" for long; it is the ambiguity of possession that she expresses.

The origins of courtesan portraiture in the Renaissance are lost in shadow since we no longer have Leonardo da Vinci's painting or drawing of Flora and his painting of Leda. In addition, his erotic mythologies were destroyed in the eighteenth century. Leonardo may well have explored other erotic themes during his lifetime that were adapted and copied by disciples. The burnt sheets alone would have extended his range to Persephone ravished by Pluto, a nymph and a satyr, a young girl embraced by an old man, and Aurora and Tithonis. Leonardo also conceived and may have executed a Bacchus.

Nevertheless, the master's exploration of such figures as Flora and Leda, fusing with his innovative three-quarter-length, life-size female portrait presentation as used first in *Cecilia Gallerani* and then in the *Gioconda*, opened the possibilities for paintings of courtesans and mistresses by Raphael, Palma Vecchio, Paris Bordone, and Titian. The boldness and scale of these works suggests the important social role assigned to the sitter. As the century progressed, courtesan portraits took their place beside those of royalty, nobility, popes, prelates, and *condottieri*.

Among the most popular mythological subjects of the time was Leda and the Swan. Leda was the daughter of a King of Aetolia and wife of a King of Sparta. The primary version of the myth places Leda on the bank of the Euphrates, where Jove approaches her in the form of a swan and seduces her. It was this union that produced Castor and Pollux and Helen of Troy. Some variations of the myth also appear in art.

All that remains of Leonardo da Vinci's lost painting of the kneeling Leda is a sketch in Rotterdam showing a crouching Leda (possibly inspired by ancient depictions of a crouching Venus), her head curved toward the swan; a drawing in Chatsworth in which Leda's head faces the spectator avoiding the beak, and a copy in Munich of the original painting in which Leda's head faces front and, where, in the words of a Leonardo scholar who has traced these developments, there is a "tense resistance to the swan."[25] As for the standing Leda, in addition to a

Joseph Heintz, *Venus*. 16th century. Kunsthistorisches Museum, Vienna

Joseph Heintz, *Venus*. 16th century. Musée des Beaux-Arts, Dijon

School of Leonardo, *Leda and the Swan*. 16th century. Galleria Borghese, Rome

Anonymous, *Leda and the Swan* (sculptural relief). 3rd century B.C. Museo Archeologico, Venice

drawing of the head and braided hair arrangements and a copy drawing in the Louvre, there are several School versions, including one in the Galleria Borghese and another in the Galleria degli Uffizi, Florence.

The replicas of the standing Leda are small paintings, and it is thought that the original may have been small as well. Since Leonardo took the painting to France, at some point giving it to Francis I, it can be assumed that the painter painted the canvas for his own pleasure rather than on commission. Whether commissioned or not, both the *Leda* and the *Gioconda* seem to have had a personal significance for the artist, and it was natural for him to keep them close at hand. These were women who traveled well, even if they were not "his" women in the sense that some of Raphael's were.

There have been two principal ways of imagining Leda and the Swan from ancient times to the Renaissance—as a couple in situations of tender love, or else as participants in scenes of violent copulation. A third possibility existed, of course, of mutual indifference in which the two pose more or less side by side. In the Museo Palatino in Rome, there is a relief illustrating the first type; in the Museo Archeologico in Venice (Grimani Collection) there is a sculptured relief that is clearly a celebration of the sexual act, as well as an example of a successful endeavor of a swan.

Leonardo's crouching Leda is one of the first type, domestic in feeling due to the protective gesture of the swan. This is a tender demonstration of love expressed among other things in the downiness of the bird's wing. Definitely an imitation of nature, Leonardo's portrayal was not necessarily an imitation of the antique.

Followers of Leonardo, such as Cesare da Sesto, Bugiardini di Giano, and Andrea del Sarto, painted his crouching and standing Ledas, while Raphael, Baldasarre Peruzzi, and others did drawings after them; but Leonardo imitation also encompassed paintings that seem to represent a curious fusion of Flora and Leda motifs.

Abstruse cosmic myths and theories relating to fertility and the interplay of natural elements invest some of the School of Leonardo Floras, Pomonas, and Ledas with an air of mystery. In Melzi's *Flora*, for example, through the centrally placed columbine plant on a pedestal, the sky-blue drapery, and the flowers in her lap, the painter has created a configuration in which the woman is almost an attribute of the flowers

Reflecting on Leonardo's continual preoccupation with the natural sciences, we may assume that in his Ledas the artist is remarking on the organization of the universe and not simply offering a pleasurable juxtaposition of curvilinear features in a woman and swan. In the painting in the Uffizi known as the ex-Spiridon Leda, the mythological scene is given a more profound erotic meaning by its contamination with Flora motifs. Leda is shown holding flowers, and many distinct flowers are sprinkled through the garden in which she is standing. This horticultural interest not only reflects a general concern for nature, but it also broadens the significance of the female figure.

A fusion of myths has occurred because the real focus of the artist's attention is elsewhere. First of all, to create a Leda-Flora figure is to demonstrate that one is not a slave to tradition. Second, the artist evidently wishes to universalize the female figure and to connect her to nature through her mystically regenerative powers that also make her akin to Venus. This tendency to synthesize goes hand in hand with Leonardo's physiological theories of the circulation of elements in the cosmos. In light of such concerns, narrative accuracy becomes secondary, as does sexual definition, permitting and sanctioning the rise of the androgynous character of many figures in Leonardo that has persistently disturbed and stimulated so many viewers.

This diffusion of the image under scientific pressure may be the explanation for the unsettling masculine "cut" of the Chantilly *Nude Gioconda* and a perverse nuance in the *Gioconda* herself (one recalls that Walter Pater called her "an insidious sphynx"). But even if the results of such experimentation are odd, they are linked to some of the most seminal concepts in Leonardo's development.

There is quite a contrast when one turns to Marcantonio's engraving after Giulio Romano in which Leda and a man-sized swan actively engage in love-

Anonymous (Jan Bruegel the Elder?), *Nude Gioconda*. 17th century. Accademia Carrara di Belle Arti, Bergamo

School of Leonardo, *Nude Gioconda*. 16th century. Musée Condé, Chantilly

Marcantonio Raimondi, *Leda and the Swan* (engraving). 16th century. Graphische Sammlung Albertina, Vienna

Maître à l'Oiseau, *Leda and the Swan* (engraving). 16th century. Cabinet des Dessins, Musée National du Louvre, Paris

making in a landscape. In this realistic Renaissance fantasy, Leda sits leaning against a tree, her head thrown back in ecstasy, holding the large swan on her lap, his beak near her mouth. A related scene appears in an engraving by the Maître à l'Oiseau (French, sixteenth century). Here, the swan has cleverly coiled his neck all the way around the woman's head in order to kiss her on the mouth with his beak. These skillfully entangled forms might have provided one of Giulio Romano's postures in *I modi*. Other erotic versions exist: one anonymous sixteenth-century print has the swan triumphing over a Leda completely stretched out on her back. A half-reclining pose was used by Veronese, whose lovely rendition of the scene was destroyed in Dresden during the war. In Veronese's painting, many features—the elegant hairstyle, the jewelry, and the luxurious bed—indicate that Leda is a Venetian courtesan in her boudoir. Surely Leda knows that her unusual partner is, in reality, a royal guest. So in control is she of the situation that the swan no longer appears as a formidable divine force, but rather as an affectionate pet.

Rosso Fiorentino's *Leda and the Swan*, based on a lost painting by Michelangelo, acts as another bridge to the world of the courtesans. Half reclining against cushions on a bed, this voluptuary, with her massive curves, wears on her head a curious raised, bejeweled headdress. Not only are the design, the muscularity of the hip, buttocks, and long thigh Michelangelesque but also the form and gesture of the expressive right hand, which are reminiscent of certain hands on the Sistine Chapel ceiling. Leda's arm artfully cradles the neck of the swan, which moves up between her breasts almost as Cleopatra's asp does in some northern Italian erotic paintings of the period. This is the kind of taste that, through the internationalization of Mannerism encouraged creations such as the monumental nude Venuses of Joseph Heintz, favorite court painter of Rudolph II of Hapsburg.

During the siege of Florence in 1530, which once more brought the Medicis back into power, Michelangelo painted his *Leda and the Swan* for Alfonso d'Este, duke of Ferrara, for whom Titian soon after produced a series of erotic allegories, group scenes

Veronese, *Leda and the Swan*. 16th century. Staatliche Kunstsammlung, Dresden

with classical settings called "the poetries." However, the duke never received the painting due to a mistake on the part of the person who was to deliver it to him. Michelangelo then gave his pupil Antonio Mini both the painting and the cartoon. Mini took them to France in 1531 in order to sell them to Francis I for his palace at Fontainebleau, where erotic mythologies were greatly in favor, but somehow the painting never arrived.

Both Correggio's and Michelangelo's *Ledas* were commissioned by great connoisseurs of erotic art. Like Leonardo's lost *Leda*, each had a dramatic history, one mysteriously disappearing and the other circulating restlessly through half of Europe as though its potent content could nowhere be properly located. Correggio's *Leda* was probably meant to form part of a cycle of erotic paintings done for Federico di Gonzaga II of Mantua. Like Titian's paint-

Giampetrino, *Cleopatra's Suicide*. 16th century. Musée National du Louvre, Paris

ings for Alfonso intended for the *studiolo* at Ferrara, these were meant to be placed on the walls of a private room. Correggio's cycle, including *Leda*, *Danae*, *Antiope*, *Io*, and *Ganymede*, was possibly to have decorated the walls of the Ovidian Hall in the Palazzo del Te, the duke's summer residence built by Giulio Romano and designed to be the living quarters of Isabella Boschetti, the duke's official mistress.

Federico di Gonzaga, Giulio Romano's great patron, was quite accustomed to erotic art, since Giulio had filled Mantua and especially the Palazzo del Te with it, and many of Giulio's erotic designs were being translated into the medium of engraved prints by Marcantonio Raimondi and others. Correggio, for his part, painted erotic frescoes for the *parlatòrio* of the abbess Giovanna Piacenza in Parma. In this most unlikely place Correggio rendered nude figures with his characteristic soft sensuality. There is a Juno "bondage" figure of great charm and a delectable Apollo.

Correggio's *Leda and the Swan*, strongly influenced by Leonardo, is the fourth painting of this theme to suffer an injurious destiny. Veronese's refined erotic account was annihilated by the collective forces of society; Correggio's *Leda* was spoiled by a single powerful individual. In 1731, before he retired to an abbey, Louis d'Orléans cut it into pieces and destroyed the head, presumably in a fit of religious mania after the death of his wife. The painting was patched together again, and Leda was given a new head, which was further restored at a still later time. The painting can be viewed today in the Staatliche Museen Preussischer Kulturbesitz, Berlin (Dahlem). What could have been so offensive to the young Duke?

Correggio's *Leda* is a hybrid allegory of music as well as a representation of the mythical encounter of a god and a mortal woman. It is said in one version of the story that Eros had enchanted Leda through the song of the swan, and so on the left we are shown two cupids with wind instruments and a winged Amor with a lyre. On the right are nude female figures variously interpreted as Leda herself in three successive stages of the event, or else her companions. According to one writer, the intent is lofty: "Jupiter and Leda are united in heavenly love

Correggio, *Leda and the Swan*. 16th century. Gemäldegalerie, Staatliche Museen Preussischer Kulturbesitz, Berlin

. . . while the cupids and Leda's playmates with the small swans embody earthly love."²⁶ A vague link to the Diana and her nymphs bathing configuration also contributes to the strangeness of the scene. The presence of a maidservant dressing (or undressing) one of the companions can be explained by the fact that Leda was a princess. Often when there are maidservants, as in Bathsheba and Susannah pictures, the situation very likely depicts a rich honest courtesan at her toilet or bath attended by maids.

Evidently the whole combination in its complex iconography was too erotic for the duke, yet his anger was directed mainly at one part of the painting. In the history of the repression of erotic art, going hand in hand with official censorship but also involving individual violence, mutilations have frequently been practiced, most conspicuously on engravings (cf. Giulio Bonasone's *Danae*, where the woman's sex has been "erased"). Usually the male organ and the female pubic zone are obliterated or covered over. It is more unusual and, in my opinion, far more significant when an expression on a face is

Giulio Bonasone, *Danae*. 16th century. Bibliothèque Nationale, Paris

noteworthy as the odyssey of an erotic artwork. It helps to explain how and why so many erotic paintings from the Renaissance were lost or came into private collections, where they are inaccessible to the general public. After the death of Federico di Gonzaga, the paintings were taken to Madrid for Philip II. At his death, in 1598, they passed into the hands of Philip III. From Madrid the paintings went to Prague where Emperor Rudolph bought the *Leda* and the others in 1603–4. After that, the *Ganymede* and *Io* went from Prague to Vienna, *Leda* and *Danae* (two beautiful women) were taken as booty by the Swedes. At the death of Queen Christina in 1654, a cardinal inherited the *Leda*. He sold it to Prince Odescalchi, whose collection was eventually purchased by Philip, duke of Orléans, regent of France. This is when his son Louis intervened.

Curiously enough, Louis turned the damaged artwork over to his favorite court painter and gave him permission to restore it. Charles Coypel changed Leda's pose and, as I have said, painted a new head for her. Then, although she was like Humpty-Dumpty who was never satisfactorily put back together again, Leda began once more to travel. Frederick the Great had her in his picture gallery in Sansouci along with other erotic works. Napoleon took her to Paris. Eventually she was returned to Berlin. One would like to ask Leda what it felt like passing from hand to hand. Alatiel, the heroine of a tale by Boccaccio, after having been possessed by pirates and princes all around the Mediterranean, arrived home as fresh as she was when she set out, symbol of a constantly renewed sensual force. Allowing for the deleterious effects of time (and an occasional mutilation), this may be true of the erotic image as well.

attacked. It means that it must have been extremely powerful. In essence, since this feature, here and elsewhere in Correggio derives in the main from Leonardo, one can imagine that it was the *Gioconda*'s ineffable smile become sweetly orgasmic that the French prince attacked. Was there not always inherent in the mysterious smile the self-satisfaction of the sensually organized and realized female?

The fate of this painting, both before and after the violence it underwent, is an incredible saga,

· THE GIOCONDA ·

Certainly no image of this kind has endured more powerfully than Leonardo's *Gioconda*, culmination of all of his explorations into the erotic up to that point. Much more went into it, however, than went into the *Flora*, the *Ledas*, and the already mentioned new genre of the mistress portrait exemplified by the master's *Cecilia Gallerani*, a painting that will be commented on shortly when we come to review the history of mistress portraits in this period.

Few subjects in the history of art have caused so much ink to be spilled as the seemingly insoluble problem of the identity of the sitter in Leonardo's portrait in the Louvre called *Mona Lisa* or the *Gioconda*. What kind of role she might have played in society is suggested by the existence of drawings and paintings of the *Nude Gioconda*, a three-quarter-length nude probably done after a lost original by Leonardo and possibly—as we have seen—having been conceived as a Flora. Whether the first *Nude Gioconda* was a study or a finished painting is impossible to determine, but whatever shape it took there are enough similarities to link the two works both formally and subjectively.

At least ten versions of the *Nude Gioconda* exist, each of them different. In several, the suggestion of the setting of a loggia before a distant landscape is retained. The Chantilly drawing has a neutral background. Despite a small variation in the position (some of them are frontal rather than slightly turned), the shape of the head and face, the intense gaze under the finely drawn eyebrows and, above all, the mysterious, ambiguous, seraphic, upturned smile and the hands carefully folded in front of the waist seem at least to this viewer, convincing evidence that the *Nude Gioconda* is a variant of the *Gioconda*. When the *Gioconda* was taken to France by Leonardo in 1517 for Francis I, some version of the *Nude Gioconda* may well have accompanied it there.

According to an eyewitness report, a portrait by Leonardo of a mistress of Giuliano de Medici was in the master's studio at Cloux in France soon after his arrival in that country. Whether this was the *Gioconda* or not is still debated, but if it was, we are strongly encouraged to think that the *Gioconda* might be a portrait of a Renaissance courtesan. Vasari's identification of the sitter as the wife of an obscure Florentine gentleman counters this assertion, but he had never seen the painting and his description not only has several important lacunae, but is considered by some to be referring to an entirely different painting.

To consider the *Gioconda* a courtesan portrait, it would be convenient to date it late in Leonardo's career (as one distinguished scholar does), seeing it as a happy product of the master's days with Giuliano in Rome in 1514–16.[27]

When Leonardo and his disciple Francesco Melzi stopped in Florence in 1513 to join the entourage of this dissolute, but extremely cultured member of the Medici family, a new vision of the social scene awaited them in Rome. Very much a part of the political and artistic life for which that city was celebrated were the courtesans, soon to be seen across the canvases of Europe. Cesare Borgia's Fiammetta was about to become a treasured memory while the image of Agostino Chigi's mistress Imperia continued to haunt the Villa Farnesina, where, as we have seen, her features appear in the *Psyche and Cupid* loggia and in the *Galatea*, painted while Raphael's own woman—as Vasari tells us—"hung over his

Leonardo da Vinci, *La Gioconda* (Mona Lisa). 16th century. Musée National du Louvre, Paris

Raphael, *La Donna Velata* (Portrait of a Woman). 16th century. Palazzo Pitti, Florence

shoulder." Many courtesans were willing to offer their charms to pose nude for important artists.

Leonardo da Vinci and Francesco Melzi must have marveled at the ubiquitous presence of courtesans in social and cultural life, including the humanistic circles around the curia. As he took up his rooms in the Belvedere of the Vatican—where, only ten years later, Giulio Romano, in the Sala del Constantino, would produce the refined pornography of *I modi*—Leonardo may well have felt, in this fast-moving urban atmosphere, the center of the world that was also a bordello, the urge to shake off just a trifle of the slight provincialism of the court painter.[28] Great artist that he was, open to the universe, did he attempt, even a little, to adapt himself to the reality around him? Under Giuliano's tutelage, surely he sensed that he was now in a far less dreamy atmosphere. Or should we say that the dream was now calculated to make men desire on a

concrete, earthly basis. Having been in the vanguard of the Flora revival if he sketched one in the first years of the century, he was now further encouraged to complete (or to invent *sur place*, as the case may be) the real-life courtesan portrait of the type that would soon fill drawing rooms and hang on the walls of boudoirs throughout Europe.

If the portrait of Giuliano de Medici's mistress seen in Leonardo's studio in France in 1517 was the *Gioconda*, who could that mistress have been? It would be idle to speculate. Giuliano's affair with Pacifica Brandano, which led to the birth of Ippolito de Medici, had already taken place in Urbino in 1511. In 1514–16, it could have been any of the elite courtesans in Rome. Giuliano's nephew Lorenzo and their friend Filippo Strozzi had been nurturing a group of Tuscan fledglings who were coming to Rome exactly in those years. Beatrice of Ferrara, Lorenzo's mistress, modeled for portraits by Raphael and Giulio Romano. Certainly any one of these women would have been an appropriate subject for Leonardo as well.[29]

If not before this date, surely the *Nude Gioconda* was invented at this time. Probably it sprang up as an interesting alternative to the dressed version of a mistress portrait. Although perhaps not a full-blown genre, the notion of showing complementary aspects of the same human reality became a mode in sixteenth-century portraiture. Raphael, whom Leonardo's female portraiture deeply influenced, followed suit. They are not the same woman, yet his *Donna Velata* and *Fornarina* have more than a tenuous connection, and the Fornarina herself is an example of an image tantalizingly suspended between the dressed and the undressed. Fontainebleau exulted over the undressed version, and the mistresses of the kings of France were quickly disrobed from their elegant gowns and even shown in their baths. The dressed and undressed mistress figure appears full length in what is now considered to be a marriage picture—Titian's *Sacred and Profane Love*. In this puzzling allegory, there is a double portrait of a woman in which the nude figure has as much if not more dignity and status than the dressed one. This has been interpreted as a contrast between the "celestial Venus" aspect of a woman and the "earthly

Venus"[30] one, but if I am not mistaken the nude could also be a nymph dreaming she is a real woman, as the real woman dreams she is a nymph. As we shall see, another enigmatic Titian painting presents an analogous situation.

Probably it was Andrea Doria who himself posed in the nude who commissioned from the Flemish Jan Massys the idealized *Flora* in Palazzo Rosso, Genoa, and in Stockholm, whose pubic area is hidden from us by the most transparent of veilings. No dressed female figure vanquishes this nude in dignity or composure. Leonardo's interest in the nude and his explorations of Flora, so congenial to a man with

an overriding mystique about creation, may have been reinforced by the novel idea—soon to become a convention—of showing a mistress dressed and undressed.

If Lisa del Giocondo was the sitter of the *Gioconda* and even if (heaven forbid) she was a *donna per bene* and not the mistress of Giuliano, Leonardo, or any other man, then Leonardo, after having worked for some time on her costumed image, decided to undress her. It is unlikely that a respectable Florentine merchant's wife would have posed as an ancient Roman courtesan in the first place, unless she had taken up a loose life in the spirit of Magda-

Jan Massys, *Flora* (Venus Cytherea). 16th century. Nationalmuseum, Stockholm

François Clouet, *Portrait of François I*. 16th century.
Musée National du Louvre, Paris

lena Offenburg. In the *Gioconda*, columns and a parapet allude to the same classical world evoked in *Lais Corinthiaca*.

Something morally unsettling by Leonardo's hand must have existed in France if Pierre Dan, in his *Trésor des merveilles de la maison royale de Fontainebleau* (1642), tried to correct the opinion of those of his readers who believed that the *Gioconda* was the portrait of a courtesan. Indeed, the unequivocal term *une courtizène* (*une courtizène* in *voil de gaze*—"a courtesan wearing veils") is found as a description of the Gioconda in an early seventeenth-century inventory at Fontainebleau. Evidently, the French gave sway to their fantasies, since one ver-

sion of the *Nude Gioconda* bore an inscription identifying it as the mistress of Francis I. Another is mistakenly called *La Belle Gabrielle*, alluding to the mistress of Henry IV, often portrayed in paintings by Clouet and the School of Fontainebleau. Given these indications, it appears likely that some kind of *Nude Gioconda* arrived at the court of Fontainebleau, but it also seems clear that its connection to the *Gioconda* was so well-known and/or so obvious, that people called the *Gioconda* outright a courtesan.[31]

Whoever the *Gioconda* was, she exists as an image perilously suspended among various roles. No merchant's wife, yet no Flora modeled after the antique either, she is a modern woman who belongs to someone while commanding his respect and enjoying his devotion. At the same time she is a muse and model who belongs to the painter who creates her and to all who possess her with their gazes.

Leonardo was eventually willing to share his private viewing of an icon such as the *Gioconda*, whereas many rulers, ecclesiastics, and gentlemen who commissioned or came into possession of such pictures often desired to keep them to themselves. Cassiano del Pozzo writing about the *Gioconda* in 1625, claimed that when the duke of Buckingham sent to the French court to ask for the hand of Henriette of France for Charles I of England, he confided that his lord very much wanted the portrait of the *Gioconda*, but the courtiers around Louis XIII refused to let the king part with it. Significantly, before putting it on display at the Napoleon Museum in 1804, Bonaparte kept the painting in his private bedroom in the Tuileries. Various documents of the Renaissance cite examples of the jealous possession of talismanic female images.[32]

Consideration of the *Gioconda*'s unique status and history leads us to an important question—namely, what position the mistress of a ruler or powerful figure held in the first part of the sixteenth century. Was she the same as a concubine? Certainly her image was hoarded as real concubines often were by their lords. Nevertheless, the mistress and courtesan figures greatly evolved and to some extent converged, while a wide gulf began to separate them from the concubine as traditionally conceived.

·THREE MISTRESS PORTRAITS·

The concubine is a concept inherited from ecclesiastical practice. In contrast, the courtesan is the realization on a concrete plane of a kind of love originally generated and sanctioned in Provençe for which an adulterous liaison (or at least one outside of marriage) was essential; this kind of passion was conceived of as a discipline involving progressive stages toward the satisfaction of desire; acts were buttressed by the imagination (in other words, by culture).

Concubinage was an accepted habit, a necessity tolerated especially in the case of celibates, and it was widespread in Rome well before and throughout the fifteenth century. As long as single men took women to them, this custom had a semblance of respectability, but when husbands openly made visits to courtesans' dwellings or houses set up for erotic encounters, and the remunerated women displayed themselves openly in public, society itself underwent a dramatic change.

Unlike courtesans, concubines were seldom heard from. In Pasqualigo's *Lettere amorose*, a 671-page Renaissance novel in epistolary form containing code language, secret signs, and fetishistic objects, a concubine in Venice carries out extradomestic affairs in great secrecy. Living in the house of a lord she fears, the female letter writer has other liaisons, and hence is a kind of "adulterous" concubine. The form of punishment she might be subjected to were she discovered is not specified, but her fear (and the thrill it produces) characterizes the many hundreds of letters of this fascinating and until now entirely unexplored document.

Two engravings of concubine dress show us at least what they looked like: Cesare Vecellio's *Bolognese Concubine* and Jan II van Grevenbroeck's eighteenth-century watercolor illustrating a sixteenth-century Venetian concubine. Grevenbroeck's concubine in a watercolor version is almost identical to another showing a courtesan. The two categories are one in his text, so perhaps by that time they had merged, but there are clues to an earlier distinction. According to this artist, concubines "came from outside Venice and could not im-

mediately change their way of dressing." It seems they went around like ladies because they did not know better and were previously used to that. Probably the implication is that, in places where feudal and ecclesiastical traditions persisted, concubinage was still an accepted practice, but in Venice concubines risked being identified with the new phenomenon of the courtesan, far more threatening to society because of her high position and pretense to economic freedom. Through open adultery and displays of pomp and luxury, the courtesan rivaled wives as well as mimicked the patrician class. Evidently, Grevenbroeck saw concubines having to find a new identity even while they continued to dress as they had in their previous situations. Concubines were once better defined and hence better protected; now they had become an amorphous transitional group classed together indiscriminately with courtesans and prostitutes.

Concubines may have had to change their style in Venice, but there were places where they triumphed. Cecilia Gallerani of Milan, mistress of Ludovico Sforza, Il Moro—if this is indeed she in Leonardo's portrait—has about her all of the dignity of the traditional kept woman. In Ferrara, where the highest aspects of feudal culture were lovingly preserved in the new age, Duke Alfonso d'Este gave his heart to Laura Dianti, a courtesan who apparently mirrored the most virtuous qualities. In Cologne, Katarina Jabach became the concubine of a great churchman and posed for an important court painter. Each of these portraits has its own fascination.

The image of Leonardo's *Cecilia Gallerani* comes to us out of another world. There is still the feeling of Quattrocento portraiture about it. It is a formal portrait: the ermine is equated with the woman, both of them precious status symbols. (The artist has exploited the fact that the woman's last name is similar to the Greek word for this animal, *galé*.) The woman's sexuality curled up and coy is yet present.

Isabella d'Este, striving to be the most brilliant woman in Europe, was dazzled by this portrait and asked Leonardo to make one of her exactly like it.

Concubina Bolognese.

Cesare Vecellio, *Bolognese Concubine* from *Habiti et moderni di tutto il mondo*. Venice, 1590

Jan II van Grevenbroeck, *Venetian Concubine* (watercolor). 18th century. Museo Correr, Venice

Leonardo da Vinci, *Cecilia Gallerani* (The Lady with an Ermine). 16th century. Muzeum Naradowego, Cracow

Evidently, she too wanted to be ornamented with these qualities, that were a simulation, but also a synthesis, of the aristocratic pose. She seems not to have been alarmed by Cecilia's equivocal position. As a matter of fact, a few year later, Isabella was extremely curious to hear about Tullia d'Aragona's triumph in Ferrara, where the courtesan outshone even the marchioness of Pescara, the poet Vittoria Colonna. Isabella's envoy Battista Stambellino's letters to her from her native city are full of evaluations of the remarkable Tullia.

Ferrara itself produced an outstanding mistress on its own soil. Laura Eustochio Dianti was the daughter of a hat maker of Ferrara. After the death of Lucrezia Borgia, the second wife of Alfonso d'Este, in 1519, she became Alfonso's mistress. The two sons she bore him, Alfonso and Alfonsino, are described in their father's testament as natural sons of an unmarried woman, and it is on this basis that many distrust the story circulating after Alfonso's death, in 1534, that Laura had become his duchess. Whatever the truth, the Ferrarese populace referred to Laura during her lifetime as "wife" and "duchess." Both Aretino and Vasari (the first in a letter to someone of the Este family, the second in his biography of Titian), refer to her this way. Laura died in 1573. Her portrait reveals her to be a dignified woman, who was not without a hidden sense of humor.

Titian's striking portrait of *Laura Dianti* has been seen in an exotic light, perhaps because of the olive-hued skin of the sitter and the turbanlike headdress she wears, although this exquisite tulle fantasy with its enameled red brooch is in another category from the turban of the Fornarina or those of odalisques. This is no "Turkish Woman," although some have given it that title. The portrait has been considered a pendant to a lost one by Titian of Alfonso. Not especially dynamic, another portrait by Titian shows Alfonso as a plain military man, quite different from the exquisitely groomed, pleasure-loving Federico di Gonzaga immortalized in his blue doublet in Titian's stunning painting in the Museo del Prado. Laura's portrait has a similar splendor.

The most startling fact of this portrait besides the subject's being a concubine is the Ethiopian slave.

This was the first introduction of the Moorish page or servant into a portrait, and it was soon widely imitated (for example, by Frans von Mieris). Another noticeable quality is the brilliant array of colors in the clothing of the sitter and her page—the ultramarine velvet dress, the white sleeves, the light yellow scarf partly covering the bodice, the blackamoor's striped green, blue, lavender, and yellow silk outfit. A detail—Titian's signature applied in red letters on the bracelet Laura wears on her upper right arm—manifests the master's satisfaction with the effect of these radiant colors. It also shows, significantly, that Titian views Laura as a mistress in the classical style, like the *Fornarina*.

It is tempting to ascribe the yellow shawl Laura is wearing to the category of yellow veils courtesans in some cities in Italy were required to wear even into the sixteenth century, but it is unlikely someone in Laura's position would have allowed this aspect of her past to be so flagrantly displayed, unless, of course, she had a secret pride in her own ascent.

But the psychological aspect of the painting is far more interesting than any artistic or biographical documentation it contains. A great social distance separates the duchess (or, more accurately, the woman appointed to play the role of duchess) from her Ethiopian slave, yet how affectionately, how protectively she places her hand on the little boy's shoulder, and how adoringly he looks up at his mistress while holding with great care her luxurious gloves. The familiar, domestic, and human relationship between these two figures speaks volumes for the character of Laura Dianti who, as history tells us, became a good mother to her people. Indeed, it seems that during her reign, hardly a word was spoken of Laura's past, and no shadows darkened her usurpation of the post of legitimate ducal consort.

The Florentines were a bit more hypocritical than the Ferrarese regarding Bianca Cappello, a Venetian noblewoman who was not a courtesan but who resembled a courtesan in her attitude and in the shape of her career: it is not known which, or if any, of the several portraits of Bianca attributed to Titian and Bronzino, is the authentic one. Skepticism has been aroused by the fact that Bianca, who after the murder of her lover, married Francesco de Medici (she was already his mistress at the time) and finally as grand duchess of Tuscany was "absolved" by the Venetian Republic for political reasons, was known to be quite plump. In the painting by Bronzino shown here, Bianca wears a gown with ribbon inserts and braid decoration, the V-neck bordered with scrolled lace.

Katarina Jabach was the daughter of Tringin Jabach, an envoy of a man soon to be archbishop and prince palatinate, Johann Gebhardt van Mansfeld. When he took Katarina as his mistress, he was already the leading prelate of Cologne. Katarina had two daughters by her lover, who eventually set her up in a house on the Glocke in Waidmarkt. Just before 1565 she was married off to Wilhelm von Muhlheim, an honorable canon of Saint George.

In a portrait of her by Barthel Bruyn dated to 1535–36, a nude half-figure sits with the hands gracefully folded in a significant position, right over left, the index and third fingers opened. She faces front, her body just barely turned to the left. Rather startlingly, the sitter's nude upper body appears in all its muscular strength. Her hair is parted in the middle as the Gioconda's and rather closely bound around her head. The face is strikingly individualized and there is a trace of a well-controlled yet impish smile on the slightly upturned lips and in the intelligent eyes.

Katarina wears costly jewelry that distinguishes and identifies her—a heavy jeweled pendant on a chain around her neck prominently placed between the breasts, along with rings and earrings. Part of her mistress's garb is a rich fur cape dropped down on the left side and slipped over her right arm. She rests her hand on a scroll-shaped chair arm. Although a heavy curtain fills three-fourths of the background, a Leonardesque landscape is prominently shown past the windowsill on the left side of the picture.

What could seem conflicting elements add up to a valid mistress portrait. The beautifully ornamented room and expensive jewelry, the landscape of the formal portrait, the dignified pose and serene gaze of a woman who clearly thinks of herself as powerful, or as in a powerful position, are only slightly jarred by the stark nudity of the sitter that,

Bronzino, *Portrait of a Woman* (Bianca Cappello?). 16th century. Palazzo Pitti, Florence

unlike that in many courtesan paintings, is only to some extent idealized.

Katarina is a concubine, but she has had the courage to do something a mistress did not usually do in the north—that is, to pose nude as herself. It seems that Bruyn arrived at the portrayal through the mediation of Joos van Cleve, who had made a trip to the French court in 1529. Joos painted a portrait considered by some to have been of a royal mistress, which derived from the French interpretation of the *Nude Gioconda* type, showing the nude half-figure in the frontal position. Since Joos's painting is lost, Bruyn's portrait survives as a pivotal work in the history of mistress portraits.

If, by the 1530s, the nude bust had become fashionable in female portraiture in Germany, something new must have occurred. This was the arrival of the courtesan on the social scene. The powerful influence of her personality and the liberties artists

Titian, *Alfonso I d'Este.* 16th century. Palazzo Pitti, Florence

painted (before 1520), the courtesan, already active at the Borgia court, but not yet defined as a formidable entity, seems to have taken on and absorbed for herself the privileges and, to some extent, the manners of the medievalizing concubines of rulers and high level prelates.

No sooner have Italian courtesans reclaimed and renewed the noble prerogatives of the mistress, than they add to their luster the prestige of being followers of Phryne, Lais, and Campsaspe, who posed for the great artists of antiquity. But now the search for an image begins, for there had not been until then a realistic courtesan portrait tradition—it had to be invented. *Cecilia Gallerani* and the *Gioconda*, the *Nude Gioconda,* the *Fornarina,* the *Portrait of Katarina Jabach,* and *Diane de Poitiers in Her Bath* are all various stages in this development, representing the apotheosis of the mistress figure, the transition to the courtesan, the courtesan's taking on a new decorum, and various fusions of the mistress and courtesan images. There is no linear chronology, and any description of what happened is bound to be sketchy. Nevertheless, a revolution took place, and a new visual "type" emerged that underwent further changes (and became somewhat generalized) in the hands of the Venetian masters.

felt free to make with her image radically transform the traditional mistress portrait. Interestingly, the process is reciprocal, for by the time the *Fornarina* is

· *THE FORNARINA* ·

Leonardo made the first major move, Raphael the second. It was Raphael who created the image of the full-fledged courtesan, although he may not have admitted the identity of his subject. Raphael delighted in veiling the source of his inspiration—for example, in a letter to Castiglione in 1514, he gives a tongue-in-cheek explanation of how he came to conceive paintings such as his *Galatea:*

In order for me to paint a beautiful woman, I have to look at many different beautiful women. In any case, you, my excellent man, would have to be present to choose the most beautiful one. But since there is a current lack of good judges and of beautiful women, I necessarily turn to a certain idea of my own. I myself cannot say whether this idea is an artful one, but I strive very hard to arrive at it.[33]

The fantasy of taking single qualities from many beautiful persons in order to compose an ideal one continued to intrigue Renaissance artists. They no doubt developed the notion from the classical tale of Zeuxis, who assembled a likeness of Helen of Troy by combining features of several beautiful women.[34] Vasari painted this scene, as did Dutch and German artists.

Raphael knew that he could not conceive of a portrait without using the "reminiscences" of features of beautiful women (and perhaps used as models), so he merely paid a compliment to a fashionable concept and at the same time indicated his sincere striving for the ideal. Raphael's *Galatea,* supposedly inspired by the courtesan Imperia, does manage to be an original creation and a revival of

Titian, *Laura Dianti*. 16th century. Hans Kisters Collection, Kreuzlingen

Alfonso Raspigiari, *Courtesan and Admirer*. 16th century. Victoria and Albert Museum, London

the antique. This could be said about his *Fornarina* as well, although she is much closer to reality.

The idea that the *Fornarina* might be a specific Roman courtesan is an old one. The coy appearance of the artist's name in gold letters on the *armilla* (upper-arm bracelet) has always inspired speculation that the sitter was Raphael's mistress. Fabio Chigi, who saw the portrait in the Boncompagni palace in 1618, was the first person to identify the sitter with Raphael's beloved. Curiously, he also calls her a prostitute (*meretricula*). On the basis of a passage in Vasari stating that the master did a portrait of her, art historians were led to speculate that she might be Beatrice of Ferrara.[35] As mentioned earlier, Beatrice seems also to be the woman in Giulio Romano's *Woman at Her Toilet* and the subject and narrator of the long poem about the Ferrarese courtesan in which her coral lips, alabaster neck, and crow-black eyes are described.

The *Fornarina* represents a fusion of classical motifs typical of Raphael with Leonardo's naturalistic portraiture. Was Raphael rivaling Leonardo when he set himself to paint it? Influenced by Leonardo's nude and dressed courtesans, Raphael may have felt encouraged to create his own version parallel to, but different from, these. Significantly, his woman is brunette as well, in contrast to the blond Venetian types, and classical elements alluding to Rome also appear, such as the *armilla* and the pose with one hand displaying an exposed breast. The veil twisted around the head, which photography reveals in the underpainting, becomes, in the final version, a vaguely oriental turban decorated with a precious jewel; and a parapet in the foreground and a landscape to one side in the background make way for a garden setting of luxuriant laurel and myrtle, perhaps in reference to the ancient *hortus* the humanists had revived as a setting for intellectual exchange.

The *Fornarina* is one of the most intimate portraits ever made. Some of the effect is created by the placement of the garden foliage almost to the edge of the picture plane, crowding the figure toward the viewer and trapping her in an enclosed space, making her fully available to our delectation. Although she yields with a slight irony, there is no way she can escape us, no landscape or interior of a house into which she can flee. She must remain there eternally as an icon of pleasure, self-created but also perfectly rendered by the painter, who may or may not be her current lover, yet who certainly has been complicit in her presentation—the necessity and the intensity of it.

The *Fornarina* already offers herself from, and in, an exclusive pleasure garden connected both to cultural enterprise and to fertility; the viewer's private encounter with her was meant to be further enhanced by a pair of actual wooden shutters designed to protect the painting but also to conceal it from the gaze of the profane. Evidently, this portrait which Vasari called "so alive, so alive," formed a kind of double portrait with the viewer whenever he opened the shutters. A medal by Alfonso Ruspigiari shows a courtesan full-face with an admirer in profile off to one side. Certainly, looking at the *Fornarina*, one enters a magical place.

The question of the Fornarina's identity has inspired much conjecture. Even today, art historians, unwilling to relinquish the sentimentalized tradition of Raphael's loves and reluctant to see her as a professional mistress, a mercenary of love, attempt to make the Fornarina into a full-fledged "Venus" on the basis of the myrtle in the background and the upper armband that the Venus of Cnidus also wears, in addition giving her the qualities of a wife.

For example, Konrad Oberhuber, who offers an excellent reconstruction of the history of the painting, comments that "while Leonardo's *Nude Gioconda* proudly shows her body, Raphael represents his sitter in a more modest pose deliberately fashioned after the type of the *Venus pudica*, a gesture that is particularly appropriate in a bridal context." Yet this portrait of a courtesan, with her brazen expression and playful indecency, mocks the very notion of a bridal context.[36]

This is a portrait that has disconcerted viewers for centuries, perhaps because it has not been properly understood that courtesans were effigies of aristocratic women. Given their real purpose, they constituted an insidious simulacrum. Everything this scholar calls "nuptial," chaste, pure, and devoted can be seen as no more than a kind of facade or veil that the sitter can sweep away with one gesture when she wants to. Is the *Fornarina's* pose really "more modest"? Is it not more lascivious than the frankly nude bust would be? As for the *Venus pudica* gesture, one could reasonably argue that the sitter's left hand is resting in her lap, not hiding her sex, which is already covered by her garment. It is the right hand that, as Oberhuber also notes, makes a significant gesture, displaying a breast.

As an alternative to his nuptial proposal, this scholar offers a second possibility stating that, if the *Fornarina* is not the *sponsa* (wife) type, the portrait would have to be considered "a vulgar exposure of a woman of ill repute." This is a notion he instantly

repels. But why a "vulgar exposure" one wants to ask, why not a presentation of an honest courtesan—the kind who wrote poetry (hence the laurel), modeled herself after Venus (hence the myrtle), divided her devotion between the shrines of Apollo and Venus, as Veronica Franco tells us in her poems she did, and wore precious rings on her fingers? If Beatrice of Ferrara did not write poetry, her bosom friend Camilla of Pisa, mistress of Filippo Strozzi, did, since she sends a book she has written to Francesco del Nero, presumably to be scrutinized by his critical eye.

The complex messages this portrait conveys (is the Fornarina's right hand holding up modestly, or slightly letting dip down, the transparent veil between her breasts?) result from her provocative gestures and her consciousness of who and what she is. This communication is even stronger than the sight of her flesh and the inviting pose. It is my idea that the Fornarina is very much her own woman, and this suggests that the painter has included the possessive armband almost as a sign of futility, of delicious self-mockery. Yes, Raphael created her: she knows that; she has deliberately made herself into his ideal courtesan. Yet is she a woman who can ultimately be possessed at all?

Another legitimate question is whether, in the case of the Fornarina, the artist is putting the courtesan in a pose or, rather, attempting to capture her *posing as herself*. The Levantine touch of the turban emphasizes that she is a courtesan in an exotic costume, and therefore not herself. She uses such props, however, only for the revelation of her own personality.

·ANTEA·

Her eyes hold the tragic past; the formal elements of the painting predict the future. This is *Antea*, one of Parmigianino's most elegant portraits but also one difficult to decipher. The solemnity of the presentation and the full dress—almost a costume—of the sitter might raise a doubt about whether this is a courtesan or lady. However, the little surprise of the dividing and dipping point of the breasts above the

severe bodice together with the at-once bold and frightened look in the woman's eyes offer us a clue that this is someone who has lived and continues to live in a devastatingly unprotected manner, or perhaps under a protection that threatens or crushes. It seems she has become somewhat like her fierce-toothed but immobile weasel handsomely draped over her shoulder.

Parmigianino, *Antea* (Portrait of a Young Woman). 16th century. Museo Nazionale di Capodimonte, Naples

Barthel Bruyn, *Portrait of a Young Woman* (Katarina Jabach). 1535–36. Germanisches Nationalmuseum, Nuremberg

Parmigianino's portrait, dating to 1535–37, depicts a Roman personage; it was painted about eight years after the Sack of Rome, not long enough to permit the horrors of that episode to be forgotten—the destruction of part of the city, the pillage and the rapes, not least of all the partial extinguishing of the brilliant cultural life Rome was enjoying, magnet to which humanists, painters, writers, and beautiful women had been drawn from the entire peninsula and from abroad. Many are the laments on the part of fictional courtesans in prose and poetry from 1530 on, telling us how their Golden Age was now over. The theatrical space in which they appeared was diminished, and the public on whom they depended dispersed; a psychological crisis had set in that would deepen as the century proceeded.

Is it a collective or a personal anxiety that emanates from the expressionistic oval of Antea's face and her larger-than-life eyes, the pursed lips that seem they would never open to utter a word explaining her condition, which she wants us, however, to realize? Obviously something had changed since the time of insouciant, hegemonic *Galatea* and winsome, witty, and self-conscious *Fornarina*.

Antea does not appeal for help; rather she stands frozen as if wounded, even mutilated—a victim or effigy of a victim—and yet she lives. Her ceremony, or rather the ceremoniousness with which her lovers—and the painter—have surrounded her is like that of certain high-placed ecclesiastical functionaries. She bears the weight of it with intelligent resignation, as if it were part of her duty to be beautiful. Beautiful she is, with a rare melancholy beauty. But her melancholy is as inaccessible as her beauty, inward and aristocratic; precisely that quality would elude him who hired her and made love to her. The florid Venetian courtesans of Palma, Paris Bordone, Titian, and their followers, if they do not offer "all," indicate that what they have and are is candidly presented on the surface of the painting. Antea, on the other hand, is hidden; hers is an ambiguous promise.

Clues are given, however, if not to the nature of the disturbance (which one analyzes in retrospect as a disturbance of society), at least to its presence. The unnaturally small head, the suggestion of

shoulders of a different size, the illusion of a slight twist to the sitter's lower left body that does not correspond to the basically frontal position of the bust and head, create a sense of disproportion and incongruity, as if the painter had deliberately and arbitrarily fitted it together for his own expressive purposes, which in part elude us. In addition, as Sydney Freedberg has pointed out, "the tapering shoulders, high waist, and wide hips conveying a sense of suave maturity subtly contradict the almost childish delicacy of the head."[37] Further, the oval form of the scaled-down face accentuates the rigid rectangular form of the body created partly by the straight lines of the gown and overgown Antea is wearing. Each geometrical shape reinforces the perception of the subject as an abstraction, sign of the artist's obsession with form itself, which is one of the essential meanings of the painting.

It is surely an exaggeration to say that this sixteenth-century portrait presages in its strong elements, the twentieth-century movements of Expressionism and Constructivism, as well as Surrealism. Yet the head of the weasel, with its fierce look, resting in a knotted and confused area lying quite near the woman's pubic area, appears as an almost surrealistic element. Antea's gloves are tightly held in one hand, which emerges from an arm with a monumental quality: it is no longer a realistic arm; it is the necessary human scaffolding on which the whole edifice of gown and *schiratto* (fur throw) has been laid. The woman's right arm has been burdened; the weasel's head lies menacingly near her sexual zone, either equated with it or reminding us of aggressions that can take place in relation to it; and the wide-open, perhaps humid eyes seem to be full of the thought of some hurt past or to come. Nevertheless, what Antea is and what has happened or will happen to her is not shared. She communicates instead on some partly conscious level, where perhaps we do not want to be aroused.

Antea, if this is indeed Antea, was an honest courtesan in Rome in the 1530s, named after a classical hetaera. She was notorious for having been brutally scarred by a jealous lover. She was for a while Parmigianino's mistress. It is tempting to imagine that here we see her already involved in the turbid intrigues that will lead to that event so fear-some for courtesans because of the devastating ef-fect it could have on their careers. Her eyes emanate a timid prescience that will fuse, like weasel's head and woman's pubis and gloved hand, into something indistinct but palpably present that can be called "her life." Whoever the woman is, her existence is so portentous, so like a cascading dark fabric, that the painter, fascinated by distortion and confusion, but intent on his own "neurotic" need for elegant lines, attenuated forms, and solidified clothing, ex-presses this drama in geometrical and symbolical forms, half—but only half—emptying eyes and lips, schematizing head and face, and aggrandizing the body while giving it a vicious twist, thus distancing sitter, spectator, and the artist himself from "reality" but offering, as substitute, a beautiful object for con-templation.

Antea is the philosophical opposite of the *Gio-conda*. In the *Gioconda* a female figure is so im-mersed in the atmosphere around her that they be-come a single homogenous entity. No longer is the woman separate from nature, in particular no longer is she distinct from the almost unnaturally natural light that reveals outlines and penetrates face, hands, lightly clothed body, and even eyes, as well as spreads diffusely and tenuously over the land-scape. Light for Leonardo is a kind of amorous vapor akin to the humanized clouds in paintings from Ven-ice and Parma, in which Jove descends to Danae and Io.

In *Antea*, the subject, isolated from nature, be-comes a nature of her own—a hardened, opaque ob-ject set into relief neither near nor far from the neu-tral dark background, at an ambiguous distance. Light is projected directly onto the figure so that it appears almost a hostile force, cruelly revealing the rigid doll's skirts and definite oval of the face. The pleats of the dress and other surface elements are tactile, but they do not invite touch. She keeps her feelings behind glass, although they appear poi-gnantly ready to spill over into our realm and be-come comprehensible. The *Gioconda's* smile and smiling eyes may be mysterious, but they contain the assurance of her own (and our) continuity with the created universe, above all with a society that considered individual human beings the radiant center of that universe.

In short, the Gioconda is in control, whereas An-tea is under control, or at least has lost some of her potency. It has been instead transferred to her out-ward appearance and thus become as easily remov-able as clothes. Cecilia Gallerani too lived in the Gioconda's assured sphere, whereas her Spanish costume and ostentatious pet remotely signaled the dangers that lay ahead for the mistress-courtesan.

· THEORETICAL INTERLUDE ·

Is there an answer to Antea? A lost painting of an-other Renaissance courtesan, Jacopo Tintoretto's portrait of the Venetian courtesan Veronica Franco, would undoubtedly have provided clues. Since she was one of the most vigorous self-publicists of the age and a proud woman who battled the streams of history, Veronica would surely have radiated out from that canvas.

Veronica was the intellectual courtesan, a six-teenth-century Diotima with a sense of humor. I as-sociate her with Dosso Dossi's *Circe*, a benevolent sorceress surrounded by the most contemplative an-imals ever created. One of them has been given a human face by the artist, since according to Homer the beasts were originally men transformed by Circe's powers. In this humanistic painting, Circe seems to have humanized the animals. Similarly, Veronica attempts to domesticate and civilize her lovers. One of them, Marco Venier, praises her "ma-ture intellect in a young body." (For her part, Veron-ica hastens to assure us that she worships Apollo as well as Venus, although she would not want her am-orous talents underestimated.)

Gaspara Stampa and Veronica Franco are the liv-ing proof that the cultural pose is something not necessarily forced on the courtesan; it emanates from her. The quality and demeanor of the courte-san are infused into Circe, Salome, and other representations. As she posed in mythological guise, her personality emerged.

In a sense she was "nothing" until she was Flora or Venus. The courtesan had no name until she gave herself names. It was a self-creation. One is almost able to catch her in the instant before she becomes what she is, before she knows what she is, before she chooses what she is. It is this self-fashioning of a personality that allows the pose. She loses nothing, and the myth or legend she embodies gains.

An interesting question comes to mind: does the courtesan's portrait reflect this awareness that she becomes herself only when she poses? To answer that, courtesan portraiture needs to be viewed in the perspective of the illusionism of Renaissance art in general.

Until the triumph of Mannerism, the artist attempted to divert attention away from the artificial toward the natural, although art often came to replace and to surpass nature. The idea was to conjure up the natural by means of the greatest artifice, but without calling attention to artifice (something already implicit in Giambattista Alberti). Who better to accomplish this end than the courtesan, a mercenary of love who adopted the decorum of lasciviousness?

The illusionism of courtesanry was a practical expedient, an experiential analogue to the theoretical illusionism of art. Logically, the first preceded the second, but in fact, in the case of portraiture, the two processes occurred simultaneously.

To create an illusion of naturalness, the artist often has to draw on previous representations. Lucian, a Greek writer of the second century A.D., offers a parable about this concept. Fascinated by the thought that figurative representation cannot arise from "nothing"—that is, from the purely ideal or from material reality alone, when he was asked to create a portrait in words of the mistress of an emperor (probably Lucius Verus's Panthea), he did not turn to the actual person as the gods had created her, but rather to art. Scouring the land for the most beautiful statues and paintings, he produced a composite picture of ideal female beauty, using "the languid eyes and gracious smile" of the *Venus of Cnidus*, along with "the cheeks and soft, tapering fingers of

the *Venus* of Alcamene," in addition to "the symmetrical nose of Phidias's *Lemnia*" (a statue of Minerva in the citadel in Athens). The shades of color came from different paintings and included "that hue not too white but of a light flesh color" Apelles used in his portrait of Campsaspe. Needless to say, Lucian encountered difficulty in perfecting this obsequious homage to feminine beauty, and the result was felt to lack some essential quality. Nevertheless, the story makes an important point. By suggesting that only art could have fashioned such a beautiful woman, Lucian encouraged artists to imitate an imitation of nature.

This "triplicity"—the imitation of art that is in turn an imitation of nature—fascinated Renaissance artists and their sitters. When Andrea Doria posed as Neptune, he saw Neptune as depicted in ancient art, even perhaps—taking the notion one step further—as emperors, generals, and admirals had imagined themselves in the guise of Jove, Mars, and Neptune. A man thus portrayed was intended to appear as himself and not himself—that is to say, as something more than himself, this more being an extension, an interpretation, or a projection.

The concept is illustrated in a somewhat naive way in Leone Leoni's life-size, naturalistic bronze bust of Emperor Charles V in ancient armor. The artist devised a panel opened with a set of keys that removed the armor to expose a naked Mars underneath. The result is a modern emperor seeing himself as an ancient Caesar who strove to be a Mars or at least a symbolic representation of him.

Similarly, we are asked to "unbutton" Flora in order to find the naked courtesan underneath, but at the same time are encouraged to adorn our concept of the courtesan with the accouterments of Flora, hoisting the unloosened chemise an inch or two over her breasts and shoulders and thrusting a small nosegay into her hand—"This and this, too," not "this instead of that."

Like Andrea Doria and others in powerful roles, the courtesan depended on such identifications and extensions of her significance, although in her case sometimes the metaphor, the other embodiment, becomes the real one, and the person herself stands in the shadow of it. Fiction has a resemblance to

Dosso Dossi, *Circe*. About 1525. Samuel H. Kress Collection, National Gallery of Art, Washington, D.C.

truth, and art is a natural resource as inspiring to artists as nature itself. The imitation of imitation can result in something real. In this sense, the Renaissance courtesan offers herself to art as a "second nature," an accomplished paradigm but one that needs to be halted in its flux, fixed for a moment, in order to exist at all. For in life she prefers not to be entirely grasped.

There was another reason for the artist's involvement in the illusionary process of the courtesan. Both artist and courtesan were marginal and central at the same time. The artist was in essence a courtier for his patron. The struggles of giants like Michelangelo and Titian indicate to what extent art-

ists' freedom was limited, although they tried to exert their wills as much as possible. Like Aretino using his phallic pen or courtesans using their sex, artists used paint brushes and chisels in order to present their personalities to the public.

A painter commissioned to paint a courtesan's portrait had no choice but to paint the woman's own presentation of herself, the artifice of which already gained his complicity and consensus and in which—whether he wanted to or not—he saw his own image narcissistically reflected.

Those familiar with Castiglione's *The Courtier* will not be surprised to see *sprezzatura* (a sophisticated casualness, a feigned indifference) in courtesan portraiture. The sitter making a "high-cultural" presentation of herself becomes a work of art to be contemplated, yet she is also something natural; she has only been further "realized" by human hands and offered up theatrically to the public as a kind of hypothesis or proposition. She wants you to know that *she* knows this. Beneath the pose or in the next moment, a natural being in the world could spring to life.

The iconography of courtesans is crucial to Renaissance image making. The infusion of courtesan qualities into Magdalenes, Floras, and Venuses and the envisioning of these figures as projections of and "frames" for the courtesan not only conditions the depiction of the female presence in art in general; it also allows a slight, deliberate fracture between appearance and reality to be felt. Another way to view this phenomenon is in terms of transparency, of seeing one thing under or through another as in a palimpsest in which both the surface and the ground beneath are "true."

But an interesting question comes to mind. If, in her self-presentation, the courtesan passes through several phases in rapid succession, when does the artist intervene—during the "foreplay," the immersion, the ironic reflectiveness on it, or the abandoning of it? Does he combine these phases? Is this combination possible? Sometimes the woman seems to be mocking art—the artificiality of what she is and what "it" is. In this mockery there may be the implication that she knows she can do what the artist is doing and has done it better, simply by becoming what she is. In this case, the mistress rivals the artist, who may sometimes be her lover. The artist encourages the rivalry by offering and demanding to paint her portrait. By doing so, he forces the courtesan to reflect on her identity and his limits.

In her glance and smile, however, mockery is mixed with gratitude, for until the artist has conceived of and crystallized her "type" and poets have framed her thoughts and those she inspires, the courtesan has been merely a generalized desire on the part of society. She needs the artist's keen acu-

men, delicate sensibility, and bold apprehension of the sensual in order to be truly "seen" and felt. Now she can be "adored," and her admirers come forward as artists mold the viewing public. But first the courtesan must please the artist, externalizing the qualities required of her by the ideology of the time. Hence the artist can be seen as endowing the courtesan with her decorum at the very moment she becomes aware of needing it. Supposedly by dressing her in his imagination, he reveals her natural self.

This is precisely what renders the artist's labor difficult. It is one matter to paint a landscape, or a figure based on an antique statue of Venus or Bacchus, but the courtesan was a complex subject. To capture the spirit and fugitive appearance of a woman whose borrowed role was in turn modeled on concepts and tangible forms of beauty and refinement, the artist pursued a dizzying series of images mirrored in other images. Yet in the hands of great artists such as Leonardo or Raphael, this chain of imitation produces something at once exquisitely natural and culturally relevant, a vision that is the artist's own and yet, at the same time, the reflection society demanded—a private and public image.

The courtesan may have felt she was a better artist than the artist since her work preceded his; she may also have been amused or dismayed by the fact that, no matter how skillful he was in fixing her image, she could change in the next moment, being almost as elusive an artistic subject as she was an erotic object in life. Still, she depended on the artist, and it may be dependency and familiarity, and the rebellion these states produced within the courtesan, that appear in the *Gioconda's* face. Her wistful smile contains a mocking smugness, the willingness—the spiritual necessity—to *épater l'artiste*, almost as though the beautiful woman mocked God who created her but could never sleep with her. Long before she acquired the various mustaches painted on her, the *Gioconda* "defaced" Leonardo's painting by letting her own consciousness of the situation shine through like a rainbow out of a rain-misted sky.

THE COURTESAN IN VENETIAN, FRENCH, AND NORTHERN PAINTING

· PALMA VECCHIO, TITIAN, AND CARIANI ·

Palma Vecchio, born around 1480 in a town near Bergamo, painted in Venice beginning in the first decade of the sixteenth century. He was influenced by Giovanni Bellini, Cima da Conegliano, and Carpaccio. In the 1520s he became drawn into the magical circle around Giorgione, devoting himself to the creation of dreamy landscapes and pastoral scenes. The third great influence on him was Titian, whose monumental figures become rounded and softened in Palma's hands. Although Palma's religious pictures are beautiful, his portraits of courtesans and courtesan types are especially characteristic. These women often display their breasts, while luxurious clothing, expertly loosened, drops down from their shoulders. Milky skin, glittering blond hair, intense glances, and curvaceous bodies beckon discreetly but candidly.

Especially precious is the young *Violante*, a portrait in Vienna sometimes attributed to Titian and called "Little Cat," where voluptuous promise is indistinguishable from robust health and ingenuous insouciance. The same charming ease invests a group portrait traditionally called *The Three Sisters*,

again presenting Violante with her identifying flower and two sisters-of-the-trade. A similarly young, fresh, mischievous courtesan appears in Giovanni Cariani's *Portrait of a Young Woman* in Budapest. Cariani, also from Bergamo, was influenced by Palma, but has his own distinctive style. As we shall see, one of his paintings gives us an unusual view of Renaissance courtesan life.

There is nothing sharp or harshly modeled in Palma's work. His paintings reveal the perception of a universe of florid but never vulgarly displayed female forms. His colors—as, for example, in the *Woman in Blue*—are vivid and intense; the treatment of flesh and hair sometimes arrives at the ineffable vanishing point between the material and the immaterial—as in his Flora. Sometimes a kind of spirituality of carnality appears in his work; at other times, he uses women's worldly charms in a somewhat more exterior fashion as window dressing, thus encouraging comparison with Paris Bordone's more stereotyped renderings of these Venetian mercenaries of eros. In a third variation, *La Bella* in the Thyssen-Bornemisza Collection, the in-

TOP LEFT: Palma Vecchio, *Three Sisters*. 16th century. Staatliche Kunstsammlung, Dresden

BOTTOM LEFT: Palma Vecchio, *Woman in Blue*. 16th century. Kunsthistorisches Museum, Vienna

ABOVE: Giovanni Cariani, *Portrait of a Young Woman*. 16th century. Szepmuveszeti Museum, Budapest

PALMA VECCHIO, TITIAN, AND CARIANI ———————————

Attributed to Bonifacio dei Pitati or Giovanni Cariani, *Venus and Cupid*. 16th century. Ex collection Hans Kisters, Kreuzlingen

telligent look in the sitter's eyes suggests that she is a valuable person, but one not asking, at least at this moment, to be exalted or seduced.

There is no such look in the eyes of the courtesans of Paris Bordone, a painter whose oeuvre reflects the pin-up side of the courtesan image. Although he repeats the same figures and poses sometimes to the point of tedium, Bordone's brilliant coloration and concern with the display of womanly beauty make his courtesan portraits important. The *Woman in Red Velvet* with her pet squirrel relates to the Carpaccio rooftop loggia scene with courtesans and their menagerie and Andrea Calmo's descriptions. The *Young Woman at Her Toilet* shows us an elegantly brocaded dress worked with

gold thread and an interest in long hair elaborately waved and plaited that could almost be called fetishistic. The hair returns in other portraits of courtesans, as do the elegant clothes, many of stiffened and embossed materials that seem to have a life of their own or of richly hued taffetas.

Bordone, who enjoyed placing mysterious narrative scenes in the background of his portraits, usually having to do with love—the delivery of love notes, for example, to someone on a loggia in a courtyard, created a double composition of this kind for a Genoese nobleman, Ottaviano Grimaldi. At least a portrait of himself was to have been sent to him along with one of "an extremely lascivious woman." Since there are so many resemblances between his portrait and one of a woman in red taffeta in the National Gallery, London, it is thought that the person in red is the lascivious woman. This would bolster my contention that sometimes the dressed courtesan can be more seductive than her nude counterpart.

Paris Bordone painted many mythological scenes, and his Floras and Venuses are today flung far and wide across Europe. His work is often considered conventional and superficial; still, the cumulative effect of all those ample breasts and blond tresses is quite powerful, if slightly abstract compared to some more individualized interpretations by his Venetian contemporaries.

Quite in the opposite direction are two Venus paintings of the Venetian School that are definitely courtesan portraits and exhibit a striking, almost disturbing realism. One is a *Venus and Cupid* attributed to Bonifacio dei Pitati or Giovanni Cariani, which features the incestuous kiss that appears often in Renaissance art, both in the south and the north, in both Venus and Cupid, and Madonna and Child configurations. Another one is Bernardino Licinio's

Venus, in which a very real woman whose face is strikingly shown in profile reclines in an extremely private boudoir. It is a surprise to find works of art so *hors de catégorie*. The Licinio has an almost nineteenth-century quality about it, the self-sufficiency of the waiting figure absorbed in her own seductiveness.

By the third and fourth decades of the sixteenth century, painters such as Titian were promoting a newly imagined ideal type. The sources for this vision can be found in a convergence of "high culture" based on Petrarch, Bembo, and Castiglione, with Platonic overtones, and the Venetian ambiance of courtesans and polygraphs ("bohemian" writers associated with the printing presses), where individual personalities held sway and customs were perhaps freer than anywhere else in Europe. A revival of Provencal courtly love—involving the cult of an elite adulterous passion—lent its special quality to the ideal.

As one critic put it, "at the time of Titian, flesh did not ascend toward the idea, but rather ideas proceeded to incarnate themselves." The medieval as-

Bernardino Licinio, *Reclining Venus*. 16th century. Temporarily at Palazzo Vecchio, Florence

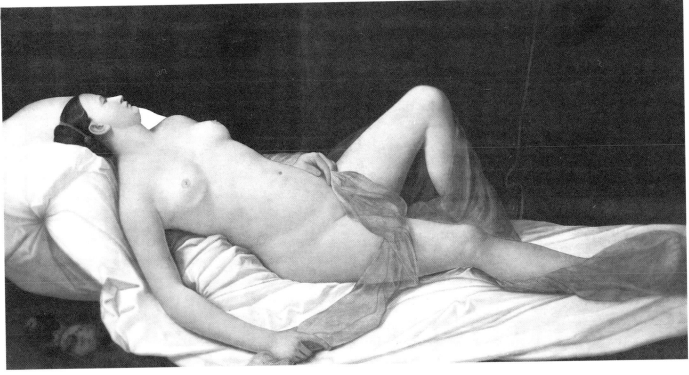

Paris Bordone, *Woman in Red Velvet*. 16th century. Thyssen-Bornemisza Collection, Lugano

THE COURTESAN IN VENETIAN, FRENCH, AND NORTHERN PAINTING

Titian, *Flora*. 16th century. Galleria degli Uffizi, Florence

piration to dissolve material reality had been replaced by the impulse to give primacy to the natural world. A spiritualized naturalism resulted, in which everything erotic played a major role. Courtesans, posing for paintings by Titian and his circle, became vehicles to convey this ideological message. In short, carnality became imbued with a new value, and thus courtesans, their venality lying just below the surface, offered an image that reflected the patricians' highest dreams of disinterested beauty.

The great rulers of Europe craved and commissioned such images, filling their bedrooms and baths with these palpitating visions of imagined beauty. Letters by Giovanni della Casa and Ludovico Dolce tell us how intense the desire of men such as Cardinal Alessandro Farnese and Philip II of Spain was to possess paintings like Titian's *Danae* (one in the Museo di Capodimonte, Naples, and the other in the Museo del Prado, Madrid). There are so many replicas of certain female types in set poses because the market demanded them; it was the trend of the time. Literature too played its part. Plays, novellas, and above all the poems of Ariosto and Tasso offered stimulating portraits of beautiful, tender young women susceptible to love and elegantly conceived in classical and/or pastoral settings.

Titian fuses a number of conventions—for example in his *Flora*, a painting as meltingly tender as it is provocative, one finds the dreamy contemplativeness and allegorizing of Giorgione, the half-figure poses of Leonardo, and Palma Vecchio's taste for large-scale, curved female forms, together with the artist's own subtle coloration. If Leonardo is the first to develop the female portrait on a life-size, major scale in an intimate rapport with the viewer, Titian finally humanizes it. All the currents are gathered into a *summa* of courtesan portraiture, testimony to the purity of carnal love if cast in Platonic terms.

With Titian's work, different poses and conceptions overlap or rather allude to one another as well as to the past. The Violante motif recurs in the *Bacchanale of the Andrians* as the seated woman in contemporary dress, violets tucked into her bosom. Together with a female companion, she provides a strange contrast to the mythological figures intent on their revels or sleeping. Violante and the reclin-

ing nymph could well represent two different moments or aspects of the same person; indeed, one might be dreaming the other. Titian's signature on the most gossamer bit of veiling just above the border of Violante's bodice links both paintings to the *Fornarina*. The ostentatiously placed signature returns on Laura Dianti's sleeve in Titian's portrait of her.

Another individual portrait of a courtesan is the justly celebrated *Venus of Urbino*: an honest courtesan in her boudoir with maids and a dog stares at us with a sweet impudence barely masking the indifference that becomes a touchstone expression in paintings by artists such as Goya and Manet. *La Bella*, with her finely arched eyebrows and elaborate, prudent dress, could be "one of them," or has she perhaps stumbled into the group simply because her name is not known? The courtesan inspiration persists in Titian's representations of *Venus at her Toilet* and *Venus Binding the Eyes of Cupid*, as well as of *Danae*, alluding to the *Venus of Urbino* with her drooping braceleted arm, and a whole gamut of mythological figures including even Diana, only an arrow's flight away from the unleashed Bacchic.

With the Venus and Musician paintings Titian removes to a slightly different terrain; here the sixteenth-century social setting comes into play, and one finds oneself in intimate rooms that are also the open loggias of palaces. In *Venus and the Organist* in Berlin (where the musician is thought to have the features of Philip II of Spain for whom it was commissioned), the landscape is generously revealed. The fabulous and the mythological come to invest this domestic interior, just as music "transports" elsewhere the musician and his audience of one who is also muse and inspiration. Although the music is inaudible, the experience is conveyed visually through the beautiful forms of the arrayed woman, carnal equivalent to the harmony of the spheres.

Beauty, writes the Renaissance philosopher Leone Ebreo, is only a revelation on earth of the highest categories of being. The beautiful woman naturally delivers to her lover or to those who gaze at her the most rarefied spiritual experience. Every aspect speaks of love; apparently she is carrying on a sacred conversation with the universe to which she co-responds. Her body "speaks," and the intimate, unspoken and yet implicit response is mystically conveyed to those of us who look on and who have nurtured within ourselves "gentle hearts" (to use the Provençal-Stilnovist term for the naturally elite sensibility).

Contrasting Titian's work with Bordone's frequently more impersonal renderings of female beauty as delicate as they are cold, scholars of the old school speak of this artist's "ingenuous goodness and simplicity that veils evil and impurity" and his "almost childlike innocence."[38] The meaning of such pronouncements is clear, but it is hard to consider the *Flora* ingenuous or childlike, and the terms are even less apt for the woman in Vienna posing with a fur cape provocatively draped down one side of her nude body. In a version of this painting now in the Hermitage, a man's plumed hat and cape reinforce the ambiguity of the figure. *Woman in Fur* in turn inspired Rubens's *Hélène Fourment in Fur*, one of the most daring and yet tender conjugal portraits ever made.

Giorgione's *Laura* is another ambiguous painting that can hardly be described as "ingenuous." There is nothing innocent about this woman, even whose pout is provocative. The deliberately revealed naked breast and the laurel leaves suggest that the figure is a courtesan who wrote poetry, not simply a woman named "Laura." Likewise, Vincenzo Catena's *Portrait of a Young Woman Posing as a Magdalene* does not imply that the subject was saintly. More problematic is Lorenzo Lotto's *Lucretia*, which shows a buxom woman in an elegant decolleté gown exhibiting her name on a piece of paper. Lucretia was a favorite name for courtesans; in identifying with the historical heroine, surely her namesakes intended more to enhance her depiction with the beauty of their breasts than to imitate her virtue or ill-fated life.

On the surface, but only on the surface, Giovanni Cariani's *Courtesans and Gentlemen*, traditionally called *Seven Portraits of the Albani Family*, has an ingenuous quality. This is one of the rare Italian paintings to show a group of courtesans and their lovers—in this case, three men and four women—posed together. Another candidate—

Vicenzo Catena, *Portrait of a Young Woman Posing as a Magdalene*. 16th century. Gemäldegalerie, Staatliche Museen Preussischer Kulturbesitz, Berlin

Dosso Dossi's *Allegory of Hercules*, presenting two contrasted types of courtesans seated at a gaming table behind which stand several men—offers a somewhat formal view of the interior of a casino, but the artist has hidden his meaning in a series of symbols difficult to decipher, and this distracts from a realistic interpretation of the work. The unusual *Society Scene* by the Flemish-Venetian painter, Ludovico Pozzoserrato, shows us couples and single figures of courtesans in the living room of a high-class brothel, possibly but not necessarily in Venice, since the clothing reflects both Flemish and Venetian fashions. All of these sixteenth-century examples anticipate the genre scenes of seventeenth-century Dutch painting.

In Cariani's group scene, *Courtesans and Gentlemen*, the arrangement of the figures is formal but subtle. This is a salon, a Venetian *ridotto* where gentlemen, writers, artists and courtesans gathered together carried on high-toned conversations, lis-

Titian, *Danae*. 16th century. Museo Nazionale di Capodimonte, Naples

Titian, detail from *Bacchanale of the Andrians*. 16th century. Museo del Prado, Madrid

Peter Paul Rubens, *Hélène Fourment in Fur*. 17th century. Kunsthistorisches Museum, Vienna

Titian, *Portrait of a Young Woman*. 16th century. The Hermitage, Leningrad

Giovanni Cariani, *Courtesan in a Landscape*. 16th century. Gemäldegalerie, Staatliche Museen Preussischer Kulturbesitz, Berlin

tened to music and flirted in specific socially approved ways. Probably the men are visiting the women, rather than the other way around, since there are still vestiges of the preparations the women have made in order to appear at their best.

A courtesan seated on the right holds a mirror in her hand, which she would do most naturally in her own home. Indeed, she seems to be discreetly grooming herself or perhaps admiring the effect after she has just ceased grooming, for the man standing behind her, undoubtedly her lover, cannot resist touching some of the fine golden strands with his fingers as he gazes down intensely on the rounded head embraced by its precious golden band.

There is much to observe in this scene, for centuries considered a portrait of members of a distinguished Bergamasque family. The cumulative presence of significant objects and gestures is not alone responsible for the picture's unique atmosphere, but contributes to it. There is a squirrel, which could mean lust or greed but might simply be a pet; a feathered fan gripped in an enticing way; and a handsome small mirror also held delicately but in full display. The painting is rich with details, such as the single index finger that is still gloved (partly removed gloves were especially modish, even seductive), the hand of the courtesan on the far left that tightly holds her gloves behind her back, as well as the attractive bracelets of gold and precious stones.

Titian, *Venus of Urbino*. 16th century. Galleria degli Uffizi, Florence

Titian, *Venus and the Organist*. 16th century. Gemäldegalerie, Staatliche Museen Preussischer Kulturbesitz, Berlin

Titian, *Woman in Fur*. 16th century. Kunsthistorisches Museum, Vienna

School of Giorgione, *Seduction*. 16th century. Detroit Institute of Arts

School of Giorgione, *Lovers*. 16th century. Casa Buonarroti, Florence

The personages in Cariani's painting are the epitome of contemporary fashion. The procuress is distinguished by a characteristic plumed hat. Each woman's hairstyle is different, but all have artfully crimped, curled, braided, and waved blond hair. The gowns are luxurious underdresses with applied voluminous sleeves, except in the case of the woman on the left who wears a dark taffeta overdress, her exposed back adorned with one of those heavy golden chains seen again and again in Cranach's many depictions of Lucretia.

Elaborate hairstyles, caps, and hats are not limited to the women. The most sharply drawn male member of the group wears a fashionable beret with a medal on it that seems almost to mirror in modified form the turbanlike braided coiffure, also adorned with a brooch, of the courtesan on the left. The young man on the left wears a precious dangling earring; his outfit is made of four or five different luxurious materials fitted together. Our attention is also drawn by the high-necked batiste pleated blouse of the youth next to him whose beret

has already been noted. The third man, who is older and has a touch of the cynical about him (while the youth in the beret romantically gazes) wears beautiful gloves and a large brimmed hat gentlemen and knights often doffed; his white collar is impeccable.

Each person has cut out a space for him- or herself and stands or sits like statuary, a composition apart and yet a participant in the group that has gathered for some purpose, no matter how oblique; for, as we know, afternoon formal conversations could be quite not-to-the-point anticipations of what the French would call salons of *précieuses*. A remnant of Giorgione-like atmosphere circulates around the solitary figures, encouraging the notion that each is lost in a dreamy contemplativeness, aspiring to the idea of love as much as to a concrete, earthly manifestation of it, or at least affecting this concern as a preamble to heartier pleasures.

This secular version of a "Sacred Conversation" has much in common with Giorgione's amorously mystical concert scenes that Cariani, Licinio, and others inherit and duly reinterpret. The solemn expressions and pose of the company combined with the sensual realization of details and coloring produce a witty, sophisticated effect that is yet extremely idealized. Cariani spent important years of his artistic life in his native city, Bergamo. Although he was greatly influenced by painters of the the Venetian School, he has qualities distinct from theirs. Clearly he sees his courtesans' salon as elegant as any in that city and perhaps even more so. It is this "more so" that comes through in the picture—the exasperation of fashionableness, of affected attitudes, gestures and poses, the extenuated romantic gazes, and the feigned indifference of the courted ladies. All of these features produce a delightful scene, but one that might have seemed just a bit overdone.

Is the flower tucked into the bosom of the seated courtesan on the right yet another allusion to the Violante type? Lacking that softer human quality of Titian's *Flora* and nymphs, Cariani's courtesans are nevertheless marvelously conceived real persons in their own right, deserving to be linked to both Palma's and Titian's representations. They have most in common, perhaps, with Palma's *La Bella*, who, as I have suggested, adds the quality of a penetrating intelligence to a perfectly composed demeanor.

There is a genre related to the group portraits: that of lovers shown together, often with a third person present—male or female. A formidable example is the couple in Paris Bordone's *Venetian Lovers* also called *Seduction* (where the man ostentatiously offers a golden necklace to the woman). Several triangles have a vaguely erotic air, that might represent situations such as those narrated in

School of Cariani, *Seduction.* 16th century. Galleria Borghese, Rome

Dosso Dossi, detail from *Allegory of Hercules*. 16th century. Galleria degli Uffizi, Florence

THE COURTESAN IN VENETIAN, FRENCH, AND NORTHERN PAINTING

Giovanni Cariani, *Courtesans and Gentlemen*. 16th century. Private collection

Felicitas Sartori, Portrait of Gaspara Stampa. 18th century. Civica Raccolta delle Stampe Achille Bertarelli, Milan

Felicitas Sartori, *Portrait of Collaltino del Collalto.* 18th century. Civica Raccolta delle Stampe Achille Bertarelli, Milan

novellas. Like the Bordone painting, they have been attributed titles such as *Seduction.*

Unfortunately, we shall never be able to view the Venetian couple *par excellence* of Collaltino del Collalto and Gaspara Stampa; the portrait Titian painted of Collaltino del Collalto is lost. A pair of eighteenth-century prints offers an imaginary double portrait of the lovers. Fortunately, we have Gaspara's portrait in words, where we learn that Collaltino was fair-haired but also that he was cruel. In addition, Gaspara's lyrical effusions provide an ongoing self-portrait, although one scarce in physical details. Thus the lovers live on—he as she conceived him, and she as she impresses herself and her endless plight on our consciousness. Since luckily

art generates art, Gaspara's spirit endures as well in Rilke's and d'Annunzio's devoted lines.

One of the mythological situations surely foremost in Gaspara's mind as she waits eagerly for her lover to return from the battlefield (or from amusing himself at the French court) is that of Venus and Mars. One thinks of Lambert Sustris's mannered but extremely elegant *Venus Awaiting Mars,* or the many varying depictions of the scene in Veronese's work. Especially appropriate for a courtesan are his *Mars Undressing Venus* in the National Gallery of Scotland, the bedroom scene below stairs, in the Galleria Sabauda in Turin, in which Mars has his back suggestively turned to us, the more formal depiction in Chantilly where Venus is shown with her fan, and

THE COURTESAN IN VENETIAN, FRENCH, AND NORTHERN PAINTING

even the gloriously conjugal Venus, now in the Metropolitan Museum of Art in New York, pressing milk from her breasts.

Collaltino was a country gentleman. His family, of Langobard origin, owned castles near Treviso and in the Friuli regions. A warrior, he was also a man of letters and frequented the ambiance of the polygraphs. His secretary, Giuseppi Betussi, wrote two treatises on love, one of them centered around the figure of Franceschina Baffo, a poet who was probably also a courtesan, and he also published a continuation of Boccaccio's annotated list of illustrious women, adding many contemporary examples. In this appendix, a relative of Collaltino's, Bianca del Collalto, is praised for her chastity, but there is not a single word about Gaspara the poet, whose skills exceeded those of most of the other women of her generation.

The final apotheosis of the courtesan image in Venetian painting occurs in Titian's *Danae* paintings. Fortunately there are two of them. The second one places us firmly on the earth by inserting the courtesan once more in a recognizable social context.

·THE THEME OF DANAE·

Danae has long been the symbol of the woman whose love can be purchased. In the Greek legend she was a virgin princess whose father, Acrisius, locked her in a tower for safekeeping. It did not take long for writers to perceive in her a symbol of the venal courtesan. As pictured in Renaissance paintings, Danae can be an innocent maiden or, more usually, a ripe, beautiful woman alluringly arrayed on her bed, as the god comes to her in one of his most enigmatic material forms—a rain of gold, for the most part shown as actual coins.

Jan Gossaert's *Danae*, the very image of intense expectancy, is a young courtesan of Flanders romantically posed in a handsome classical loggia. It is she who makes the connection to the earlier iconographic tradition equating Danae with Mary of the Annunciation. At the opposite extreme is Correggio's painting, which refers to nothing outside of itself. In this painting, one of Correggio's masterpieces, a palpable light seems to come from both within and without.

The first impression conveyed by Titian's *Danae* in Naples is lustfulness, but further examination suggests that Danae's face is absorbed in an idea, perhaps a contemplation of the divine. Hence, a potential contrast exists between the voluptuous body, the right hand with the bracelet making the gesture that relates the woman to another of Titian's courtesans, and the rapt gazing. Our eyes are attracted by the gaze but do not stop there, inevitably returning to the more physical aspects that, however, "vaporize" themselves as we look on—for example, the shadow moving down along Danae's left side or the hair disappearing into the left armpit and indistinguishable from it, or the contour of the left breast that descends to the nipple below.

Florentines accused the Venetians of poor modeling techniques, of being weak in form, though strong in coloring. Here a lovely line is used, however, in order to achieve an expressive indistinctness. The left shoulder is concealed in a veritable nest of hair. The nipple of the right breast resembles a tiny mass of slightly darker hair, but at the same time is dematerialized.

Gradually, as the luminosity of the body diminishes, the face largely in shadow seems to lift toward the divine, moving into another world. This woman seems to have two natures. She thinks one thing and does another: on the one hand, she is contemplative, on the other she makes herself available to the god descending in the form of money. Evidently, this is the only way that he can have and know her and she have and know him.

This mutual having and knowing—if that is what is happening here before our eyes—conditions the atmosphere of the whole room, which is not a room at all but an immense loggia open to the sky, the contradictory inside-outside habitation appropriate for the Venetian Venus, who is at once a ritualistic-public and a private phenomenon.

Lambert Sustris, *Venus Awaiting Mars*. 16th century. Musée National du Louvre, Paris

THE COURTESAN IN VENETIAN, FRENCH, AND NORTHERN PAINTING

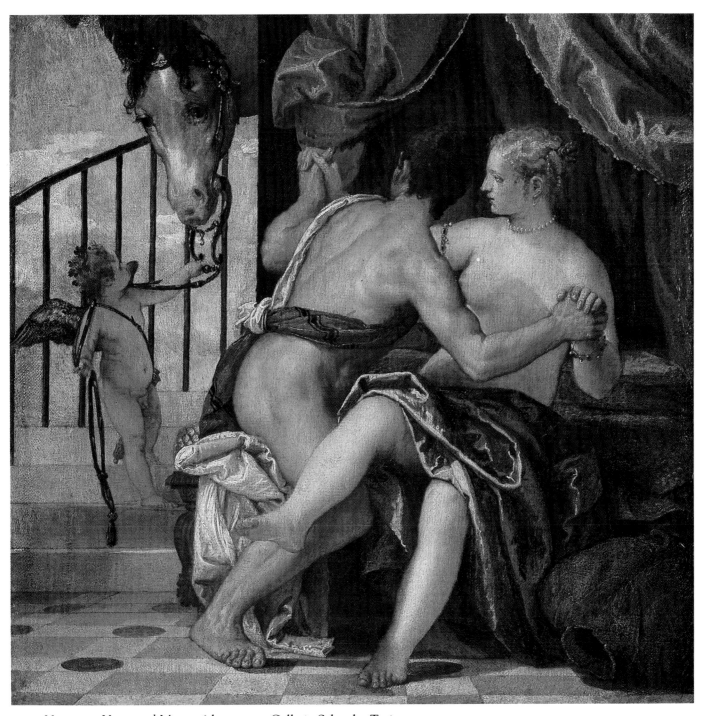

Veronese, *Venus and Mars*. 16th century. Galleria Sabauda, Turin

As the raincloud lowers into the room that is not a room, there is a symbolical contrasting of elements—of divine and mortal, masculine and feminine, light and shadow, outside and inside, even flesh and materials and (in the Prado version) the old woman and the younger one. But now the shadow it casts begins to take possession of and alter the materiality. Irregular and fantastic, it is the shadow of a moving object.

The brushstrokes that follow the curves of Danae's body and seem to mark where it ends and space begins do not form a real contour, rather this is more like a condensed shadow. If the hand is the hand of the *Venus of Urbino*, the face is the face of the "other" aspect of that woman distant and idealized. It is the dream of love that one sees here, not orgasm, or is it perhaps both? Uncertainty is of the essence. Danae is immobile while love descends, yet she too engineers the scene, her active passivity vaguely reminiscent of Mary's.

If Danae is made of shadow, it is not because she is some portentous figure of religious allegory. Still, the mystical fringes of Renaissance thought permit a certain speculation. The woman presented here is not the object—the possession—of a man, she is the object of God. He has created her, and she is the best example of his work, the very fashioning of an example. Therefore, how can he help loving her and moving close to her (or moving her close to him) in order to mirror in her his own reality, his own power, that here is indicated in an ingenuous way in the shower of gold? (And what if God were the patrician class mirroring itself in the honest courtesan, seeing there, appropriately framed, an exaltation of its own true nature?)

Shadow is still "the idea." The woman is immersed in shadow; all of her is shadow in the sense that she really is divine beauty that can be only partially grasped. Yet every once in a while, through a transcendent grace, beauty crosses over into our visual space. Titian renders what he can of it, the maximum beyond which limit it is impossible to proceed. Hence it is *limit* we see when we gaze at that line rounding the left breast and descending to the nipple, or that ineffable fusion of hair near the left armpit.

Thus Danae as Titian conceives of her perfectly embodies the contradiction between venal acquiescence and heavenly aspiration. If she were only the sign of limit (and hence of death) she would have to stay forever inside her tower. But this is a courtesan who lives and who is only posed here, her loggia of the huge columns rising invisibly into space an homage to Venice, city of courtesans.

Can that explain the little wrinkles also seeming of shadow of her stomach, the fine, fleshy lips, the hand that drops in lassitude? This is all languor on the alert for the "event." The hybrid symbolism no longer worries us: Titian's *Danae* is also Venus with Cupid, a woman of her time available for love, sublimely indifferent to the material negotiations, attached to her freedom, but when she is fascinated by a beauty outside of herself, willing to make herself a slave, if only for a moment, to a god or the idea of a god.

Titian's *Danae* in the Prado, originally sent to Philip II of Spain in the mid-1550s, precipitates this more rarefied version into the real world, for here finally the procuress appears as the indispensable companion to the courtesan.

In classical literature alluding to the Danae story, the old nurse is rarely mentioned, and attention is focused instead on the venality of the prison guards whom Jove bribes.[39] In the Renaissance, however, the go-between played too important a social role to be overlooked. In addition, she provided a way to siphon off some of the blame from the idealized, Venus-like princess who, nevertheless, accepts Jove's amorous advances (thus becoming the ancestor of Perseus, but this later history is mostly irrelevant to the scene). Formally, the presence of the procuress could be an advantage, setting into dramatic relief the pale, smooth flesh, delicate features and presumably more spiritual outlook of the younger woman, or a disadvantage, distracting attention away from the solitary reclining figure.

In complex paintings such as this one, the procuress cannot be identified too patly as an allegorical figure of Avidity, freeing Danae to play a more or less neutral role. What the artist has done is to conflate successive phases into one. Danae experiences the phase of sublimation involving an initial fasci-

Titian, *Danae*. 16th century. Museo del Prado, Madrid

nation with the other, as well as the rather fabulous invasion of her room by a golden cloud; yet, as Jove returns to his, she will return to her other nature, either during or after the copulation, and she will have her money and her memories.

The possibility of a momentary metamorphosis of the courtesan figure into her "better" half intensifies the interest of the picture. In depictions of *Danae* by other artists, there is often considerable emphasis on the sheerly worldly side, and there the central role of the procuress is set into relief (just as in the version in Vienna the mediating function of the procuress already has a formal analogue in the placing of the pan in the center of the pictorial space).

Primaticcio's *Danae*, a fresco in Fontainebleau,

shows the procuress moving to catch the gold in a large vase as Cupid attempts to hold her back (his motives can be variously interpreted). In Tintoretto's painting, a maidservant no older than Danae, and quite attractive herself, gathers coins in her apron as she kneels and looks up wonderingly. There is a slight reversal of roles here, for the maidservant has an ingenuous expression on her face and a respectable air, while Danae, leaning toward the left in a pose as studied as those of the French royal mistresses, looks knowingly sideways, poised and ready. Her luxurious courtesan's chamber is adorned with rich velvet bed hangings; an overturned lute on the windowsill connects the scene to the Vanity theme; and, not least of all, a charming dog awaits

Jan Gossaert, *Danae*. 16th century. Alte Pinakothek, Munich

Tintoretto, *Danae*. 16th century. Musée des Beaux-Arts, Lyons

A COURTESAN RECOUNTS HER WILES

Even if sometimes I became infatuated, whoever wanted to have me for his Danae had to rain like Jove into my lap in the form of gold. Once a merchant of considerable fortune, while strolling by, caught sight of me at the window talking with my neighbors and became so enamoured of me he thought his life depended on possessing me. I laid out my snares, but it took a while to get him exactly where I wanted him. Again and again he sent messages, together with gifts, but I scornfully sent them back; yet, at the same time, I held out little glints of hope to lure him on. When, finally, I let him know that I would see him for a short while he rejoiced as if a new era of his life had begun. The opening up of a stronghold of armour or a treasury was no less ceremonious than the admittance to my chambers. Once there, my suspicions, accusations, and threats (for example, my saying that one of my lovers might take us by surprise) drove him into a fearful state. . . . So intoxicated was he that he became a Tantalus whose lips touched water without his being able to drink a drop. Each day the spasmodic desire to have me near him grew. Eventually, after he gave me a hundred doubloons as down payment, I consented to go around with, and devote myself to, him for a few weeks. We fixed my salary at twenty-five gold ducats a month.

This man lived alone with a maidservant and a boy servant. As soon as she stuck her head through the door, I managed to quarrel with the maid and get her fired. The next step was to persuade the merchant to assume my mother, whom I painted as the wisest woman in the world. At my urging he gave up his boy servant as well, whom I replaced with a friend of mine. Now, with great satisfaction, I ruled over the whole household. Try to imagine the sea of luxury I floated in. Our kitchen resembled that of Apicius [wealthy gastronomic expert in Rome of Tiberius, author of a famous

cookbook]. All day, partridges with cloves and pheasants with cinnamon simmered away. It was no small advantage that my lover was a trader in spices from the East. The first flowers and fruits of the season, the rarest game, the most unusual fish were the order of the day, along with rich fabrics and lovely jewels. So dazzled was he by my caresses, that scarcely an instant transpired between my viewing something I liked and my having it. All his energies were bent toward satisfying the immense range of my desires. In a few weeks, he was reduced almost to a skeleton, had very little money left, and was in debt. This is the true alchemy of a courtesan, who transforms stones and turns wood into precious twigs of gold. A courtesan who fails to look out for herself, and lets her lovers give her only what they wish, quickly goes to her downfall.

Such were the nooses and chains I used to capture and drag my lovers towards my chamber—the sticky traps catching those birds. Once seized, they never got away again, except by leaving their finest feathers behind. You should have seen a lover struck to the very heart, spellbound and immobile, by the sight of my laughing mouth; and if, by chance, his gaze met mine, I possessed him more effectively than if I had drawn around his feet the Witch Ismeno's magical circles [witch in Tasso's *Jerusalem Liberated* who tries to foil the Crusaders with her black arts]. I discovered in myself the marvelous powers of the witch Circe. Some men I changed into lions, making them ferocious, others into dogs who obeyed my slightest gesture and guarded my doors, or who became rabid with jealousy. Others were timid hares, so afraid were they of displeasing me or of being abused by my other lovers; still others became filthy beasts attracted to nothing but Venus's pigsty. Thus I saw it was possible to change men into animals.

Francesco Pona, *La lucerna*, pp. 105–11

his mistress. As if the woman's occupation were not clear, Tintoretto has spread out the golden coins over Danae's hips and thighs where they tip over into the pubic area (the golden rain symbolizes semen), and she holds out her right hand to display a coin held between thumb and forefinger while pointing to it with her left hand. Is she explaining the action to her servant, or justifying to the world the role she has agreed to play, or warning her companion, us, and herself, of the dangers of material greed? The answer is probably none of these things and all of them.

·COURTESANS AT THEIR BATH·

Diana would seem to be a less likely incarnation than Danae for a courtesan, but she came to play that role briefly in Renaissance painting. This was because Courtesans at Their Bath constituted a pleasing variation on the theme of Courtesans at Their Toilet. In Italy, women at their bath appeared primarily in Diana and Her Nymphs depictions taking place outdoors, or in scenes featuring Venus in the sea, Galatea and Nereids. Often these were small-scale frescoes decorating intimate spaces such as palace baths. In France, painters of the School of Fontainebleau developed the special subject of the royal mistress at her bath. The effect is a curious one in *Diane de Poitiers in Her Bath* by François Clouet, the formality of the pose contrasting with the action. Diane de Poitiers (1499–1566), whose father descended from an old family of Aquitaine, was at thirty-two the widow of a grand-seneschal of Normandy. It is thought that she gave herself to Francis I in order to save her father. The duke of Orléans, subsequently Henry II, although twenty years her junior, fell in love with her and continued to be devoted to her all his life (d. 1559). As duchess of Valentinois, Diane became extremely powerful in France, her influence due to her remarkable personality and strength of character as much as to her beauty—the fine hair, smooth skin, and regular features we see in portraits of her.

In some versions of another Clouet painting, "fancy" allegorizing allows another royal mistress, Gabrielle d'Estrées, to dally as the mythical Diana, standing with nymphs in a landscape while Henry IV, her lover, the royal voyeur, happens to ride by on horseback and espy them.[40] According to the Greek myth, Actaeon, accidentally coming upon the sight of Diana bathing, fell in love and was transformed into a stag as a punishment. But Henry, enjoying "diplomatic immunity" is allowed to return to the scene of the crime, viewing his already well-known mistress over and over.

Unlike Diane de Poitiers, Gabrielle was born to a disreputable mother whose many daughters seem to have taken up the trade of prostitution. At sixteen Gabrielle was handed over to Henry III for the known price of 6,000 *scudi*. A series of lovers followed, the last of whom personally arranged the affair with Henry IV. On the occasion of Henry's solemn entry into Paris in September 1594, Madame de Liancourt (Gabrielle had been married off to a gentleman from Picardy named Liancourt) was carried ahead of him dressed as a queen, in a bejeweled litter surrounded by torches. Nicknamed L'Etoile, Gabrielle assumed the titles of marquise of Monceaux, then of duchess of Beaufort, and came to own rich domains in France.

In a work by an artist of the school of Fontainebleau, Gabrielle is posed, as in Clouet's *Diane de Poitiers at Her Bath*, in a large-scale double nude bust portrait along with her sister, the duchess of Villars, who tweaks one of Gabrielle's nipples with her fingers in a gesture that has its own symbolism. This was a way of displaying and acknowledging beauty, but there may be a hidden substratum of humor in this painting, one that is enjoying a new popularity today.[41] A variant of this scene shows the nude sisters in a different pose, one delicately proffering a ring to the other.

Certainly the "mistress at her bath" theme gained favor in French art of the sixteenth century primarily because of the prominence of Diane de Poitiers and the connection through her name with the Diana myth. But the forest, too, plays its part, for

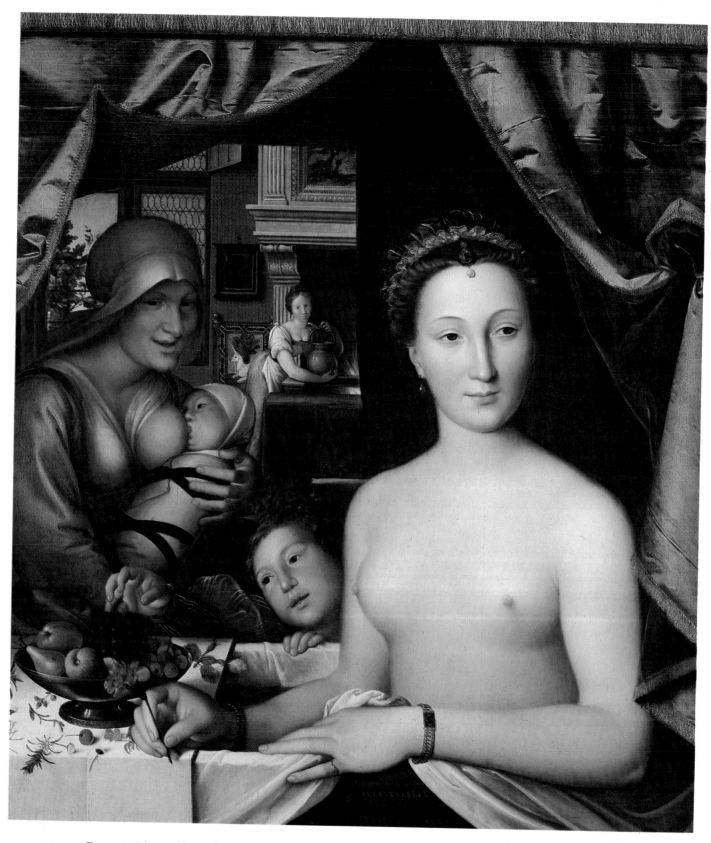

ABOVE: François Clouet, *Diane de Poitiers in Her Bath.* 16th century. Samuel H. Kress Collection, National Gallery of Art, Washington, D.C.

TOP RIGHT: François Clouet, *Diana with Her Nymphs in a Landscape.* 16th century. Musée des Beaux-Arts, Rouen

BOTTOM RIGHT: School of Fontainebleau, *Gabrielle d'Estrées and Her Sister.* 16th century. Musée National du Louvre, Paris

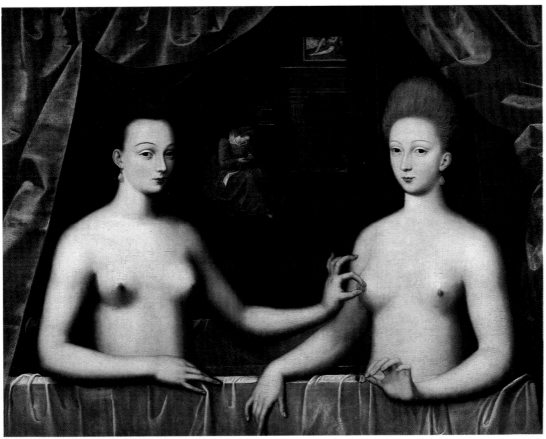

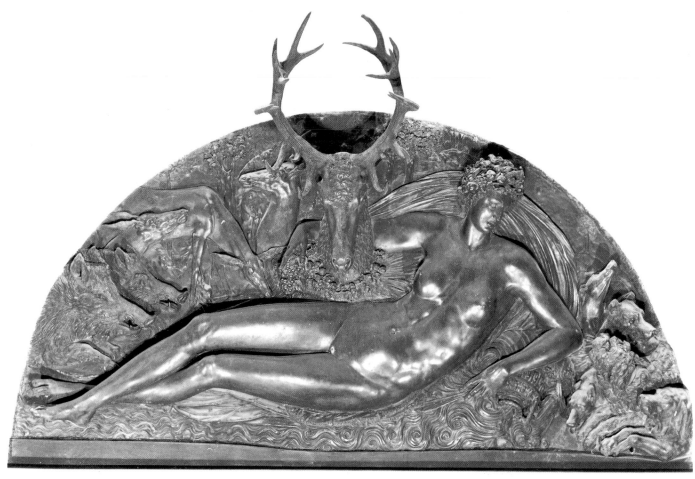

Benvenuto Cellini, *Nymph of Fontainebleau.* 16th century. Musée National du Louvre, Paris

the nymph of Fontainebleau, the presiding spirit of the spring that is supposedly at the origin of Fontainebleau itself, came to lend her charms to the conception. The nymph is blended with Diane de Poitiers in Cellini's bronze relief that was originally placed over the doorway at the Château d'Anet, Diane's private residence to which she retired after Henry II's death.

Diana Hunting continues to haunt the French imagination along with Diana at Her Bath, where the landscape lends itself to the guises of mythology, allowing nymphs to disport in the most natural way. In a painting probably by Luca Penni, obviously conceived in homage to Diane de Poitiers, who was an excellent horsewoman, a woman wearing yellow (the courtesan's emblematic shade, but undoubtedly a coincidence) sets out on a solitary hunting expe-

dition. The figure corresponds to a French ideal that has been consistent through the centuries—a type of woman who is slightly masculine in a jaunty way and, if not intellectual, at least self-sufficient. But the huntress image is not exclusive to France. Lucas van Leyden, perhaps drawing on an obscure legend, depicts the Magdalene hunting. It is as though, in both cases, we were being allowed a glimpse of the woman's precourtesan days when, conscious of her charms but unaware as yet of the ways of the world, she rode out fresh and uncontaminated as Eve into the woods of her own delight.

The forest can be seen, of course, in psychological terms, as the feminine element itself, and it is possible that Henry IV risks losing himself there when he pauses, in his urbane way, to gaze at the naked ladies. The hunt, too, can be viewed erotically, for Diane de Poitiers was an extremely aggressive woman who went after what she wanted and obtained it and seems to have played with role-reversal possibilities in order to keep her grip on Henry II.

In the sexualization of the landscape that takes place in French and Italian paintings of the Diana myth, there is also room for lesbian asides, for women frolicking together in the sensual pleasures of the bath are notoriously drawn to each other's beauty, in admiration or beyond. At least this is what various artists, such as Palma Vecchio, tell us as they delight in painting and engraving the Diana and Callisto myth. This is a particularly interesting story that in today's terms could easily seem to have been generated by a male lover's fantasy about how his mistress and another woman might caress each other, were they to find each other alone in a secluded place. According to the myth, Jove, in order to seduce the nymph Callisto, disguises himself as the goddess Diana. In art we are offered both the initial seduction with the two women and the scene in which Callisto's pregnancy is exposed, to the horror of the others, whom we presume are all still virgins. In a related instance Jove becomes a woodland creature, transforming himself into a satyr in order to gain more intimate access to the nymph Antiope. Sixteenth-century engravings of subjects such as these can be quite audaciously erotic, as for example Jacopo da Caraglio's *Jove and Antiope* in his Loves of the Gods series.

Titian seems veritably obsessed with the themes of forest, baths, and the hunt during the 1560s, when he produces major paintings around the figures of Diana, Callisto, Actaeon, and also Venus and Adonis. Some of the most mysterious paintings ever executed, they offer us allusions to courtesan portraiture but never the thing itself. For example, there is the unforgettable image of Diana in *Diana and Actaeon*, seated on the right of the painting, her body partly turned away from us in profile, yet well visible, as she lifts her left arm seemingly in outrage covering half of her face. A spaniel that would be just as happy in a boudoir as in the wilds sits near her feet, and a Moorish servant makes gestures of protection from behind. Diana's entire body ex-

presses simultaneously reluctance and invitation; her leisurely position—the free and open disposition of her charms, corresponding to her attitude in the few moments preceding the event—cannot be so quickly abandoned that we, the artist and viewing public, do not see her beauty for what it is, the effort of concealment making it only that much more enticing.

Another female presence reminiscent of courtesan portraiture appears in Titian's *Jove and Antiope*. The woman in contemporary dress, seated with the naked satyr whose head is wreathed in vine leaves, is clearly the first cousin of the dressed, seated woman in the *Bacchanale of the Andrians*, who seems the other self of the nymph stretched out luxuriously on the ground uncovered by a satyr in as civilized a gesture as woodland creatures ever make. Perhaps the clothed women are dreaming the nymph. The nymph also has the possibility of "precipitating out" into reality as a lovely Venetian woman dedicated to love in the highest manner.

It is a far cry from the idealized depictions of Diana and nymphs in a landscape to the realistic indoor bath scenes, often with men and women together, of northern and French engravers. Although sometimes, in an attempt to raise the tone, Venus, or Venus and Mars, are shown stepping into a wooden tub; at other times what appear to be orgies take place in a Renaissance *stufa* conceived by the artist in terms of ancient ones. In prints by such engravers as Jean Mignon, the bath is often merely a pretext for revealing naked women enjoying various pleasures together. Sometimes these can be morally neutral genre scenes (in one startling case the event is an initiation of Anabaptists). In other prints, such as Heinrich Aldegrever's *Venus at Her Bath*, the brutal display of the woman's sexual zone can only mean that Venus herself was a whore, a theme of satirical literature throughout Europe. Of great interest to the present subject is the background of some bath scenes, which contains a bedroom with lovers on the bed. In one case, a porcelain stove is covered over presumably with erotic figuration.

Bath scenes almost always imply a sense of violation. Spying on Diana and her nymphs in a land-

Crispin de Passe, bath scene from Prodigal Son series. 17th century. Folger Shakespeare Library, Washington, D.C.

Jean Mignon, *Women Bathing*. 16th century. Bibliothèque Nationale, Paris

Luca Penni, *Diana Hunting*. 16th century. Musée National du Louvre, Paris

scape, Actaeon does not meet his death but is transfigured to a lower form of existence. For the sight of naked bathing women had something of the taboo about it. Meditating on the significance of bathing scenes through the centuries, one arrives at the idea that Actaeon can be no other than the anonymous spectator of art, but there is another way to look at it. Could Actaeon not be better seen as the artist who locates and isolates from the rest of nature beautiful forms and lets them register on his consciousness? As such, he is always in danger of transgressing the threshold of the sacred, that which the cosmos has tucked away for its own enjoyment. The artist looks and, in that looking, perceives everything, the whole in the part, the divine in the apparently mortal. The look itself is a kind of possession, already a daring performance. But the actual translation onto canvas or into stone is an act that, in various societies, has always been considered forbidden or at least cloaked in mystery because of its resemblance to the creative act of God. The depiction of courtesans and mistresses at their bath draws on this archetypal situation rich in meaning, for until she is *seen* the courtesan does not exist as such. She depends on the spying, the violation, as much as she depends on her individual patrons for material welfare.

How almost obscene, then—but charming—when a regent of France, Henry IV, is shown portrayed in place of Actaeon, in the guise of a knight riding by, fully dressed in his historical role, while Diana bathes with her nymphs nearby. Not only does he coyly usurp the place of a legendary figure, he sets himself up as the artist's rival. Could one argue that the real lover, no matter how powerful in society he is, can be just as much an "intrusion" in erotic scenes as the men and women who commissioned sacred paintings sometimes were?

·THE BIBLICAL POSE·

Largely idealized in Venetian and realistically depicted in northern painting, Susannah and Bathsheba are two more figures visualized by artists as courtesans at their bath, albeit courtesans with private living quarters rather than brothel whores. Interestingly, in both episodes, an element of taboo, of the forbidden operates: the men gazing at and lusting after Susannah are inappropriately old (sometimes they are even portrayed as fatherly, in a reverse image of Lot and His Daughters); David, who is married, should not let himself be tempted by another woman. In each of these cases—Susannah, Bathsheba, Diana and her nymphs—the "difficult" or "impossible" allows the action to be permanently suspended, to enter the world of art, where the contemplation of desire is a higher form than desire itself.

Who would deny that the artist is like David in the David and Bathsheba configuration? He sees himself seeing Bathsheba, whereas David sees what is squarely placed before his eyes. Bathsheba stepping out of her bath is a favorite Renaissance subject, lending itself to displays of the female nude and luxurious toilet articles or even unusual bathrooms, as in Hans Memling's painting where the elegant black slippers, little white dog and classical architecture leave no doubt about who the protagonist of this scene (or at least her model) really is. Paris Bordone creates two lovely Bathsheba at the Fountain scenes.

Susannah, like Bathsheba, can be shown in a temptress type bathing scene. In Tintoretto's exquisite rendering, we are dazzled by the display of beautiful objects. Susannah is the courtesan *par excellence* in an engraving by Jean Collaert: sitting at her toilet in a garden by a fountain she preens herself as she is being insidiously opportuned. But biblical poses related to courtesan life are not limited to these two figures.

Just as in the temples of antiquity there were sometimes portraits of courtesans, perhaps as a group propitiation to the gods who it was thought would be persuaded by anything so beautiful, in Christian churches in the sixteenth century, courtesans' images also found their place. As Cupids and other pagan elements mingled in abstract decora-

VERSES ON TITIAN'S *MAGDALENE*

Young woman who made your eyes fountains
to wash His holy feet; clothed in your hair,
Your lovely features become humble and sad,
Your wild senses disciplined,
Tell me, are these the eyes that hills and dales
Once filled with joyfulness?
Are these the tresses that, braided
In myriad fashions, delighted the world?
Or did Titian perhaps go up to Paradise
To render you with his brilliant palette
Chaste, wise, pleasing, beautiful, lively?
It must have been so—this is no merely human
Work: flesh here expresses both
Chaste lasciviousness and lascivious chastity.

Francesco Maria Molza, *Rime*, XLVIII

tive patterns, so the radiant faces and curvaceous bodies of these women, arousing a sense of awe in whoever gazed at them, loomed or beckoned from apses, cupolas, niches in the most varied imaginable postures, handsomely clad or shown nude as suavely tortured female saints. One of the most beautiful of these is Palma Vecchio's *Santa Barbara* in Santa Maria Formosa in Venice. One of the most bizarre is Palma Giovane's *Santa Cristina*, now in the Museo Civico in Padua, showing a naked woman tied to a column, a halo on her head, in what is surely one of the most suggestive of the Renaissance "bondage" scenes.

The erotic scenes suggested by both Old and New Testaments were many. In particular there came to be delineated the couplings of famous biblical heroes and heroines, even if little or nothing in the sacred scripture authorized the legends that grew up. These meanings can be "read" directly from the paintings, although occasionally there is literary evidence that such traditions existed.

The first couple is Adam and Eve, who are usually presented as fairly chaste figures, perhaps because

their nakedness was originally imposed on them by God—in other words, they found themselves in a natural boudoir and did not have to engage in the rituals of courtesans and lovers, but sometimes they were depicted in amorous attitudes. Christ and the Magdalene, as well as occasionally Christ and the Adultress, who sometimes appear side by side almost as lovers, are portrayed with even more ambiguity. The fact that in many scenes the Magdalene is dressed in fashionable contemporary garments makes the seduction she has used and—it is implied—still could effect all the more powerful.

The Magdalene shown half-undressed, her hair loose around her shoulders, with a book or skull or other emblem of her new life, is a pretext for the display of sheer feminine beauty, particularly of breasts and hair. Palma Giovane offers a whole panoply of undressed Magdalenes, one more fetching (and artificial) than the last, while Titian's in Palazzo Pitti is infused with a great human softness and tenderness, slightly intimidating us as we enter her into the annals of courtesan art in the Renaissance. She almost convinces us that she is what she is supposed

ABOVE: Tintoretto, *Susannah*. 16th century. Kunsthistorisches Museum, Vienna

LEFT: Hans Memling, *Bathsheba*. 16th century. Staatsgalerie, Stuttgart

Titian, *Magdalene*. 16th century. Palazzo Pitti, Florence

THE COURTESAN IN VENETIAN, FRENCH, AND NORTHERN PAINTING

to be—a religious image, just as this master's *Salome* in the Doria Pamphili Gallery in Rome creates in us a feeling that is voluptuous and pious in equal measure, a pleasurably disturbing emotion the painter lucidly intended us to have.

According to an underground legend dating at least as far back as the twelfth century, Salome was reputed to have been in love with John the Baptist.[42] In the Eros/Thanatos representations of this fatally skilled dancing girl, daughter of a great ruler, Salome gazes longingly at the handsome head of the man she has slain; in other representations she stares into space—an attitude often meant to be interpreted in Renaissance painting as one of amorous contemplation, distanced desire. Well might Salome long for the return of the man who no longer lives, who only rests his head as if on the final peace of her bosom or lap.

Salome is charming in the fifteenth century; in the sixteenth again she is often represented as a beautifully dressed young lady who has somehow accidentally found herself in a tragic situation. Many Salomes, by Bonifacio dei Pitati, Giampietrino, and innumerable other artists across Europe, deserve attention. Remote descendants of the ambiguous dancing girls and singers popular in Mozarabic Spain before the Reconquista, they have a distant Persian origin. Obliquely mentioned in Provençal poetry, these wandering precourtesans may have sold their charms much as the orating and acrobatic *jongleurs* did. But Eastern exoticism was reaching the West via Venice as well. Salome's was only a high-class version of what came, under the dominion of the Turks, to be a common harem spectacle. The figure is revived once more as mere picturesqueness in the eighteenth and nineteenth centuries by Ingres and Delacroix.

Moretto da Brescia's portrait of *Salome*—as legend has it, a portrait of Tullia d'Aragona—constitutes a rare example of a biblical painting constructed around an identifiable Renaissance courtesan. Courtesans must have often posed for religious pictures, and it may well be that the handsome woman kneeling in the foreground of Raphael's *Transfiguration*, one shoulder dramatically bare, is Imperia, who inspired the same artist's *Galatea*. Intended to

Palma Giovane, *Salome with the Head of John the Baptist*. 16th century. Kunsthistorisches Museum, Vienna

Bonifacio dei Pitati, *Salome*. 16th century. Kunsthistorisches Museum, Vienna

QVAE SAC...IOANIS
CAPVT SALTANDO
OBTINVIT

Moretto da Brescia, *Herodiade*. 16th century. Museo Civico, Brescia

THE COURTESAN IN VENETIAN, FRENCH, AND NORTHERN PAINTING

Tintoretto, *Joseph and Potiphar's Wife*. 16th century. Museo del Prado, Madrid

Hendrik Goltzius, *Tamar*. 16th century. Oeffentliche Kunstsammlung, Basel

Palma Giovane, *Samson and Delilah*. 16th century. Accademia di San Luca, Rome

THE COURTESAN IN VENETIAN, FRENCH, AND NORTHERN PAINTING

be a spectator in and of the scene, the woman is supposed to be calling attention to a holy miracle but instead—much like courtesans in their theater boxes in Restoration England, one imagines—calls attention to herself.

Salome was an unusually appropriate personage to associate with a courtesan model, since her dancing—her deliberately artificial, emphatic wantonness—brought about the fall of the man whom she secretly loved (often we see her looking at the head of the Baptist, desire and regret commingled in her gaze). Salome also provided the opportunity for dragging out oriental garb, something that intrigued even Raphael, as observed in the turbans of the *Fornarina* and one of his Madonnas.

Moretto da Brescia's *Salome* reveals a lovely young woman in a blue velvet dress, a scarf knotted over her right shoulder. Her fur-lined red velvet mantle is drawn around her. In her left hand she holds a long golden scepter ornamented with acanthus leaves and a pine cone. Her hair is braided and threaded through with ribbons and pearls. In a classical gesture, her left arm rests upon a marble stand whose inscription in Latin reads: "She who through her dancing achieved the [cutting off of the] head of Holy John."

There is nothing particularly oriental about this depiction, although it exudes a vague exoticism attributable to an odd contrast between the voluptuously open mouth of the woman and slightly cocked position of the head and the grave historical role assigned to her in this moment. The long face and somewhat long nose correspond to contemporary descriptions of Tullia d'Aragona; laurel in the background suggests that the sitter was a poetess. Further encouraging the identification of the subject as Tullia only incidentally posed as Salome is an episode from that courtesan's biography—the attempted suicide of a disappointed lover.

In addition to Adam and Eve, Christ and the Magdalene, Christ and the Adultress, David and Bathsheba, Susannah and the Elders, and Salome and the Baptist, there are other amorous couples, such as Samson and Delilah, Solomon and Sheba, Joseph and Potiphar's Wife, Abraham and Hagar, Tamar and her father-in-law, and still others includ-

Palma Giovane, *Bathsheba*. 16th century. Accademia di San Luca, Rome

ing Lot and his Daughters (as already noted, a reversal of the Susannah situation, the Elders being seduced rather than distanced.) Each couple provides a pretext for numerous paintings and engravings.

Samson and Delilah is one of a series of biblical couples by Palma Giovane illustrating the theme of the seductive powers of women. In Palma's paintings of her, Delilah always wears the fashionable Venetian hairdo consisting of two high cones made out of the twisted hair itself. His *Bathsheba* in the same series is very much the *puttana*—a petit-bourgeois, rather coarse-featured woman sitting naked and cross-legged, perhaps even a bit bored, pausing by an open window before turning to the tedious matter of dressing and grooming herself.

Another instance in which a woman uses the courtesan's arts in order to seduce is that of Joseph and Potiphar's Wife. Tintoretto's charming reclining figure with her rouged mouth stretches an arm back behind and over her head. Although the stories are mostly pretexts for the display of womanly

Jan van Scorel, *Magdalene*. 16th century. Rijksmuseum, Amsterdam

beauty and the formal interest of flesh intonations and positions of limbs, there may be an underlying "moral" in Palma Giovane's and Tintoretto's representations—namely, that women such as courtesans, when too much homage is paid to them, can abuse their privileges, becoming as "lethal" as these more primitive, legendary biblical figures.

Even the Magdalene can be seen as a dangerous threat, for she has not forgotten the power she once exercised over men. In a way, she is the most potent of all of these biblical heroines, especially when dressed. Flemish artists leapt to the occasion. In Joos van Cleve's *Portrait of a Woman as the Magdalene*, the saint is sporting leopard-skin sleeves; she has a jewel on her head, a necklace and pearls, and wears an elaborate hairdo. Rogier van der Weyden's *Magdalene* is also fashionably dressed; she wears an odd hat and fancy sleeves. In Jan van Scorel's *Mag-*

THE COURTESAN IN VENETIAN, FRENCH, AND NORTHERN PAINTING

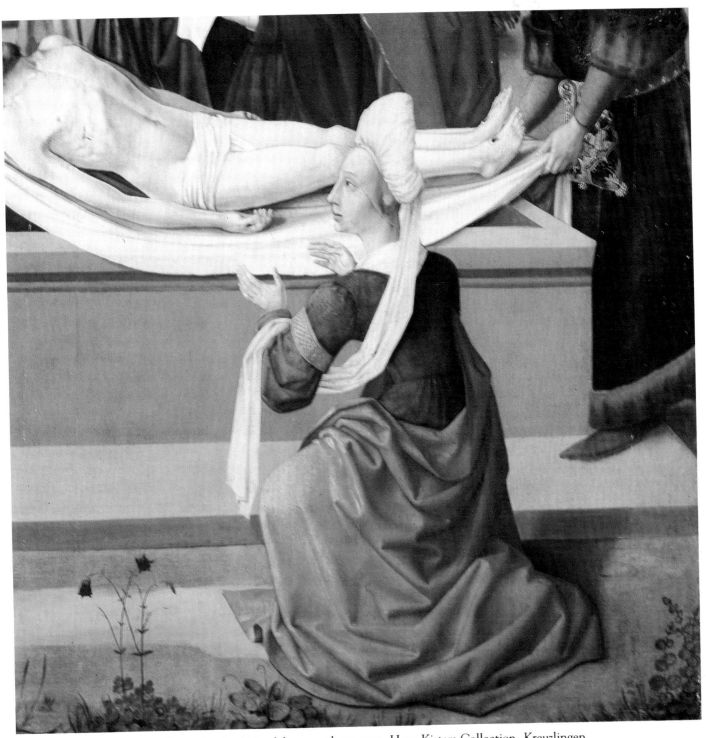

Circle of Dirk Bouts, *Pietà*, detail of Magdalene. 15th century. Hans Kisters Collection, Kreuzlingen

dalene there are lavish fabrics, pearls twisted around sleeves as if they were ribbons, all of this completed by the woman's downward but alluring gaze. Even in Jacob Cornelisz van Oostsaanen's *Noli me Tangere*, a scene usually presented in a fairly sober manner, the Magdalene wears an elaborate gown.

An interesting characteristic of some Magdalene paintings is the presence of the yellow shawl courtesans were required by law to wear as an insignia of their profession: it was similar to the yellow stars and armbands that have identified Jews through the centuries as protected or persecuted pariahs. By the sixteenth century, in Venice and many other places, courtesans no longer had to wear the yellow veil, but procuresses wore them, and painters evidently did not forget that courtesans had been subjected to this ignominy. Giovanni Girolamo Savoldo's *Magdalene*, characteristically holding an ointment jar, is

Palma Giovane, *Magdalene*. 16th century. Accademia Carrara di Belle Arti, Bergamo

swaddled in an immense yellow cloak. Another example is provided by the devout kneeling Magdalene in a *Pièta* by a painter of the circle of Dirk Bouts. The saint's face is uplifted in pious adoration, and a lemon-yellow head covering hangs down over her shoulders, attracting our gaze, which has in any case come to rest on this figure as the focal point of visual interest.

Occasionally, young girls dressed up as Magdalenes, but some of the Magdalenes are startlingly mature women who have paid their dues to a life of sin. Vincenzo Catena's *Young Girl Posing as a Magdalene*, already mentioned, just might be that very special thing, a courtesan posing as a courtesan of old.

What Renaissance courtesan prancing into church on the holy days or for an important Mass did not think of herself as a momentarily converted and fashionably arrayed Mary Magdalene? The Magdalene experiences her conversion when she accompanies her pious sister Martha to hear Jesus of Nazareth preach. According to John Bunyan's sermon "The Jerusalem Sinner Saved," when the Magdalene asked, "What kind of a preacher is he?" Martha replied, "It is one Jesus of Nazareth; he is the handsomest man that ever you saw with your eyes. Oh! he shines in beauty, and is a most excellent preacher." Mary Magdalene cedes to the temptation to go to see him. "Now what does Mary do but goes up into her chamber, and with her pins and her clouts, decks herself up as fine as her fingers could make her." Then, in church, when Jesus preached about the lost sheep, the lost goat, and the prodigal child, "she thought he pitched his innocent eyes just upon her and looked as if he spake what was now being said to her." The fallen woman feels a great emotion. Later in the day she finds Jesus at dinner at the house of Simon the Pharisee, and it is there that "she gets behind him, and weeps, and drops her tears upon his feet like rain, and washes them, and wipes them with the hair of her head. She also kissed his feet with her lips, and annointed them with ointment." The way that Jesus remonstrates with Simon, who begins to look down on him for allowing this prostitute to make such a physical show about his person, is well known: it con-

Veronese, *Apollo and Venus*. 16th century. Villa Maser, Treviso

tains an apology for passion and ardor. Her washing of the feet with tears and annointing them, together with her kisses, are taken by Jesus as a sign of her "having loved much." Those who have loved much should be much forgiven.

In a sense, the Magdalene represents another version of the "impossible" love of the Western tradition, originating in Provençe and potentially tragic. *Amor de lonh*—love from afar—is present in the Magdalene's love for Christ just as it is in Tristan's for Isolde. In this cult of love, the barriers can be temporal, spatial, social, or metaphysical. The courtesan's mercenary profession necessarily gives her a lower rank than that of her lover, but, as if to contrast the humility such as a situation should induce, the Magdalene, like the honest courtesan, is made to appear the chosen conveyer of an elite kind of love marking a superior existence. At the outer

extreme, of course, there are the merely sensual Magdalenes, usually a pretext for displaying an abundant bosom, and the ascetic ones, who, as in the case of Caravaggio's particularly misogynistic example, are emaciated and ugly. But in the middle are examples of beautiful women who look as though they have meditated long and deeply on love.

Palma Giovane dazzles us with his multifarious, often nude Magdalenes that are sometimes in dubious taste. In the case of these figures, there is no point in talking about ambiguity. The artist is simply interested in imagining different dramatic positions the converted prostitute might take. The patron saint of whores ("our defense attorney," as a character in Aretino humorously calls her) is thus shown by him in a variety of poses—standing, sitting, kneeling and with various accouterments, in-

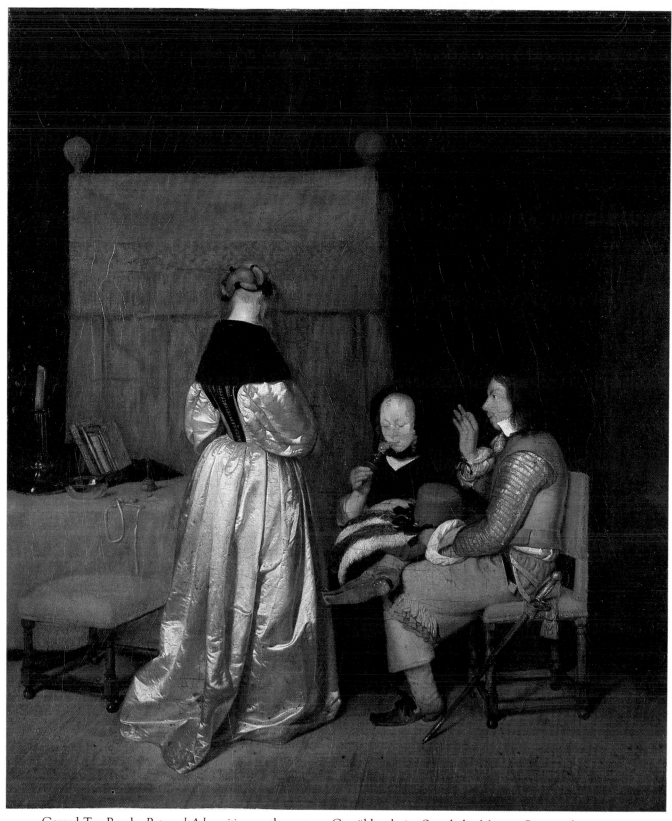

Gerard Ter Borch, *Paternal Admonition*. 17th century. Gemäldegalerie, Staatliche Museen Preussischer Kulturbesitz, Berlin

Gabriel Metsu, *The Intruder*. About 1660. Andrew W. Mellon Collection, National Gallery of Art, Washington, D.C.

cluding skulls and books. A typical painting of his is a *Magdalene* in Bergamo who kneels, her breasts fully in view, while the long trailing hair and the skull on the ground identify the figure iconographically. There are two lovely half-figures of the Magdalene by Palma in the Querini-Stampalia in Venice where the ecstatic expression of the upturned eyes is already characterized by a Baroque histrionic sentimentalism.

Many seventeenth-century Magdalenes feed off death, at least off sinister reminders of death; for what hope did the courtesan have as she grew older, other than to think that perhaps there would be another life in which values other than beauty, youthfulness and amorous skill, would be emphasized? She had been (as so many courtesans themselves, including Beatrice of Ferrara, claim) a "paradise" for her lovers, now she herself had to seek another ideal place—a *locus amoenus*—to which to direct her thoughts. But courtesans are never shown in paradise, only in Parnassus: there they reign as muses and musicians, semideities under the guiding spirits of Apollo and Venus, shown conversing together amiably in a fresco by Veronese in the lower section of a vault in a room of Villa Maser—typical villa retreat where courtesans entertained with their lutes and sweet voices. Palma gives us his version of *Parnassus* where a courtesan type displays her naked breasts as she performs on the spinet, the implication being that an equation exists between the harmony of these female forms and the beauty of the music. Earthly pleasure, the joy of the senses, are transposed to the imagination of a supernatural realm.

Coming from the Junoesque Magdalenes of Palma Giovane, suddenly we are distanced by—and made humbly curious about—Tintoretto's mysterious *Repentant Magdalene* and *Saint Mary the Egyptian*, pendant frescoes placed next to each other in San Rocco, Venice. Saint Mary the Egyptian was another saint ever present in "courtesan consciousness," since, as the tale has it, she had gained her halo by patiently subjecting herself to the sexual aggressions of a horde of soldiers.

According to Caxton's version of *The Golden Legend*, Mary the Egyptian lived an ascetic life for forty-seven years in the desert beyond Jordan. One day Abbot Zosimus finds her there, black from the sun's harsh rays. When he miraculously recognizes her, she experiences levitation, then tells her story. When she was twelve she had gone to Alexandria and become a prostitute for seventeen years, refusing no man access to her body. Encountering some Crusaders about to leave for the Holy Land, she begged to go with them in order to worship the Holy Cross, offering her body to their pleasure in order to pay for her passage. In a church in Jerusalem, she asked forgiveness of Mary, vowing to forsake the world, then proceeded into the desert beyond Jordan where she nourished herself on three loaves of bread and some herbs, but also on "the spiritual meat of the word of our Lord." When Zosimus, a year later, brings her the holy sacrament, she performs another miracle, like Christ walking on water. Zosimus wants to worship her, but she forbids him to. When he returns the next year he finds a note by her dead body explaining that she died as soon as she took the sacrament. Because the abbot is unable to do it, a lion digs up her the grave to the wonderment of Zosimus, who returns to his abbey with his faith further vivified.

Saint Mary the Egyptian regularly appears in compendiums of illustrious women printed in the sixteenth and seventeenth centuries. The sin of voluptuousness was more readily forgiven in this period than certain other ones. Luigi Dardano, in his amazing treatise in defense of women (1554), aimed in great part at combating homosexuality and sodomy in Venice, extols the converted prostitutes of history in rare tones. Of the Magdalene he says:

The steady faith of this beautiful, rich, powerful spirit was so strong she deserved to be called an Apostle.

Dardano's tenderness extends to Saint Mary the Egyptian, Pelagia of Antioch (who prostituted herself to both sexes), and even Thais, released from prison by an abbot who had had a vision of Christ's pardoning her. For Dante and the culture of his time, it was better to love too much than not at all (cf. Shakespeare's "Those who have power to hurt and will do none/ Who do not do the thing they most do show"). Tintoretto's female saints, each in her own small space, are here caught up in an intense contemplation of the natural, or should we say the divine as revealed in the natural. Surrounded by gentle trees, some appropriately tropical, these women are in a mystic harmony with the landscape. Their souls aspire to cosmic rebirth rather than to a moral redemption that might forcibly remove their eyes from the contemplation of beautiful things, or our eyes from them.

We move back now from the deserts of biblical lore to the domestic interiors of sixteenth-century Europe, to turn to one last chapter in the history of courtesans in art. Finally, we are about to see the courtesan unposed, or rather posed as herself.

· THE COURTESAN IN NORTHERN PAINTING ·

Was Goethe off the track when he described the woman whose back is turned to us in the painting by Ter Borch traditionally called *Paternal Admonition* as "that noble creature in the full-flowing, soft-pleated white silk gown?" Yes and no. It has been asserted, with good reason, that the man seated on the right and looking up at her is hardly her father, but rather a robust contemporary. He holds a telling golden coin in his hand which, since it has been partly rubbed out is thought by a contemporary critic to be a wedding ring. But would that object have been offensive enough to rub out? The expression on the face of the other woman, seated sipping her wine, is now seen to be not that of an admiring relative, a kind of youngish duenna, but rather that of a complicit procuress perhaps trying to persuade the courtesan to accept the advances of the man who has called upon this "noble creature" in order to beg her favors.

There is perhaps a moral to the scene, such as "money bends love to its will." Such emblematic lines often accompanied Dutch and German engravings, and occasionally paintings as well. Without knowing old Flemish, one can guess the point of the saying that runs under Salomon Savery's engraving of a painting by Peter Quast, in which a seated procuress takes a huge coin from the hand of a standing man. "Money talks" is used to explain one of the self-explanatory illustrations of Jacob Cats's album *Maedchen Pflicht* (Middelburg, 1628). Often titles confirm that the subject is a woman in an ambiguous situation, as in Jan Steen's *Easy Come, Easy Go* (a scene of a man eating oysters, a woman standing offering him wine, men playing tric-trac in the background). Related to such works is a series of paintings by Ter Borch showing a soldier offering a young woman coins; like many similar paintings these are at once moralistic and sensually pleasurable; this is not at all a contradiction.

Indeed, we could not be more grateful that society sanctioned paintings of scenes of debauchery behind the veils of bourgeois life. *Paternal Admonition* allows us to wallow in the opulent folds of the cream-colored satin gown, the very essence of tangibility, and to gaze marveling at the soft carmine of the four-poster bed with closed curtains that takes up a good deal of space on the canvas, the omnipresent dressing table, chair, and stool echoing the same shade, whereas the male visitor's garb is a deliberately slightly "other" red. The vertical figure of the woman whose face we die to see has something vaguely modern about it, although it is not yet a form for its own sake, abstract and distanced; it stands there pregnant, as it were, with meaning, a cipher for the viewer, as well as for the man who perhaps does not know yet whether she will acquiesce or not.

There is an unquiet, troubling air about these young Dutch courtesans in their boudoirs. They seem to be inappropriately virginal and maidenly. Such is the unsmiling girl forced from her bed in Gabriel Metsu's *The Intruder*. Again there is a seated procuress and dressing table, as well as a new touch: a handsome ermine jacket thrown over a chair. Perhaps they really are virgins—what Venetian laws referred to as *mamole*—young girls having their first experiences, but it is more likely that they are being *presented* as virgins having their first experiences (like Aretino's Nanna, who brags about the dozens of times she was offered up as innocent). Whatever the case, they are nearly indistinguishable from, say, the luminous gentlewomen of Jan Vermeer and, in fact, correspond well to Cesare Vecellio's description of courtesans as imitating aristocratic maidens and wives.

Some signs have been placed in this painting—there are the courtesan's emblematic slippers thrown casually on the floor, and the keys dangling from around the waist of the procuress together with what is probably a money pouch. This procuress is not embarrassed, but smiles, as does the woman seated in a chair who has a comb in one hand. The fingers of her other hand form a gesture that has an obscene significance in northern art. She is a coquette out to please men, and her hair is quite elaborately done up. Meanwhile, as we have seen, the young girl in white satin slipping out of the bed seems not to exist yet in the realm of the sexually symbolic.

Beds were often set up in living rooms in Dutch homes at this time, so that it could be argued that

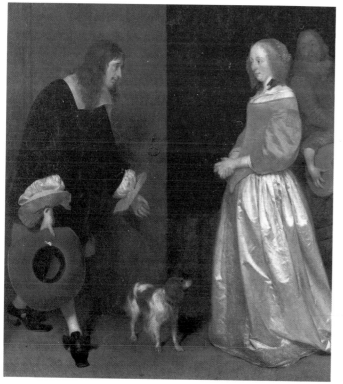

Gerard Ter Borch, detail from *The Suitor's Visit.* Andrew W. Mellon Collection, National Gallery of Art, Washington, D.C.

this is only a young girl unpleasantly surprised at an inopportune visit, the older woman being no more than a maid, but in a similar painting by Ter Borch the situation is unequivocal. In *The Suitor's Visit* the woman has stuck her thumb out, and the man makes a circle with his fingers, each letting the other, and us, know his or her intentions. The gilded leather wall coverings, a prestigious sign of luxury, are similar to those used in Venetian interiors. To stress the "Italian connection," classicizing architecture, popular in any case at this time, appears on the right-hand side of the canvas. A dog and musical instruments further set the tone.

Many Dutch genre scenes directly exhibit courtesans, others are ambiguous. Scenes apparently of tranquil family life reveal upon closer examination their real subject matter. Ter Borch and Metsu offer brothel scenes, and van Mieris an interior of an inn that is also a bordello. If we needed any other clue, the coupling dogs would tell us where we are.

A sexual symbolism extends to objects and gestures. For example, as in Gabriel Metsu's *The Intruder*, the candle and the ewer often appear together in Dutch painting signifying male and female, and a series of objects such as combs, mirrors, musical instruments, and small dogs can be seen in scenes of seduction, as well as in Vanity pictures. Coins are passed from one person to another or lie on a plate on the table, and dead birds and various other gifts also provide clues.

Beds in themselves can be quite intriguing as, for example, a tent-shaped one in Gerard Ter Borch's *Gallant Officer*, held in place by a thick cord hanging from the ceiling. Beds become the focus in many engravings of the Tarquin and Lucretia theme as, for example, one after Titian by Cornelis Cort. It is a challenge to render the softness of satin cushions and sheets in that medium and, in addition, the bed itself offers a solid architectural presence that helps give a structure to the whole space. In general, the Dutch examples are fairly simple, and there is nothing like the obsessively classical, handsome gilded bed that seems almost a miniature shrine in Il Sodoma's *Alexander and Roxanne* cycle.

Cleopatra's bed in a painting of the School of Bordone strikes a suggestive compromise, for the ex-

Carlo Saraceni, *Mars and Venus*. Early 17th century. Thyssen-Bornemisza Collection, Lugano

quisitely detailed Burano lacework of the linen and curtains—sign of local handiwork—harmonizes with the crenellated columns serving as posters. When we come to the somewhat later Carlo Saraceni *Mars and Venus*, we find a bed with painted scenes on it in the midst of a delirium of classical architecture, the room being inside and outside at the same time, seeming to have no limit. But perhaps the prize for the most elaborate bedroom fantasy along this line should go to Joseph Heintz of the Prague School and his *Mars and Venus*.

There is no lack of beds in northern art, where we are treated to both indoors and outdoors brothel-inn scenes and, occasionally, the two together. A theme from the New Testament—the Prodigal Son (Luke 15:13), interweaves with everyday genre scenes of repast and debauchery in brothel-inns to produce a collective panoramic view of the phenomenon. *The Prodigal Son Surrounded by Courtesans* more often allowed the presence of high-class mercenaries of love, in all their fashionable dress including extravagant headgear, frequently performing on musical instruments; whereas the brothel-inn became a pretext for grouping drinkers and unruly prostitutes whom artists delighted in showing pulling each other's hair or fighting (in some cases, as cold water is splashed over their heads to cool them down).

ABOVE LEFT: Frans van Mieris. *Inn Scene.* 17th century. Maurithuis, The Hague

ABOVE RIGHT: Gerard Ter Borch, *The Gallant Officer.* 17th century. Musée National du Louvre, Paris

LEFT: Cornelius Cort, *Tarquin and Lucretia.* 16th century. Calcografia dello Stato, Villa Farnesina, Rome

Braunschweig Monogrammist (Jan Sanders van Hemessen?), detail from *Merry Company*. About 1540. Gemäldegalerie, Staatliche Museen Preussischer Kulturbesitz, Berlin

One of the earliest Prodigal Son tavern scenes is Lucas van Leyden's woodcut with a motto carved into it. Later in the sixteenth century, the subject was developed by the Braunschweig Monogrammist (identified variously with Jan van Amstel and Jan Sanders van Hemessen, but also possibly another artist) and painters from Antwerp such as Joachim Bueckelaer and the forenamed van Hemessen. To the Braunschweig Monogrammist is owed a remarkable series depicting the interior structure of brothels and displaying activities engaged in within their walls. In one reproduced here, we see the characteristic stairway leading up to the higher floors, where tiny bedrooms were located, a birdcage over the front door—sign of the house, a woman playing a flute, a couple situated on and around a bed choosing wares from a peddler's bag, a quarrel among prostitutes, and general revelry at or near a round dining table.

In related paintings, bagpipers appear, servants do cartwheels, waffles are toasted over a fire, pro-

curesses make an appearance, and prostitutes exit from and go into their upstairs rooms holding huge keys; naturally there are playing-cards and dice and the inevitable tankards.

Many series of prints also relate the story of the Prodigal Son, pretext for street, courtyard, tavern, casino, and boudoir scenes. By narrating various episodes in the life of a rake, these works illustrate the habits of the prostitutes they frequented. The erotic content of the group scenes in Dutch genre painting can be even more explicit in prints, the multiple images making these racy scenes available to the very people who frequented stews and taverns.

Some striking examples of prints on the theme of the Prodigal Son are those engraved by Crispin de Passe, who lived important years of his life in Paris. These show us chamber pots emptied on importunate suitors' heads from upstairs windows, prostitutes and clients engaged in games of backgammon, and men and women bathing together while a couple in bed in a back room embrace. Some related

Micheli Parrhasio, *Courtesan Playing Lute*. 16th century. Szepmuveszeti Museum, Budapest

School of Fontainebleau, *A Woman between Men of Two Ages*. 16th century. Musée des Beaux-Arts, Rennes

Crispin de Passe, scene from Prodigal Son series. 17th century. Folger Shakespeare Library, Washington, D.C.

Italian prints and watercolors attract us by their rarity. For example, a delightful sixteenth-century Italian series of engravings with Northern influences, illustrates the downfall of a rich merchant from Cologne, who is taken in a gondola to visit courtesans in Venice. In three of these scenes we are shown the merchant arriving by gondola to the courtesans' door, a visit made through a courtyard with a staircase, and a courtesan being summoned to her window on a square where a suitor stands with a bouquet of flowers in his hands. An album of watercolors entitled *Mors italiae* (*Customs of Italian Life*, Venetian, sixteenth century) offers still more typical scenes involving courtesans, including an attractive balcony scene and another in which courtesans and their friends seem to be playing games.

The portrait genre exists as well in the engraving tradition, so that we have courtesan types posing for Lucas van Leyden's *Virtues*. The marvelous *Miroir des Plus Belles Courtisanes de ce Temps* (*A Mirror of the Most Beautiful Courtesans of Our Age*), again by Crispin de Passe, consists of forty portraits of international courtesans in typical attire—that is to say, in elegant regional dress, together with quatrains of Old Dutch, Old German, and French that relate the episodes—with the names of the seducers—that led to their initial downfall. These portraits, six of which are here reproduced are in effect no more than fashion plates, but exquisite ones. When Crispin turns to the nobility, he portrays the ladies as shepherdesses, but the effect is not half so striking.

Perhaps the most fascinating brothel scene of all

THE COURTESAN IN VENETIAN, FRENCH, AND NORTHERN PAINTING

is the frontispiece of the *Miroir* where a Dutch burgher seated comfortably in a chair smokes a pipe and chooses from portraits on the wall the courtesan who will be his for that night. Presumably the portraits on the wall are the same as those in the album. Giulio Romano and Marcantonio Raimondi produced the first of these Renaissance galleries of courtesans, possibly with ancient precedents in mind. The difference is that theirs are nude and shown copulating with their lovers. Nevertheless, the figures of the women are highly idealized, and it is only because of Aretino's sonnets that we are encouraged to identify them as portraits of specific courtesans.

An interesting variant of Crispin's series is an anonymous French imitation of the *Miroir* that sets portraits of courtesans and their lovers side by side (one thinks of the symmetrical saints of the icon tradition) and offers titillating dialogue as captions. A further step takes us in the direction of contemporary comic books: Italian engravers made broadsheets on which sequences of narrative scenes appear—with captions—illustrating "The Life and Miserable End of Courtesans."

A motif that becomes immensely popular in the north is the double portrait of a young girl and an old man, a basically comic device already observed in Andrea Calmo's *Lettere*. Artists such as Cranach, and many others as well, exploit the possibility of alternately grotesque and tender contrasts.[43] Prints that are imitations of, or variations on, the School of Fontainebleau *A Woman between Men of Two Ages* make it clear that the enticing courtesan is mocking the elderly man, by including explanatory verses: "Put this pair of glasses on," she tells him, "so that next time you can see your true situation more clearly." An interesting fusion of genres occurs in van Hemessen's *Merry Company*, in Karlsruhe, where "the three ages of man" are illustrated by a young man in a bedroom of a house of ill repute, a middle-aged man at the entry and, on the frontal plane, an old man together with a prostitute and a procuress.[44]

A further curiosity is *Amsterdamse Hoerdom* (*Whoredom in Amsterdam*), a seventeenth-century Dutch book with engravings, supposedly written by the sheriff of Amsterdam describing the sights of the

Anonymous, scenes from *Vita del lascivo* (*Life of a Rake*). 16th century. New York Public Library Print Room. Top: foreigner arriving at a Venetian courtesan's house in a gondola. Center: suitor offering flower to courtesans. Bottom: courtyard where suitor seeks a courtesan

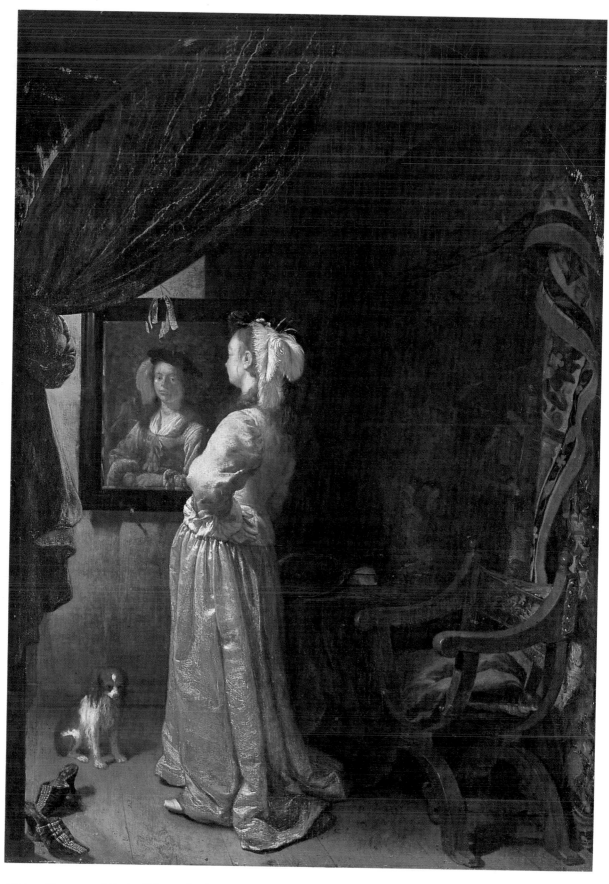

ABOVE: Frans van Mieris, *Woman Looking into a Mirror*. 17th century. Alte Pinakothek, Munich.

TOP RIGHT: Gerrit van Honthorst, *Searching for Fleas by Candlelight*. 16th century

BOTTOM RIGHT: Paul Morelsee, *Young Woman with a Mirror* (Vanity). 16th century. Fitzwilliam Museum, University of Cambridge

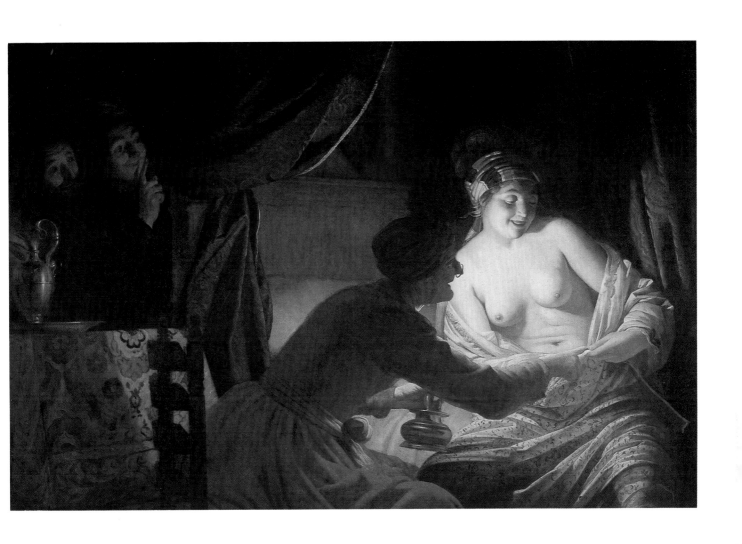

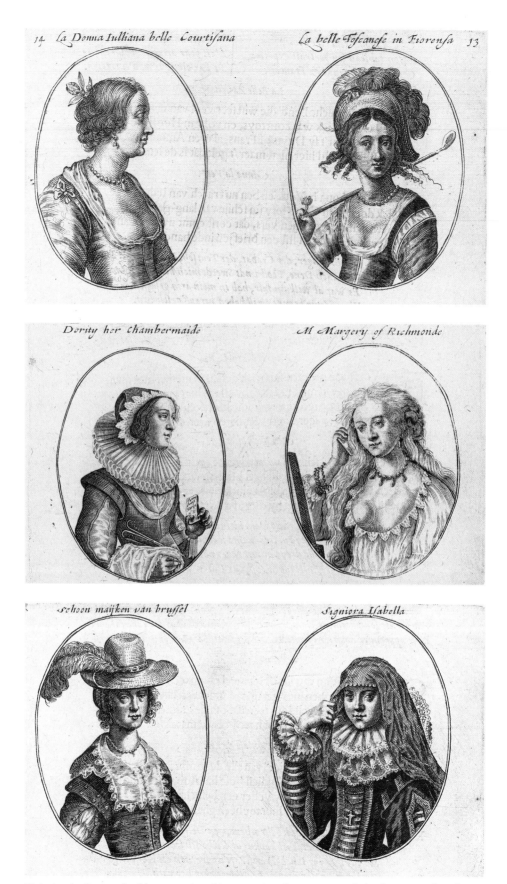

Crispin de Passe, double portraits of international courtesans from *Le miroir des plus belles courtisanes de ce temps*. 17th century. Folger Shakespeare Library, Washington, D.C.

Crispin de Passe, frontispiece from *Le miroir des plus belles courtisanes de ce temps.* 17th century. Folger Shakespeare Library, Washington, D.C.

city for his counterpart in Rotterdam. A salacious intent lurks beneath the moralism. The title page of the 1681 edition shows a young woman held by a devil at whose feet lie two men in manacles held by another devil. The woman and the standing devil each place a foot on the neck of each of the two men. The first plate depicts a woman turning a chair on one leg in a brothel-tavern, illustrating the superstition that, if a chair is spun by a prostitute, a fight is sure to take place. The second plate shows a man paying an extortionate bill, and the third something we have not yet run across—sailors and their whores.

Occasionally there is the single figure of a prostitute—for example, Paul Morelsee's telling *Blond Shepherdess* in Pommersfelden (a whole genre of shepherdess-courtesan portraits was created by the Utrecht School) and Frans van Mieris's melancholy *Woman Looking into a Mirror*, whose status is only implied. Certainly respectable women could also make a display of themselves, gaze too long into

mirrors, kick off their mules, set frivolous feathers in their caps, and doze in taverns, but sometimes one must choose, and mood often helps us to separate the professional women from those generally enjoying a good time or paying penance for it. In a category by itself is the sleeping courtesan, so beautifully captured in another Frans van Mieris painting, worlds apart from Jacob Duck's bosomy woman asleep in a tavern while her procuress attempts to wake the lover by tickling him with a piece of straw.

We have seen how writers either exalted or tried to destroy the courtesan, her image, and her reputation, and how disillusioned lovers sometimes attempted to hurt her by means of the thirty-one, scarring, and other kinds of abuses. There was still another way to get even, this time with the whole category if not with the single individual who had offended: artistic revenge. Thus, many genre paintings and prints in northern art aim at showing the courtesan in her worst aspect as a conniving, greedy, lustful, and filthy prostitute. But sometimes the in-

Niccolò dell'Abbate, *Procuress* (drawing). 16th century. Alte Pinakothek, Munich

spiration for such works, executed with moralistic intent in centuries past, was simply the more charitable and human desire to represent low life as it usually is around town and even out in soldiers' camps.

A delightful drawing by Urs Graf shows a *Prostitute Taking Her Pet Mouse for a Walk*. Clearly she has overdressed for the occasion in her beribboned overdress and long train (kept in place by the sash tied below the knee) and wide-brimmed, circular hat. The most profound of his drawings of prostitutes is one that we glanced at earlier while speaking of Isabella da Luna's early life when she was a camp

follower: *Soldier Visiting the Harlot Fortuna*. Here, the interest of the boudoir/tent scene, with its rectangular canopy over the bed, plaid cushion, table with fruit, chest, and lamp held up by the prostitute while she, adorned with only a necklace and feathered hat, undresses the young knight, is secondary only to the pensive and possibly sad expression on her face as she looks out toward, but past, us. Meanwhile the man, longing ardently, empties his gold coins onto a plate.

Many depictions are done with a savage and yet affectionate thrust of burin or pen. The large-scale, muscular, heavily jowled women who fill Heinrich

THE COURTESAN IN VENETIAN, FRENCH, AND NORTHERN PAINTING

Aldegrever's engravings of virtues like Faith, or of historical and biblical figures such as Salome, conform only remotely to the canons of proportion and the instinctively harmonious curves of Italian art of the same period. Evidently these figures are meant to represent "beauty" for their creator, as in the presentation of an Amazonic nude *Bathsheba*, where a disturbing second figure—another nude giantess, who could be either servant or procuress—stands close by. The same handsome muscular nude figure appears in a *Memento Mori*, where she holds up a decoratively framed hourglass—a skull and a shovel on the ground, Eve's apple in her hand, her hair flying in the air as witches' do, and the wicked city visible in the background.

If the northern prostitute is not always pictured as a witch, she is nevertheless a sorceress in love, and when grown old becomes the cunning procuress. The fascination with all that is commercial explains the more or less autonomous development in the north of the procuress portrait and the use of the procuress as the central focus of scenes involving courtesans. Besides Dirk van Baburen's *Procuress*, there are many more, as for example a group scene by Vermeer where, interestingly, the painter includes a self-portrait on the left side showing himself dressed in an old-fashioned, elegant Burgundian costume. Significantly, the young woman pictured with her go-between is dressed in yellow. Along these lines, one northern *Danae* is extremely interesting. In Joachim Uyteval's drawing, the gold coins fall into a chamber (a simple bedroom rather than an aristocratic loggia) tumbling directly out of an unseen lover's moneybag placed near the ceiling. Is this the divine essence that will impregnate the princess at least with dreaminess? It does not look that way. Most likely this young woman with her maid will use the profits to buy two chops and a loaf of wholesome black bread.

Sometimes an entirely original motif can appear in northern art—for example, the procuress searching her courtesan's body for fleas. The nocturnal bedroom setting in his *Searching for Fleas by Candlelight*, allows Gerrit van Honthorst of the Utrecht School to display his special talent for light effects. This painting reminds us of another work of his

Urs Graf, *Prostitute Taking Her Pet Mouse for a Walk* (drawing). 17th century. Oeffentliche Kunstsammlung, Basel

Heinrich Aldegrever, *Bathsheba*. 16th century. Bibliothèque Nationale, Paris

Dirk van Baburen, *Procuress*. 17th century.
M. Theresa B. Hopkins Fund, Museum of Fine Arts,
Boston

Giacomo Franco, *Courtesan Being Groomed by a
Maidservant* from *Habiti delle donne Venetiane*. Early
17th century. Biblioteca del Civico Museo Correr,
Venice

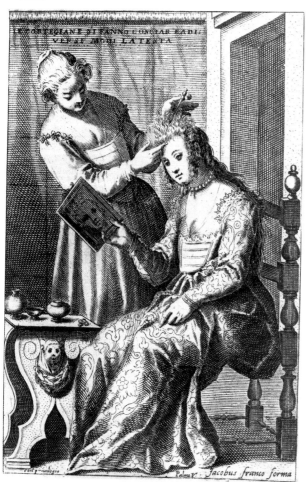

where a Caravaggesque candlelit mode is used to il-
luminate the scene of a man offering coins to a courtesan with a lute while a procuress looks on.

To be fair, there are some Italian versions of procuress portraits. Niccolò dell'Abbate, the artist who
played a crucial role in the development of art at
Fontainebleau, produced an important example,
and it is likely that *The Old Woman* by Giorgione,
an ambiguous symbol of the passage of time, is in
this category as well, given the nature of the painter's circle. All through the Renaissance, images of
shrewd, elderly women were consciously or uncon-
sciously summoned to play the role by artists.

Quite fastidious about their dress are the *macrelles*
who fill the pages of the *Miroir des Courtisanes*. An
attractive double portrait in that album is *La Belle
Dans et sa Macrelle*, in which the procuress performs
the time-honored function of holding a mirror so
that the courtesan can arrange her hair. A Venetian
courtesan in a print by Giacomo Franco uses an in-
genious system of two mirrors. In another print of
his a maidservant grooms a courtesan. In a painting
of the School of Fontainebleau, *The Beautiful
Woman and the Love Note*, the procuress plays another role, that of conveyer of seductive messages.

Another favorite genre incorporating courtesan
types is "The Five Senses," a theme requiring five related scenes—or a single compendium scene—illustrating the use of each sense. The sense of touch was
often portrayed as the most insidious. Courtesans
abound in prints such as *The Five Senses* by Cornelis
Cort and a series by Jan Sanredam, to say nothing
of the buxom and boisterous women in a set by Jacob van der Merck.

Of all the senses, the sense of sight must have
posed a special danger for the courtesan who had to
resist the temptation of narcissistically gazing at her
own image. Veronica Franco is tempted by Tintoretto's mirrorlike rendering of her (which is, alas,
lost):

I guarantee you that when I first set eyes on the portrait
you did of me, produced by your own divine hands, I remained for a long time in doubt as to whether I was looking at a painting or, rather, a phantasm conjured up by
some diabolical power—surely not to make me fall in
love with myself—I hardly think I am so beautiful as to
cause such passions—but for some other reason.

Artists naturally sympathize with those who love beauty and who strive to embody it. Perhaps that is why the transition from the portrait of honest courtesans at their toilet to the moralistic Vanity genre, also showing a lovely woman gazing into her mirror, is sometimes almost imperceptible as, for example in the Vanity painting attributed to Veronese in the Accademia di San Luca, Rome, or a painting by Quentin Massys in a private Barcelona collection·

In the latter painting a courtesan dressed similarly to those in Paris Bordone's work is presented along with classical ruins, a nude statuette, a map of the world indicating terrestrial concerns, (also the ephemerality of human science), and a lute. To these objects meant to signify futility and the passing of time has been added Vulcan's anvil, a traditional symbol for ardor. An admonitory inscription is carved into the sarcophagus the woman is resting her arm on, just in case we have not yet perceived the message.

Similarly ambivalent is the superb engraving by Jacob de Gheyn the Elder called *Vanity*, in which a courtesan sits at her dressing table in an atmosphere of refinement, surrounded by cosmetics and bibelots and accompanied by her pet monkey. More violent in its approach is Jacob Binck's engraving *Vanity* that makes the dramatic, large standing female figure with its frivolous accouterments ridiculous. Vanity depictions converge with two other representations—those of Lust (Luxuria) and Lasciviousness (Lascivia). Northern art pullulates with these putative banners of morality in the form of hefty nude seated and standing females.

But now the examination of the courtesan image in art has come to an end, for when she falls off on the one side into allegory and on the other into unadorned realism, she is no more the complex, double, illusionary figure—posing and conscious of the pose. Undoubtedly she "escapes" through this very crevice that has been created.

We have seen how the prostitute abounds in northern art; this is where she thrived, rather than in the idealizing south, or at Fontainebleau, where Italian precedents gave rise to a whole school of allegorical, exalted portraiture of nude ladies some of whom were mistresses to kings. Meanwhile, in

School of Fontainebleau, *The Beautiful Woman and the Love Note*. 16th century. Private collection

Jacob de Gheyn the Elder, *Vanity*. 17th century. The Elisha Whittelsey Fund, 1949, The Metropolitan Museum of Art, New York

Andrea Michiel (Il Vicentino), detail of courtesan holding fan (Veronica Franco?) from *Henry III Arriving at the Lido*. 16th century. Palazzo Ducale, Venice

THE COURTESAN IN VENETIAN, FRENCH, AND NORTHERN PAINTING

Jacob Binck. *Vanity* (engraving). 16th century.
Graphische Sammlung Albertina, Vienna

Anonymous, *Lascivia* (engraving). 16th century.
Bibliothèque Nationale, Paris

Velásquez's *Rokeby (Venus with a Mirror)* and Goya's *La Maya* (dressed and undressed), the courtesan figure continues to reign as "the beautiful image," almost to be worshiped, until we arrive, via the mainly decorative odalisques of Ingres and Delacroix, at the ironical effrontery of Manet's *Olympia*, aware that she is not only a compendium of all of the preceding types, but something new as well.

· AFTERWORD ·

In the Renaissance, much comes from the ancients, but is no less for that. I have found in Lucian the category of the *cortezan de lume* (candlelight courtesan) and, elsewhere, the stews, the tricks, the parties, the quarrels, even some of the clothes, but most of all the situations immortalized in plays and poems, also lived out in real life. However, I know of no Renaissance courtesan who kept an hourglass by her bed, as did Metiche—nicknamed Clepsydra —who, when the sand ran out, stopped her caresses.

Nevertheless, Renaissance courtesans must also have had a practical side, and even sometimes seemed instruments of the devil. The vicious satires of the sixteenth century in Italy and France are the equivalent of seventeenth-century Dutch genre art when it chooses to be realistic almost to the point of the grotesque. And thus the courtesan continues to escape definition through such widely disparate representations of her soul. No wonder.

The courtesan is meant to be a half-defined, float-ing figure never fixing herself surely in the imagination. She is the memory of an experience, the point at which a dream is transformed into reality or reality into a dream. The bright colors fade, her name becomes a mere echo—echo of an echo, since she has probably adopted it from some ancient predecessor. The idea of the courtesan is a garden of delights in which the lover walks, smelling first this flower and then that but never understanding whence comes the fragrance that intoxicates him. Why should the courtesan not elude analysis? She does not want to be recognized for what she is, but rather to be allowed to be potent and effective. She offers the truth of herself—or, rather, of the passions that become directed toward her. And what she gives back is one's self and an hour of grace in her presence. Love revives when you look at her: is that not enough? She is the generative force of an illusion, the birth point of desire, the threshold of contemplation of bodily beauty.

·ACKNOWLEDGMENTS·

My interest in courtesans in Renaissance culture stems from my earliest days in Italy, when Vanni Scheiwiller, son of Ezra Pound's first publisher, placed a volume of poetry by Gaspara Stampa and Veronica Franco in my hands, suggesting that I translate some of them for the English-speaking world. This gift, which took on more and more significance as the years passed, made me the custodian of more than these two precious spirits.

I began to study literature about and by the courtesans in the 1970s just after I had been a Fellow at the Radcliffe Institute (the Bunting Institute); work begun at Widener and Houghton Libraries continued in Rome, where University of Rome resources, the Vatican and, eventually, the Herziana Libraries proved useful. A sojourn at Villa I Tatti (the Harvard Center for Italian Renaissance Studies) found me sometimes running off from Florence to Venice to track down my courtesans' lives. There, the now-retired director of the Marciana Library, Giorgio Emmanuele Ferrari, lent a helping hand, as did Venetian experts in several fields.

The privilege of living for many years in the heart of Old Rome, near Chiesa Nuova in the former courtesan quarter, infused atmosphere into my days.

An invitation to give a lecture series in 1982 on the subject of "Courtesans and Renaissance Culture" for the Italian Department, Renaissance Studies Program, at Yale University and the Yale University Women's Studies Program further encouraged me to formulate the lines of this book. I am grateful to the Center for Advanced Study in the Visual Arts, National Gallery of Art, Washington, D.C., where I was an Andrew W. Mellon Visiting Senior Fellow in the winter of 1982–83, developing the visual arts side of my study while working on my *I modi* book on Giulio Romano and Marcantonio Raimondi.

Prudence suggests that I not name the distinguished persons with whom I have had contact over the years, lest they be blamed for any shortcomings that might appear in my work. Nevertheless, I should say that stimulating, if all too brief, conversations took place at the last moment with Federico Zeri, Philip Fehl, and other friends. Walter Liedtke and Otto Naumann offered interesting suggestions regarding Dutch art. Caroline Karpinski has, all along, been helpful on prints. Tracy Dick of Yale University offered generous help as my assistant in Rome in 1983–84. Special thanks go to Frau Gerlende Kisters for her hospitality at Kreuzlingen and her help in documenting "my" Laura— Titian's *Laura Dianti*.

Two Palma Vecchio paintings appear here in all their vivid coloration, newly cleaned, thanks to my friend Alessandra Molfino, director of the Poldi-Pezzoli Museum, Milan, and the staff at Berlin-Dahlem.

·NOTES·

Unless otherwise noted, translations from foreign languages are by the author.

1. Francisco Delicado, *La Lozana andalusa* (Venice, 1528; but written in 1524). Delicado was a Spanish priest who emigrated to Rome from Cordova and eventually went to live in Venice. Afflicted with syphilis, he wrote a tract on how to cure the disease. No less than 105 persons, including the author, speak in *La Lozana*. Other fictional procuresses of the time appear in Fernando de Rojas's *La Celestina* and Alessandro Piccolomini's *La Raffaella*, as well as Aretino's *Dialogues*.

2. Domenico Gnoli, *La Roma di Leone X* (Milan: Hoepli, 1938), pp. 196–97.

3. The classic sources for information about the Roman population in the early sixteenth century have traditionally been: M. Armellini, "Un censimento della città di Roma sotto il pontificato di Leone X," *Gli studi in Italia: Descriptio urbis nel 1526*, vols. IV–V (Rome, 1882), pp. 7–43, and Domenico Gnoli, "Descriptio urbis o censimento della popolazione di Roma avanti il Sacco Borbonico," *Archivio della società romana di storia patria*, vol. XVII (Rome, 1894), pp. 375–520. An important edition of the 1527 census has just been published—*Descriptio Urbis: The Roman Census of 1527*, ed. Egmont Lee (Rome: Bulzoni, 1985), drawing on the original manuscript. In this volume is presented a rich panorama of Roman society in the early sixteenth century, but also, for whoever peruses it closely (bearing in mind the circumstances and habits of the caste) fascinating information about the vast number of courtesans who lived in the city at this time. Only twenty-nine women are referred to as *cortesana*, or in Latin, *curialis*, seven of these in the *rione* Campo Marzio, but clusters of names of single women from many different lands nonetheless appear in adjacent dwellings, revealing the courtesan presence. Interspersed with an occasional jeweler, silk merchant, or notary—all men who served them—are dozens of Angelas, Lucretias, Cecilias, Beatrices, Imperias, Violantes, Fiammettas, each with a handful of servants. Spanish laundresses and shirtmakers, who functioned as procuresses, are often found living nearby. Historical figures are listed—Giulia del Sole, Camilla of Pisa, Beatrice Spagnola, Matrema-non-vole—and many others known from life and fiction—even a Pippa of Florence reminiscent of a character in Aretino's *Dialogues*. It is tantalizing to speculate that "Faustina cortesana" may be the one about whom Aretino makes a ribald comment in his *Sonetti lussuriosi*, written about the same time as the census. Interesting names—such as Iovenetta cortesana and Ieronima cortesana, as well as the literary or classicizing Pantasileas, Tiberias, Cassandras, and Honoras—supplement those already known. In the Regula district, living near Pontiana, a courtesan from Valenzia, and not far from Elvira of Sicily, are nine others not specifically called courtesans, but obviously practicing the trade. In Ponte, the situation is even more conspicuous: at numbers 2531–39 there are, again, nine in a row, including a Polish woman and a Schiavona from the Dalmatian coast, forming another courtesan enclave amid the pilgrims, adventurers, diplomats, artisans, and courtiers of the shifting Roman population.

4. The first ghetto where Venetian prostitutes were required to live had been the Castelletto near the Rialto, founded in 1360 and closed in 1498. A kind of feudal possession of its patrician administrators who took a small profit from it, the Castelletto housed a community that needed to be severely regulated in order to prevent upheaval in everyday citizen life and to protect the women themselves from abuse. This double aim continued to be pursued through the next decades.

The second ghetto was Carampane. Ca' Rampani meant literally "house of the Rampani." The Rampani family, originally from Ravenna, had long lived in an area not far from the Rialto near the churches of Sant'Aponal and San Cassian when the last descendant died in 1319. This is the zone to which the government chose, in the sixteenth century, to assign Venetian prostitutes, closing them in at night behind locked gates. The visitor to Carampane today can see how easy it would have been to create a castle of sin cut off by a system of moats—the tiny surrounding canals, one of which separates the area by a thin watery line from the Capello palace, aristocratic stronghold from which the audacious Bianca fled with her bank clerk in the autumn of 1563.

Protection of another kind and degree (as documented

by trial records) extended to the higher echelons of courtesans who, as long as they avoided San Marco and churches, could live more or less where they wished. Giacomo de Sant'Agostin, who beat Elena Balbi and tore a necklace from her neck, was prosecuted by the Senate, and Giovan Francesco Justinian was imprisoned for doing more or less the same thing to the well-known Bianca Saraton. The Council of Ten offered a reward for information about a man who, for motives of revenge, went armed to the door of Giulia Lombarda, "sumptuous prostitute," and tried to knock it down.

In 1532 a certain Viena was absolved from the charge of having taken into her service, without proper authorization, a very young girl, because, as Marin Sanudo noted in his diaries, "This famous woman . . . enjoyed powerful connections with our patricians." Sanudo's diaries (*Diarii di Marino Sanuto*, ed. R. Fulin, F. Stefani, N. Barozzi [Venice, 1879–1902; repr. Bologna, 1969]) consist of fifty-eight volumes containing letters, documents, economic news, ambassadorial reports, social gossip, and comments about cultural events. Hence they provide considerable information about courtesans, both judicial and frivolous.

If one wanted to distinguish the sumptuous prostitute from the Carampane whore, one could do no better than to cite a letter of April 22, 1531, from a Venetian envoy to a member of the Tiepolo family in Venice, reproduced in the diaries (vol. LIV). It seems that at a supper party in Anversa offered by the papal legate, attended by merchants and dignitaries from Venice, the former ambassador from France to Venice, wishing to extol the Republic, exclaimed: "I don't believe one can find here a certain kind of merchandise I found in Venice; at least it is not so abundant or exquisitely fashioned." Then he began to name Cornelia Griffo, Giulia Lombarda, Bianca Saraton, the Ballerini sisters, and others. Nevertheless, all of these names appear in the infamous *La tariffa delle puttane principali di Venezia* (Venice, 1535), where fine distinctions are blurred.

5. See also Armand Baschet and Félix-Sebastien Feuillet de Conches, *Les femmes blondes selon les peintres de l'école de Venise* (Paris, 1865), which includes an anthology of French Renaissance poetry paying homage to blond hair.

6. Quoted in Emmanuel Rodocanachi, *La femme italienne à l'époque de la Renaissance* (Paris, 1907), p.174.

7. Venetian sumptuary laws are gathered in a handy compendium: Giulio Bistort, *Il magistrato delle pompe nella Repubblica di Venezia: Studio storico* (Venice, 1912; repr. Bologna: Forni, 1969).

8. See Lynne Lawner, *"I Modi" nell'opera di Giulio Romano, Marcantonio Raimondi, e Jean-Frédéric Maximilien de Waldeck* (Milan: Longanesi, 1984). Reproduced in this modern edition are the original fragments and fourteen (originally sixteen) woodcuts of a pirated edition printed in Venice in about 1527. Pietro Aretino's original sonnets appear below the designs.

9. Vettori's letter, in a Codex of the Biblioteca Palatina in Florence (today Biblioteca Nazionale Centrale), is quoted extensively in Guido Biagi, *Una etera romana, Tullia d'Argona* (Florence, 1897), pp. 87ff.

10. Luigi Ferrai, *Lettere di cortigiane del XVI secolo* (Florence, 1884), letter XX.

11. For a more extended analysis of Gaspara Stampa's poetry along these lines, see Lynne Lawner, "Gaspara Stampa and the Rhetoric of Submission," *Renaissance Studies in Honor of Craig Hugh Smyth* (Villa I Tatti: The Harvard University Center for Italian Renaissance Studies 7) (Florence: Giunti Barbera, 1985), vol. 1, pp. 345–62.

12. Veronica's name, in the form of V. FRANCO in block letters also appears on the lining of a courtesan portrait in the Worcester Art Museum, listed in the catalogue as "by a follower of Jacopo Tintoretto," which Paola Rossi attributes to Domenico Tintoretto. The painting has been lined onto another canvas, the signature visible only under ultraviolet light. According to the museum director, James A. Welu, who kindly reexamined it at my request, the signature is impossible to date. Martin Davies, in his study of European paintings in the Worcester collection, claimed it was "fairly old but clearly not very old" (pp. 480–81). The inscription was accepted, with doubts, as authentic by Berenson, and in fact the canvas could have been relined at any time from the sixteenth century on, and the signature removed from the back of the painting to the lining.

From a letter by Veronica we know that Jacopo painted her portrait in 1580. One might speculate that the portrait resembled this idealized portrait, in which a piece of jewelry composed of precious gems crosses the woman's chest diagonally, reminiscent of a traditional ornament of Venus's. The woman's left nipple is half exposed beneath the puckered border of a rich chemise, and an elaborate costume and a blue shawl elegantly fastened in the jeweled chain and held by the right hand over the right breast give a slightly heroic feeling to the portrait.

The sitter of this portrait seems to me to be the same woman who appears in a School of Tintoretto bust portrait in the Museo del Prado, exposing her right breast, her face in profile, and possible a second portrait there, where the head is turned more toward the viewer and the right breast is again exposed. In all three portraits the women wear pearl necklaces. The hair arrangement (modified horns) in the Worcester portrait is similar to that in the 1575 engraving of Veronica Franco and a figure I call attention to in Il Vicentino's *Henry III Arriving at the Lido* (see page 58); however, the face is fuller and the lips somewhat tumid. In the past, it has been thought that some of the Prado portraits (a series of five numbered 381–85) were by or of Marietta, Jacopo's daughter and also a painter. One is a *Flora*.

13. *Aretino's Dialogues*, trans. Raymond Rosenthal (New York: Stein and Day, 1971). All citations (with a few corrections by the author) are from this English language translation of Aretino's *Dialoghi* and *Ragionamenti*, combined under the title *Le sei giornate* in Giovanni Aquilecchia's standard modern Italian edition (Bari: Laterza, 1969).

14. Anna Pallucchini, "Il ritratto di Caterina Sandella di Jacopo Tintoretto," *Arte Veneta* 25 (1971), pp. 262ff. Rodolfo Pallucchini has informed me that the portrait has recently been sold to a German collector and is no longer in a private collection in Venice. One sees from the reproduction in Pallucchini-Rossi that Caterina is wearing a yellow gown with white veils. The band around her hair suggests that she may have just now bleached it in the sun. A version of this painting, certainly wrongly entitled *Irene of Spilimburg*, was once on the New York art market.

15. The well-known sixteenth-century translation of Plutarch's *Lives* by Thomas North, *Lives of the Greeks and Romans* (London, 1579), is appropriate for this context but has to be amended in at least one place. Cf. *Plutarch's Lives*, trans. Perrin, vol. 5 (Cambridge, Mass.: Harvard University Press, 1968), pp. 118–21.

16. Alessandro Tassoni, *Dieci libri di pensieri diversi* (*Ten Books of Various Thoughts*) (Venice, 1620), vol. X, chap. 19: Pliny XXXV.119. Vasari draws on the Pliny passage in his *Life of Raphael*. A curious variant of the theme appears in an anecdote recounted by Leonardo concerning a patron of his who bought a painting, then, having fallen in love with its "divine subject," requested the master to remove the most sublime attributes so that its owner would "feel free to kiss it." (*Treatise*, ed. McMahon [1956], vol. I, p. 22).

17. Paul Ganz, *The Paintings of Hans Holbein* (London: Phaidon, 1950), p. 231, credits Woermann as the first to point this out.

18. The display of one partially exposed breast became prominent in classical art in the late fifth century B.C. in the works of a Greek sculptor, probably Callimachus, who showed Aphrodite in what came to be called (to use the Latin name) the Venus Genetrix pose. The exposed single breast also appears in representations of Amazons, who were reputed to have cut off one breast so that it would not interfere with their bowstrings. A rich imagery in art involving the presentation and holding of breasts dates to ancient Middle Eastern practices

regarding such figures as Ishtar and Astarte. Similarly, the Madonna Lactans pose may hark back to Egyptian depictions of Isis Lactans.

19. Desiring to have a Flora of its own, the Renaissance obtained one through the efforts of Guglielmo della Porta, who creatively reconstructed an ancient statue to which he added Flora's attributes—the so-called *Flora Farnese* presently in the Museo Nazionale, Naples.

20. Philetaerus, in the play *Playing the Corinthian*, quoted in Athenaeus, *Deipnosophistae* XIII.559 (trans. C. B. Gulick, *Athenaeus* [Cambridge, Mass.: Harvard University Press, 1937]), vol. VI, p. 21. An impressive amount of literature existed in the ancient world on the subject of courtesans. Our word "pornography" derives from the Greek and means literally "writing about courtesans." The references in Athenaeus to poems, plays, treatises, and lists of courtesans are dazzling, giving one some idea of what the Greeks produced along this line, and there are also such important documents as Lucian of Samosata's *Dialogues of the Courtesans*. Taking their cues from Greek dramatists of the New Comedy, Plautus and Terence portray many courtesans in their plays, and the Roman poets, above all Horace, Tibullus, Propertius, and Ovid, sing their praises and condemn their bad habits.

Anyone interested in this subject must begin with the K. Schneider entries in Pauly-Wissowa, *Real-Encyclopädie*, on "Hetairai" and "Meretrix," vol. 8, pp. 1331–72, vol. 15, pp. 1018–27. See also C. Charbonnier, "La courtisane de Plaute à Ovide," *Bulletin de l'Association Guillaume Budé* 4 (December 1969): 451ff.

21. *Lupa* (she-wolf) was the term used for prostitute in Roman times. Brothels in Italy are still called *lupanari*.

22. Julius Held, "Flora, Goddess, and Courtesan," in *Essays in Honor of Erwin Panofsky* (New York, 1961), vol. I, pp. 201–18, offers a reconstruction of the history of the iconography of Flora up to and beyond the Renaissance that takes into account many examples of illustrations and literary sources.

23. See Carlo Pedretti, *Leonardo: A Study in Chronology and Style* (Berkeley: University of California Press, 1973), pp. 137–39.

24. Ibid., p. 138.

25. Cecil Gould, *Leonardo: The Artist and the Non-Artist* (Boston, 1975), pp. 117–22. See also Kenneth Clark, *Leonardo da Vinci: An Account of His Development as an Artist* (Cambridge, 1952), pp. 121–23.

26. Egon Verheyen, "Correggio's 'Amori di Giove,'" *Journal of the Warburg and Courtauld Institutes* 29 (1966): 188–91. Nevertheless, the painting succeeds in being "an allegory of sensual ecstasy," as Kenneth Clark terms it (*Leonardo da Vinci*, p. 124).

27. See Pedretti, *Leonardo*, pp. 133–37. He believes

that the elaboration of mythological figures such as Flora can be dated, in the master's work and that of his disciples, to 1510–11, the period in which the Gioconda would also have been developed as an idea. Many other scholars resist this idea, insisting that the Gioconda was more or less realized by 1503–4, influencing Raphael soon thereafter.

28. This remark is obviously meant to be a bit tongue in cheek. Along this line it is interesting to note that the Giampietrino *Nymph Egeria* (presently in the Annibale Brivio collection, Milan) where the notorious Gioconda-type smile graces a voluptuous nude, is thought to have been painted in homage to a mistress of the French governor of Milan, Charles d'Amboise. Scholars have also wondered whether the mysterious early *La Belle Ferronière* by Leonardo might not represent another mistress of Ludovico Sforza, Lucrezia Crivelli.

29. Antonio de Beatis remarks, on his visit accompanying Cardinal Luis d'Aragona to the artist's studio in France, that Giuliano's mistress portrayed by Leonardo was "Florentine." Pedretti (*Leonardo*, p. 136) brings up a curious fact—namely, that in his report of another visit the following day de Beatis compared a portrait of a Milanese woman unfavorably with the "Signora Gualanda" he saw the day before.

30. The "two Venuses" hypothesis was first proposed by Erwin Panofsky, *Studies in Iconology: Humanistic Themes in Art of the Renaissance* (New York: Harper and Row, 1962), 2d ed., pp. 150ff., then discussed again in his *Problems in Titian, Mostly Iconographic* (New York: New York University Press, 1969), pp. 114ff., incorporating new speculation on the part of scholars that the painting called *Sacred and Profane Love* might be a marriage picture.

Just as Venus does not belong entirely to courtesans, Venus and Mars were sometimes painted on bridal *cassoni* or, as in the ancient world, given the features of husbands and wives. Similarly, respectable women came to pose as Flora. (Rembrandt's portrait of Saskia as Flora is a particularly ambiguous example.) It is unusual to find this in the sixteenth century, however. For the Bartolommeo Veneto *Flora*, see Panofsky, *Problems of Titian*, pp. 137ff; also pp. 126–29.

31. As if to complicate matters further, Giovanni Paolo Lomazzo, in an intriguing statement in his treatise of 1584, claimed that there existed in France a pair of Gioconda portraits by Leonardo, both posed as smiling Floras. The complex history of the literature about the *Nude Gioconda*, which, to make a point, he refers to as the *Monna Vanna*, is exhaustively drawn in David Brown's portion of David Alan Brown and Konrad Oberhuber, "Monna Vanna and Fornarina: Leonardo and Raphael in Rome," *Essays Presented to Myron P. Gilmore*

(Villa I Tatti: The Harvard University Center for Renaissance Studies 2) (Florence, 1978), vol. II, pp. 25–86. One does not necessarily have to agree with his conclusions, however. Brown would dissociate the *Nude Gioconda* from the *Gioconda*, seeing them as portrayals done in a completely different spirit.

The fact is that, for one reason or another, all of the sources—from the Anonimo Gaddiano, Vasari, de Beatis, and Lomazzo to Cassiano del Pozzo and even the palace inventories—can be discredited, so that one ends, finally, with only one's personal perception of the evolution of a style but, just as important, the sense of a motif's or a constellation of motifs' belonging to a historical moment. It is not necessary to see Leonardo undressing the woman who became the world's idol, for lubricious motives: obviously, curiosity about structural elements and position in space were the overriding concerns. (Surely that is why Kenneth Clark suggests that Leonardo's first sketch for the *Gioconda* was a *Nude Gioconda*.) Yet the fact remains that the model and inspiration offered herself to the artist as someone who could and should be undressed in order fully to reveal to the public her beauty.

32. The habit of keeping portraits of courtesans and statues of Venus in private places for the enjoyment of the single viewer and/or his circle seems to have been widespread and international. One of the literary letters by the Spaniard Antonio de Guevara, dated May 16, 1531, and addressed to Enrique Enriquez, reveals that it could even be something of a learned game.

Enriquez asks Guevara, who was Bishop of Mondonedo, to tell him about the three saints whose images Enriquez possesses and worships every day. Replying to his friend, Guevara explains that Lamia, Flora, and Lais are not saints at all, but "three beautiful, celebrated whores . . . gifted with all the graces—that is to say, pretty faces, tall figures, high foreheads, large bosoms, narrow waists, long hands skillful in playing instruments, and gentle singing voices." The picture he presents of them is the usual dignified humanistic one: "While they lived, they were the richest courtesans, and when they died, they left behind many memories; statues were raised in their honor and writers wrote great things of them" (*Epistolas familiares* [Madrid, 1850], pp. 177–80). Also quoted in Held, "Flora, Goddess, and Courtesan," p. 214.

According to a document written in November 1800, Manuel Godoy, Prince of the Peace, favorite of Queen Maria Luisa and apparently lover of the duchess of Alba, kept the *Naked Maya*, along with Velázquez's nude *Venus at Her Mirror* and other Venuses, in a secret room of his palace—an inner room or study—where forbidden paintings were hung. This sequestering of the seductive female figure was all the more desirable in this period since pictures of nudes were hunted by the Inquisition. Pierre Gassier, in his *Goya* (Secaucus, N.J., 1983), pp. 142–45, says he believes that the *Maya* was painted for Godoy, that the duchess probably posed for it, and that it was also she who gave the Velázquez *Venus* to Godoy. Gassier remarks that there was an erotic link between the painter, the patron, and the duchess-model that still needs to be explored.

33. "Lettera al Castiglione," in *Scritti d'arte del cinquecento*, ed. Paola Barocchi (Turin, 1979). The letter is neither dated nor signed but is generally considered to be from around 1514.

In similar fashion Bernardo Tasso, in the poem "Ben potrete con l'ombre e coi colori," invites Titian to paint a picture of his, Bernardo's, mistress, which the poet has already painted in his mind (*pensiero*).

34. The source of this *topos* may lie in a conversation in Xenophon's Socratic *Memorabilia* III, 10.1–kv, between the painter Parrhasius and Socrates, in which the latter suggests that the artist who finds it difficult to discover the perfect person to model for him should not hesitate to combine the beautiful features found in many persons in one entirely beautiful body. See Otto Kruz and Ernst Kris, *Legend, Myth, and Magic in the Image of the Artist* (New Haven: Yale University Press, 1979), p. 43.

35. Vasari-Milanesi, vol. IV, p. 357: "Raphael painted Beatrice of Ferrara and other women and especially his own." E. Ravaglia, "Il volto romano di Beatrice ferrarese," *Roma* 3 (1923): 53–61, believed it was again Beatrice of Ferrara who appears in two versions of a portrait of a woman, probably a courtesan, by Sebastiano del Piombo in the Galleria Nazionale d'Arte Antica (Corsini), Rome, and the Galleria degli Uffizi, Florence. A tradition had grown up whereby this portrait too had been called "the Fornarina." C. Cecchelli, "La 'Psyche' della Farnesina," *Roma* 2 (1923): 9–21, believed that Raphael's Fornarina was Imperia, Agostino Chigi's mistress, who died in 1512; whereas F. Filippini, "Raffaello e Bologna," *Cronache d'Arte* 2 (1925), no. 5: 222–26, identified her instead with Albina, another noted courtesan of Renaissance Rome.

36. Oberhuber, in Brown and Oberhuber, "Monna Vanna and Fornarina," p. 48.

37. Sydney J. Freedberg, *Parmigianino: His Works in Painting* (Cambridge, Mass.: Harvard University Press, 1950), p. 119.

38. Luigi Bailo and Girolamo Biscaro, *Della vita e delle opere di Paris Bordone* (Treviso, 1900), p. xxviii.

39. August Heckscher, "Recorded from Dark Recollection." In *Essays in Honor of Erwin Panofsky* (New York, 1961), vol. I, pp. 187–200, cites the relevant classical, medieval, and Renaissance sources for this and other aspects of the Danae legend, his intent being to relate it to German folklore.

40. Four versions of this painting exist: Rouen, São Paulo (Metayer), Sulzbach collection, Tours. Sylvie Béguin, in her entry for François Clouet in *L'Ecole de Fontainebleau* (exh. cat.) (Paris, 1972), informs us that scholars now agree that the identity of the knight in the Rouen version—the oldest one—is uncertain (in any case, he is not Henry II, as had been speculated, although he wears the colors of Diane de Poitiers); the knight in the Sulzbach and Tours versions is definitely Henry IV, and Diana is Gabrielle d'Estrées.

Identification of the subject of the Clouet portrait that I have called *Diane de Poitiers at Her Bath* (National Gallery of Art, Washington, D.C.) is an even more tangled affair. Colin Eisler devotes a lengthy entry to it in the catalogue *Paintings from the Samuel H. Kress Collection: European Schools Excluding Italian* (Oxford: Oxford University Press, 1977), pp. 253–57. Many have thought it represented Diane, although a late dating (1570s) renders this unlikely, since she retired from court in 1559 at the age of sixty. One curious interpretation would make the painting a political satire, with the lady in her bath representing Mary Stuart. Eisler speculates that "this approximately life-sized bath scene may have been executed for installation in a *trompe l'oeil* setting within a lavish bathing chamber."

41. Sylvie Béguin, *L'Ecole de Fontainebleau* (Paris, 1960), p. 107, suggests that the gesture honors the recent birth of the duke of Vendôme: the duchess would still be nursing her baby. Nevertheless, she calls it "ambiguous." In her entry in *L'Ecole de Fontainebleau* (exh. cat., 1972), she brushes aside that interpretation as well as the lesbian one in favor of seeing the gesture and setting as "signs of frivolity and royal misbehavior." There is also the comparison of two different kinds of beauty—blond and brunette. Béguin reminds us that a miniature exists in the Louvre showing Henry IV peeking at the two women at their bath.

42. See Panofsky, *Problems in Titian*, pp. 42–47.

43. Alison Stewart, *Unequal Lovers* (New York: Abaris Books, 1977), offers many illustrations of this theme in northern art. In Italy a striking example occurs in a print by Annibale Carracci.

44. This observation is made by Konrad Renger, *Lockere Gesellschaft* (Berlin, 1970), pp. 120–28.

·BIBLIOGRAPHY·

This bibliography has been selected according to the following criteria: I have listed historical studies and original literary documents of the Renaissance (and, in a few cases, of the classical world) that have been important in the writing of this book, some of which are cited in the text. I have included printed works—books, few articles, and, in one instance, a manuscript. I have listed long poems and anthologies of poetry, many of which are quite rare, dialogues, collections of novellas, and two plays. However, courtesans also appear in single poems by Firenzuola, Berni, Campana, Aretino, and others, in novellas by various authors not listed, including Boccaccio, as well as in plays by Contile, Domenichi, Dolce, Aretino, Salviano, Ruzante, de Torres Naharro, Venetian dialect playwrights of the period, and the dramatists who wrote the *canovacci* (plot sketches) for the *commedia dell'arte*. They are also present in French drama after the antique and to a lesser degree in English plays, such as John Marston's *The Dutch Courtezan* (1605).

Since the reader can readily turn to monographs on the artists dealt with in this book, it did not seem necessary to list these here. However, I have appreciated the writings on art of scholars such as Pallucchini, Rossi, Freedberg, Wethey, Béguin, Rinaldi, Canova, Mariacher, Brown, Oberhuber, Pedretti, Gould, Kemp, Clark, Held, Heckscher, Panofsky, and many others. Two studies of Dutch art that touch on the subject of courtesans are referred to in the Notes, and one more should be mentioned: Alison McNeil Kettering, *The Dutch Arcadia* (Montclair, 1983). An exhibition catalogue—*Raphael Urbinas: Il mito della Fornarina* (Milan, 1983) was helpful.

Aragona, Tullia d'. *Rime*. Ed. Enrico Celani. Bologna: Romagnoli, 1891.

———. *Dialogo dell'infinità d'Amore*. Bari: 1912.

———. *Il Meschino, detto il Guerrièro, di Tullia d'Aragona*. Venice, 1838.

Aretino, Pietro. *Aretino's Dialogues*. Translated by Raymond Rosenthal. New York: Stein and Day, 1971.

———. *Le sei giornate*. Edited by Giovanni Aquilecchia. Bari: Laterza, 1969.

———. *Lettere, il primo e il secondo libro*. Edited by Francesco Flora. Milan: Mondadori, 1960.

———. *Lettere*. Paris, 1609. 6 vol.

———. *The Letters of Pietro Aretino*. Translated by Thomas Caldecott Chubb. Hamden, Conn.: Archon Books, 1967.

Athenaeus. *The Deipnosophists*. Edited by C. B. Gulick. Cambridge, Mass: Harvard University Press, 1927. Vol. 6 (containing Books 13 and 14).

Bandello, Matteo. *Novelle*. Edited by Francesco Flora. Milan: 1966.

Barzaghi, Antonio. *Donne o cortigiane? la prostituzione a Venezia. Documenti di costume dal XVI al XVII secolo*. Verona, 1980.

Baschet, Armand, and Feuillet de Conches, Félix-Sebastien. *Les femmes blondes selon les peintres de l'école de Venise*. Paris: A. Aubry, 1865.

Bellay, Joachim du. *Divers jeux rustiques*. Geneva–Paris: Droz-Minard, 1947.

Bembo, Pietro. *Lettere di M. Pietro Bembo Cardinale*. Milan, 1809.

Biagi, Guido. *Una etera Romana, Tullia d'Aragona*. Florence, 1897.

Biondo, Michelangelo. *Angitia Cortigiana*. Rome, 1540.

Bistort, Giulio. *Il Magistrato delle Pompe nella Repubblica di Venezia. Studio storico*. Venice, 1912; Bologna: Forni, 1969.

Brantôme, Pierre de. *La vie des dames galantes*. Paris, 1955.

Bravata alla bulescha, sun quel aiere de Sant'Herculano. Venice, 1556.

Burchard, Johann. *At the Court of the Borgia, being an account of the Reign of Pope Alexander VI written by his Master of Ceremonies Johann Burchard*. Edited by Geoffrey Parker. London: The Folio Society, 1963.

Calmo, Andrea. *Le lettere di Andrea Calmo*. Edited by Vittorio Rossi. Turin: Ermanno Loescher, 1888.

Il catalogo di tutte le principali et più honorate cortigiane di Venezia nel secolo XVI. Venice, 1574.

Casagrande di Villaviera, Rita. *Le cortigiane veneziane nel cinquecento*. Milan: Longanesi, 1968.

Cenni storici e leggi circa il libertinàggio in Venezia. Venice, 1886.

Cesareo, Giovanni Alfredo. *Gaspara Stampa donna e poetessa.* Naples: Perrella, 1920.

Coryat, Thomas, *Coryat's Crudities.* Glasgow, 1905. Vol. I.

Les courtisanes et la police des moeurs à Venise. Bordeaux, 1886.

Dardano, Luigi. *La bella e dotta difesa delle donne di meser Luigi Dardano gran cancelliere dell'illustrissimo senato vinitiano, contro gli accusatori. . . .* Venice, 1554.

Delicado, Francisco. *La Lozana andalusa.* Venice, 1528.

Descriptio Urbis: The Roman Census of 1527. Edited by Egmont Lee. Rome: Bulzoni, 1985.

Il dialogo di Maddalena e Giulia. [Cosmopoli], 1860.

Donadoni, Eugenio. *Gaspara Stampa.* Messina: Principato, 1919.

Doni, Antonfrancesco. *Tre libri di pistolòtti amorosi del Doni per ogni sorte generazione di brigate.* Venice: Giolito de' Ferrari, 1558.

Ferrai, Luigi. *Lettere di cortigiane del XVI secolo.* Florence, 1884.

Fortini, Pietro. *Novelle.* Florence, 1888.

Franco, Veronica. *Lettere familiari.* Edited by Benedetto Croce. Bari, 1949.

Franco, Veronica, and Stampa, Gaspara. *Rime.* Edited by A. Salza. Bari, 1913.

Franco, Niccolò. *Le pistole vulgari di M. Niccolò Franco.* Venice: Gardane, 1585.

Gamba, Bartolommeo. *Alcuni ritratti di donne illustri delle provincie veneziane.* Venice: Alvispoli, 1826.

Garzoni, Tommaso. *La piazza universale di tutte le professioni del mondo.* Venice, 1585.

I Germini, sopra quaranta meretrici della città di Firenze. Florence: 1553. Reprinted in Moneti, Francesco. *Della vita e costumi fiorentini.* Florence, 1888.

Giovio, Paolo. *Historiarum sui temporis.* Florence, 1550–52.

Giraldi Cinthio, Giovanbattista, *Gli Hecatommiti.* Venice, 1608.

Gnoli, Domenico. *La Roma di Leone X.* Milan: Hoepli, 1938.

Gnoli, Umberto. *Cortigiane romane.* Arezzo, 1941.

Graf, Arturo. "Una cortigiana fra mille. In *Attraverso il cinquecento,* pp. 177–295. Turin, 1888.

Grazzini, Antonfrancesco. *Rime burlesche.* Florence, 1882.

Labé, Louise. *Oeuvres complètes.* Maestricht: A. A. M. Stols, 1928.

Landoni, T., and Vanzolini, J. *Lettere scritte a Pietro Aretino.* Bologna, 1873–75.

Larivaille, Paul. *La vie quotidienne des courtisanes en Italie au temps de la renaissance.* Paris, 1975.

Lawner, Lynne. *"I Modi" nell'opera di Giulio Romano, Marcantonio Raimondi, e Jean-Frédéric Maximilien de Waldeck.* Milan: Longanesi, 1984.

———. "Gaspara Stampa and the Rhetoric of Submission". In *Renaissance Studies in Honor of Craig Hugh Smyth.* Florence: Giunti Barbera, 1985. Vol. I, pp. 345–62.

Lorenzi, Giovanbattista de. *Leggi e memorie venete sulla prostituzione fino alla caduta della Repubblica.* Venice, 1870–72.

Lucian, *Dialoghi delle cortigiane.* Translated by Ludovico Domenichi. Florence: Torrentino, 1548.

Malespini, Celio. *Novelle.* Venice, 1609.

Marinello, M. G. *Gli ornamenti delle donne.* Venice, 1562.

Mascharate alla bulescha de un bravazzo chiamato Figao el qual vol tor la vita a una sua Diva. Venice, 1553.

Masson, Giorgina. *Courtesans of the Italian Renaissance.* London: Secker and Warburg, 1975.

Meneghetti, Gildo, ed. *La bulesca.* Venice, 1952.

Misoscolo, Eureta [Francesco Pona]. *La lucerna.* Edited by Giorgio Fulco. Rome: Salerno, n.d.

Molmenti, Pompeo. *La storia di Venezia nella vita privata.* Turin, 1880. Vol. 2.

Molza, Francescomaria. *Poesie.* Edited by Pierantonio Serassi. Bergamo, 1747.

Moncallero, Giuseppe Lorenzo. *Imperia e i suoi cantori funebri.* Rome: Palombi, 1962.

Montaigne, Michel de. *Journal du voyage de M. de Montaigne en Italie par la Suisse et l'Allemagne en 1580 et 1581.* Rome [Paris], 1774.

Mosto, Andrea da. *I bravi di Venezia.* Milan, 1950.

Muzio, Girolamo. *Egloghe.* Venice, 1550.

Muzio, Girolamo. *Rime diverse e canzoni della Bella Donna.* Venice, 1551.

Nolhac, Pierre de, and Solerti, Angelo. *Il viaggio di Enrico III re di Francia e le feste a Venezia: Ferrara, Mantova, e Torino.* Turin, 1890.

Oddi, Sforza. *L'erofilomachia.* Edited by Benedetto Croce. Naples: Ricciardi, 1946.

Parabosco, Girolamo. *Lettere amorose.* Venice: Farri, 1560.

Pasqualigo, Alvise. *Lettere amorose del Mag. M. Alvise Paqualigo.* Book III. Venice: Farri, 1581.

Pecchiai, Pio. *Donne del rinascimento in Roma.* Padua: Cedam, 1958.

Pino, Modesto (pseud.). *Delle rime piasevoli di diversi auttori, nuovamente accolte da M. Modesto Pino, e intitolate "La Caravana."* Venice, 1576.

Pronostico alla villotta. Venice, 1558. Reprinted in Moneti, Francesco. *Della vita e costumi dei fiorentini.* Florence, 1888.

La puttana errante. Venice, 1531; repr. ed., Paris, 1883.

Rodocanachi, Emmanuel. *Courtisanes et buffons.* Paris, 1894.

———. "Une courtisane vénitienne à l'époque de la Renaissance." In *Etudes et fantaisies historiques.* Paris, 1912.

———. *La femme italienne à l'époque de la Renaissance.* Paris, 1907.

Rosati, Salvatore. *Tullia d'Aragona.* Milan: Treves, 1936.

Roscoe, William. *The Life and Pontificate of Leo X.* London, 1853.

Sansovino, Francesco. *Venetia città nobilissima et singolare . . . .* Venice, 1603.

Sant Disdier, Ms. le chevalier de. *La ville et la République de Venise.* The Hague, 1685.

Sanudo, Marin. *Diarii di Marino Sanuto.* Edited by R. Fulin, F. Stefani, and N. Barozzi. Venice, 1879–1902; repr. ed. Bologna, 1969.

Schneider, K. "Hetairai" and "Meretrix." In Pauly-Wissowa, Real-Encyclopädie der Klassicken Altertumswissenschaft. Vol. 8, pp. 1331–72; vol. 15, pp. 1018–27.

Speroni, Sperone. "Dialogo d'Amore" In *I dialoghi di M. Speron Sperone.* Venice: Aldo Manutius, 1542.

Speroni, Sperone. "Orazione alle Cortigiane." In *Orationi del Sig. Sperone Speroni nuovamente poste in luce.* Venice, 1596.

La tariffa delle puttane principali di Venezia. Venice, 1535.

Tassini, Giuseppe. *Alcune delle più clamorose condanne capitali eseguite in Venezia sotto la Repubblica.* Venice, 1892.

———. *Curiosità veneziane.* Venice: Filippi, 1915.

———. *Veronica Franco, Celebre poetessa del secolo XVI.* Venice: Altieri, 1969.

Il trionfo della Lussuria di Maestro Pasquino. Rome, 1537. Repr. in Moneti, Francesco. *Della vita e costumi dei fiorentini.* Florence, 1888.

Il vanto della cortigiana ferrarese, qual narra la bellezza sua. Con il lamento per esser redutta in la carretta per il mal franzese et l'amonitorio che fa alle altre donne, per Giovanni Bartolommeo Verini. Venice, 1532. Modern edition: Giovanni Aquilecchia, "Per l'attribuzione e il testo del 'Lamento di una cortigiana ferrarese.'" In *Tra latino e volgare. Per Carlo Dionisotti.* Padua: Antenore, 1974.

Vecellio, Cesare. *Habiti antichi et moderni di tutto il mondo.* Venice, 1590.

Vita, Alessandro del. *Galanteria e lussuria nel rinascimento.* Arezzo, 1958.

Venier, Lorenzo. *Il trentuno della Zaffetta.* Venice, 1531. Repr. ed. Paris: 1861. ed.

Venier, Maffio. "Despuò che son entrà in pensier sí vario," Codex Marciana IX. 217 (7061) fol. 84r. (Annotated List of Venetian Courtesans.)

———. *Il libro chiuso di Maffio Venier (La tenzone con Veronica Franco).* Edited by Manlio Dazzi. Venice: Neri Pozza, 1956.

Zamaron, Fernand. *Louise Labé: dame de franchise.* Paris: Nizet, 1968.

·INDEX·

PHOTOGRAPH CREDITS